The Red Web

Tom Bower has spent his life studying
politics, finance and warfare, having
graduated in law from the London School
of Economics.. He is a distinguished BBC
television producer and award-winning
documentary maker. He is the author of
Blind Eye to Murder, *The Paperclip
Conspiracy*, *The Red Web* and most
famously, *Maxwell: The Outsider*. He
frequently contributes to leading
newspapers throughout the world. He lives
in Hampstead, London, with his family.

D0893040

TOM BOWER

THE RED WEB

MI6 and the KGB MasterCoup

arrow books

To Veronica, Nicholas, Oliver and Sophie

A Mandarin Paperback

THE RED WEB

First published in Great Britain 1989
by Aurum Press Ltd
This edition published 1993
by Mandarin Paperbacks
an imprint of Reed Consumer Books Ltd
Michelin House, 81 Fulham Road, London SW3 6RB
and Auckland, Melbourne, Singapore and Toronto

Reprinted 1993 (twice)

Copyright © 1989 by Tom Bower

Maps by Richard Natkiel Associates
All uncredited illustrations are taken
by the author or from his collection

A CIP catalogue record for this title
is available from the British Library

ISBN 0 7493 1478 8

Phototypeset by Intype, London
Printed and bound in Great Britain
by Cox & Wyman Ltd, Reading, Berks

CONTENTS

INTRODUCTION

The Secret Intelligence Service or MI6 still enjoys an enviable reputation among its friends and rivals. Despite the catalogue of their well-publicised calamities, SIS officers throughout the world are generally regarded as professional and committed. Undisturbed by political revolution or military surrender, their organisation has benefited from a historical continuity which has garnered tradition and generated myths. Not surprisingly, it is an image carefully fostered by the British government, willingly aided by Hollywood, television dramas, novels and newspapers.

Spies and clandestine operations have fascinated laymen since time immemorial, not least because exposés of their deeds reveal hitherto passionately guarded secrets. After 1945 that preoccupation increased, because historians and others could for the first time disentangle the results of the unprecedented resources devoted by all combatants to their intelligence services during the Second World War.

A second stimulus to the growth of interest was the knowledge that during the Cold War all governments relied increasingly upon their intelligence services. Yet our understanding of these recent activities has been severely limited, because the secret war between East and West continues without abatement. For forty years the most diligent researchers who have probed into the world of espionage have met walls of silence, have repeated ingeniously planted disinformation or have at best successfully secured snippets of the 'truth', while being denied the overall context in which to place the new facts.

While the veil of secrecy is justifiable because governments require intelligence to formulate their policies and their sources demand discretion, there are instances where governments' demands for secrecy serve not to guard the sanctity of the service but to protect the intelligence organisation from embarrassment. The circumstances exposed in *The Red Web* fall into this category.

The catalyst for this book was the surprise appearance on Latvian television of Kim Philby in autumn 1987. In a brief excerpt sold to British television, the Soviet spy alleged that the nationalist unrest which was then sweeping the Baltic States was not prompted by general dissatisfaction or the Kremlin's new Glasnost policies, but was deliberately provoked by SIS and the British government. It was simply, claimed Philby, a repetition of policies and strategies pursued by SIS in the Baltic States at the height of the Cold War.

In February 1988 Barrie Penrose reminded me of Philby's allegations, which seemed inexplicable. Published books referred only in passing to SIS's loss of agents infiltrated into the Soviet Union after 1945, while Anthony Cavendish, a former SIS officer, mentioned his limited role in the Baltic operations only in a controversial private memoir. The reason for the ignorance and reticence, it transpired, was simple. The officers responsible in both London and Washington had understandably sought to conceal an embarrassing disaster.

Prompted by Penrose and with the encouragement and support of George Carey, Will Wyatt, Phillip Knightley, Rupert Allason MP and Thomas Powers, I travelled repeatedly over the following twelve months across Europe, the USA and to the Soviet Union to discover the facts to which Philby had alluded. The research began amid an unexpected coincidence of contradictions. While in London the British government introduced measures to restrict drastically any reporting of SIS's activities, Soviet officials in Moscow and Riga, basking in the new atmosphere of Glasnost, seemed amenable to persuasion that KGB officials who were hitherto firmly beyond any approach might now be interviewed.

During the nine months while my application to visit the Soviet Union was processed in Moscow, I spoke to nearly 200 former intelligence officers, ex-agents, émigré leaders and experts in Europe and North America. Compartmentalisation of information, an essential prerequisite for security, meant that those individuals who had served in SIS, the CIA and for West German, Swedish and Finnish intelligence organisations were aware only of that aspect of the saga which directly affected their personal work. While all knew that SIS's and the CIA's operations had ended in disaster, and most could corroborate some names and details, no one in the West understood the whole picture.

Accordingly, when in November 1988 the Soviet government allowed me access to captured and surviving SIS and CIA agents and to senior officers of the KGB's Second Chief Directorate in the Soviet Republics of Latvia and Lithuania, I knew precisely the names of those whom I wanted to interview. I also knew some details of their activities.

With the support at BBC Television of Paul Hamann and Colin Cameron, I visited the Baltic States three times, checking and re-checking the accounts given by both sides in what transpired to be an extraordinary KGB deception operation. On both sides of the Iron Curtain some questions, however, remained frustratingly unanswered. Sometimes the reason given was 'security'; on other occasions that the only possible source who could provide the information was dead. Moreover, as in all human affairs, after forty years memories were selective, prejudiced or merely confused. In the spy world's 'wilderness of mirrors', perceptions can be as valuable as informed speculation and generalities are invariably as close to the truth as the most tenacious researcher can come. Nevertheless, what follows, with all its unprecedented detail, is accurate.

I could not have completed this book without the encouragement and friendship of two individuals. Michael Shaw, my agent, was generously interested and enthusiastic. My wife Veronica endured the solitariness which a writer imposes on a spouse with exemplary humour.

London
June 1989

Boundaries since 1946

One

BIRTH OF A CRUSADE

A lifetime of secrecy and professional solitude had conditioned Harry Carr to be exceptionally untroubled in the closing struggle of his life. Like most who have reached the age of eighty-eight, the final days bore vicarious familiarity. He had always understood that disciplined discretion was a professional qualification. Nevertheless, even for the brave, anticipating the end is often accompanied by recriminations, and in Carr's case they were more vehement than is usual – although most of his visitors were oblivious to his anger.

Cooped up in a cream-painted bedroom on the second floor of a genteel Surrey retirement home with an undistinguished view through the small window, the man who described himself in *Who's Who* as a former Passport Control Officer and a First Secretary in the British Foreign Service had surrounded himself with the memorabilia of a lifetime: a silver icon; a few watercolours of desolate landscapes; a pair of shirt cuffs (a personal gift from Prokofiev who had painted the landscape at a family picnic); photographs of people in snow scenes; and a clutch of silver tennis trophies in a glass-cased chiffonier. Inevitably and instinctively the souvenirs revealed nothing about Carr's forty years as an employee of the British government, although a discerning visitor might have noticed that his few books suggested an unusual preoccupation with the British intelligence services.

Throughout his stay in the retirement home, Carr had

disdained all but the most perfunctory contact with his fellow residents. Occasionally, wafting through his firmly closed door, they caught a scratched recording of pre-revolutionary Russian folk ballads sung by an old favourite, Pyotr Leschenko, but that barely afforded a reliable clue to the past of this meticulous hypochrondriac. Even when two fresh-faced but presentable young men had arrived unexpectedly from his old firm in order, as they explained, to fill in some of the gaps which had been belatedly discovered in the personal account of his activities, they encountered a polite but immovable stonewall. By arrangement, as his rationality irretrievably ebbed, other representatives of the firm returned during his last days. Both were cleaners carrying out the final checks for any revelatory documents carelessly abandoned among his private possessions: an unnecessary chore considering the subject, but an obligatory routine. Understandably, if somewhat tactlessly, they used the opportunity for a final attempt to complete his service record. But their attempt was as unsuccessful as their predecessors'.

When Henry Lambton Carr died peacefully on 19 March 1988 he intentionally bequeathed a selected vacuum. For forty years, as one of the founder members of the Secret Intelligence Service, he had waged a personal and clandestine war against Soviet Russia, for the last fifteen years alongside his 'cousins' from America. Instinctively he believed that it was best to leave the accounts unsettled, since although history recorded that his obsession for security was betrayed and his victories undermined, he remained steadfastly convinced of personal successes which he was nevertheless unwilling to explain. Carr's death cut the last links with those earliest operations.

Carr was born on 28 November 1899 in Archangel near the Czarist capital of St Petersburg. His father, the manager of five British-owned timber mills, was enjoying the fanciful and lush life of an expatriate – a large house on

2

Moses Island which boasted a unique grass tennis court, seemingly unlimited servants and constant socialising – while proudly preaching jingoistic patriotism for his distant homeland. In that long-forgotten era, thousands of British, German and French families lived near the Baltic Sea, managing and earning sizeable fortunes from factories, estates and banks in capitalist Russia. Like most of the nations of Europe and America, Russia had long attracted investment from generations of entrepreneurs. Their successors were reaping the profits, with the additional bonus that Russia's poverty enabled the Westerners to enjoy living standards akin to those of the white man under the British Raj. Carr's last image of that opulent life style was in 1914 when, at the outbreak of war, he returned to Haileybury College in England – hence among the memorabilia in his room was a Haileybury rugby cap, testimony to his passion for and excellence in the sport. As captain of the undefeated school rugby team, Carr symbolised that cadre of Englishmen whose subsequent career never quite matched up to his school days. Too young to be recruited for the trenches in France, he spent the war at school, cut off from his family but confident about his own security and his family's sanctuary, hundreds of miles behind the eastern front.

That illusion was shattered in 1917; not by the ever-escalating losses across the Channel, but by the Bolshevik revolution and the overthrow of the Romanov dynasty. While most Britons discussed the Kaiser's intentions and mourned the news from France, Carr puzzled about the implications of the tumult in Russia. The newspaper accounts were perfunctory but the revolutionaries' challenge to the very foundations of Western capitalism was indisputable. As he completed his training in the Royal Artillery, Lloyd George was recruiting loyal and dedicated volunteers prepared to undertake a mission to reverse history. Carr took the opportunity and returned to Russia in 1919 as a member of an army which was seeking to overthrow the communists. Like so many of the founding officers of the Secret Intelligence Service,

3

Carr's whole life was influenced by that venture. At the close of their careers, Carr and his generation would concede that their foe had been underrated.

Until Czar Nicholas II abdicated in March 1917, the British government, like that of France and America, preoccupied by the pressing problems of the war on the western front, had ignored the flurry of signals which warned of the impending revolution in Russia. Only in the aftermath were the causes and consequent implications belatedly recognised but, even then, the reaction in the three Western capitals was slow and confused – the casualty of inadequate information and lack of sympathy for the deposed regime. On Lloyd George's instructions, some money was sent to Aleksandr Kerensky, the new Prime Minister, but further support was withheld until an American-financed agent, the author W. Somerset Maugham, travelling via Japan and Vladivostok, could investigate and report. After meeting Kerensky, and confirming that his position was desperate, Maugham returned to Britain with the beleaguered Russian's plea for increased aid. Lloyd George's refusal did not reach Petrograd before Kerensky resigned and on 8 November was replaced by Lenin and the Bolsheviks.

Although that news was startling, the British Cabinet was more horrified by reports that just days after seizing power the new Soviet leader had opened peace negotiations with the Germans. The consequences for the Western Allies of an armistice on the eastern front were easily calculable. The German armies could be concentrated in the west for the new offensive and, if the new Soviet government collapsed, were perfectly poised to fill the vacuum at the expense of Britain's considerable investments. Lloyd George's attempts to persuade the Bolsheviks to continue the war failed. On 3 March 1918, the Bolsheviks and Germans signed a peace treaty at Brest Litovsk. Under its terms, the new rulers of Russia renounced their historical claims to Finland, the three Baltic States, Poland and the Ukraine. German troops consolidated their occupation of all these areas. It would be the subsequent Soviet attempts to reverse Lenin's renunciation which laid the battleground for many of Carr's intrigues over the next forty years.

On 6 March 1918, the Allies took their first preventive measure. One hundred and thirty British marines were dispatched to Russia under Major General C. Maynard – the advance party of what later would be described as the North Russian Expeditionary Force. Although ostensibly the soldiers were to guard the huge military stores supplied by the Allies to the Czarist armies and provide a tripwire against any German attempt to invade northern Russia, there were some in London, in particular Winston Churchill, who were already speaking about using the British soldiers as the nucleus of a future force to overthrow the Bolsheviks.

Although Churchill's was still a minority voice, especially since the British soldiers had landed in Murmansk with Trotsky's agreement, Churchill was imbued with the history of the empire. Russia was Britain's traditional rival in Asia, a source of constant conflict along the Indian frontier and in the oil-rich territories of the Middle East. For the young politician, Lenin's public pledges to spread the communist revolution throughout the Western world echoed Disraeli's fear of a 'great, gigantic, colossal, growing Russia'. The Bolsheviks, Churchill argued, would cause more aggravation than the Czars. Their removal was vital to safeguard Britain's rich investments, especially an investment which had just been obtained in Russia itself.

Coinciding with the arrival of the first contingent of British troops, Major General Frederick Poole, whose wartime responsibility was to supervise the Allied supplies, had successfully completed secret negotiations to purchase a controlling interest in all the major Russian banks. The British War Cabinet judged the purchase to be a brilliant coup because the Russian economy would be effectively British-owned. The single-minded confidence which characterised the Cabinet's interest in these negotiations in the midst of war confirmed the certainty in

5

London that the Bolshevik coup was a passing hiccup until proper government was restored. To the British, the priority in the east was to block a German advance into Russia while British agents in Moscow could mount a successful counter-coup to remove the troublesome Red rabble whose perilous control, exercised in the face of chaos and the developing civil war, extended barely beyond the capital.

Over previous centuries, a successful coda for creating and sustaining the British empire had been the deployment of astute political agents in key areas to purchase the support of dissident groups to fight against Britain's competitors. Covert action had been a cheap and effective substitute for military engagement. In 1918, there was every reason for the British government to resort to these well-rehearsed tactics and support the anti-Soviet resistance.

One of the several architects of the counter-coup was Captain Francis Cromie, the Assistant Naval Attaché who had accumulated one million pounds in cash to finance any suitable conspiracies. During the previous year, Cromie, working with other British officers and agents, had created a network of Russian sailors and workers who in return for bribes would, on British orders, flood mines, blow up munitions dumps and scuttle the Russian fleets in the Baltic and Black Sea. Officially the plan was conceived to deny to the Germans any advantages of an unopposed invasion. But unannounced and gradually co-existent with that strategy was the British intention that the same network should also be used to deny those vital facilities to the Bolsheviks. The diplomats' allies in the various plots were an uneasy coalition of various nationalist groups, eager to exploit the disintegration of Russia's centralised rule to assert their own independence, and the Czarists. For general purposes, they were known as White Russians.

Cromie's activities were supplemented by a succession of agents dispatched from London by Sir Mansfield Cumming, the head of SIS, whose broad remit was to exploit

6

any opportunity to oust the revolutionaries. The activities of three agents in particular – Sidney Reilly, Captain George Hill and Paul Dukes – combined with the presence in Moscow of the senior British representative, Robert Bruce Lockhart, rightly convinced the Bolsheviks by 1919 that SIS was their most potent enemy. That impression persisted for nearly forty years.

Reilly, who was originally called Sigmund Rosenbaum, was a linguist, adventurer and entrepreneur who had earned a fortune as an arms dealer before and during the Great War, and in the process had forged a successful relationship with SIS. At the time of the Bolshevik coup in 1917, Reilly was visiting St Petersburg as a commission agent and was quick to exploit the chaos. Blessed with a marked ability to pose convincingly in many guises (he presented himself alternately as a Turkish and Greek merchant and as a Russian Cheka commissar), he won access to Trotsky's office in the Foreign Ministry. What he saw confirmed his loathing of what he described as the 'hideous cancer' of communism. Eagerly he accepted SIS's new offer to undertake any plot which would topple the communists from power. His codename was ST1.

Since the vast expanse of the Russian empire was by then enveloped in civil war, it was entirely realistic to contemplate a successful anti-Bolshevik coup. Through Bruce Lockhart, the British government's official representative to the revolutionary government, Reilly met a group of Latvian officers, members of Lenin's bodyguard, who were ready to betray the Soviet leader. While that plot gestated, Reilly began simultaneously to plot with Cromie, on orders from London, to destroy the Russian fleet in the Baltic. Amid indiscretions, *agents provocateurs* and double-dealing, Reilly's activities did not long go unnoticed by the Cheka, the new Soviet secret service and successor to the Okhrana.

In the three decades before the communist revolution, the imperial government had expanded the Okhrana to monitor the explosion of radical and revolutionary Russians living and plotting in exile. Okhrana agents

7

penetrated, provoked and neutralised many communists and their organisations exiled in Western Europe (and allegedly even planted an agent in Lenin's household, although to no avail). During the halcyon days after the revolution, Lenin ordered the disbandment of the Okhrana as symbolic of the despised Czarist regime, but soon approved its replacement by the Cheka.

The founder of the new Soviet secret service, the 'All Russian Extraordinary Commission for combating counter-revolution and sabotage', was Feliks Dzerzhinsky, a Pole. Dzerzhinsky's staff were inbued with his robust guidance: 'We stand for organised terror . . . The Cheka must defend the revolution and conquer the enemy even if its sword falls occasionally on the heads of the innocent.' The interpretation of Dzerzhinsky's exhortations by his staff – 'The Cheka does not judge, it strikes' – left little to the imagination, especially after 25 July when the Soviets announced the death of the Czar. Ekaterinburg, the scene of the murder of the whole imperial family, was captured by Whites on the same day. The graphic accounts of the Whites' discoveries in the cellar of the royal prison encouraged the West's revulsion for the communists. Those murders were a mere foretaste of Dzerzhinsky's methods.

On 31 August one plot, probably linked to Reilly, materialised. Dora Kaplan, a socialist, fired two shots at Lenin, hitting her target in the lung and neck. Lenin barely survived. Hours later, Cheka agents burst into the British Embassy, shot and killed Cromie, and embarked upon an orgy of killing imprisoned Czarist officers and their sympathisers. Reilly escaped to Britain, but Bruce Lockhart was arrested. He was subsequently released in exchange for the Soviet representative, Maxim Litvinov, who, as a precaution, had been arrested in London. The future relationship between the Cheka and SIS was cast.

Although Reilly's plot had backfired, the British government, in common with most Western observers, remained convinced that Lenin's regime would soon collapse, the victim of chaos, destitution, famine, plague, and the White Russian armies which were assembling in Finland, Siberia and southern Russia, preparing to advance towards Moscow and Petrograd. In June, a further 600 British soldiers had landed in Murmansk. Viewed from Moscow, where the Soviet leaders had established a new capital to avoid the possibility of capture by the Germans or the Allies, the British explanation of the Expeditionary Force's arrival for mere guard duties bore little credibility. Recovering from the assassination attempt, and deluded that a huge and hostile army was encamped in the north, Lenin feared that British troops would soon be approaching the Kremlin.

The British contingent suggested less of a threat to the American diplomat George Kennan who watched their disembarkation, commenting that they were 'almost all . . . of a physical category so low as to render them unfit for duty in France'. Lloyd George would have added that they were equally valueless in Russia but had been dispatched for political rather than military reasons. Whatever the Bolsheviks believed, politicians in London could not agree whether the revolution should be contained or destroyed, but no minister was minded to stop the slide towards support for the Whites against the Reds. Finance was the biggest obstacle and the easiest solution was to unearth allies.

Potentially the most realisable ally were two divisions of Czech soldiers, about 70,000 men, who until 1917 had been fighting with the Czar's armies against the Germans. Although they were travelling home via Vladivostok, Lloyd George hoped to divert them back towards Murmansk to come under British command. Guaranteeing the Czech's safety became the pretext for all subsequent landings of Allied troops.

A second source of fit combat troops was America. Lord Reading, the British Ambassador in Washington, began urging President Wilson to commit himself to the uncertain notion of containing the Bolshevik revolution. The obstacle was the President's Fourteen Principles which encompassed non-interfernce in other nations' affairs. Nevertheless, Wilson was persuaded to send 150 American marines to Murmansk, although strictly for guard duties. On arrival, without referring back to Washington, the local officers ignored his orders and placed themselves under General Maynard's command. They were posted to the front, allegedly to forestall the German advance, but the British plans were changing substantially.

On 1 August, an Allied flotilla under General Poole approached Archangel, then held by the Bolsheviks. Soon after disembarkation, British soldiers exchanged shots with communist defenders who later fled. Poole was welcomed by the White Russians who had taken heart from reports that the Red Army was retreating both in Siberia and in the south, and that Moscow lay undefended against the counter-revolutionary armies. While Trotsky sought conscripts, President Wilson reluctantly authorised the dispatch of reinforcements: 4,500 US infantrymen, engineers and medics were to sail for Murmansk. Other American forces were to be dispatched to Siberia to assist 72,000 Japanese troops and a battalion of British infantrymen who had landed in Vladivostok, also allegedly to protect the two Czech divisions.

In the midst of these announcements and deployments, the Allies launched on 8 August a massive and successful counter-attack on the western front, which brought an end to the Kaiser's ambitions and the original excuse for dispatching Allied troops to Russia. Ignoring the new situation, on their own initiative General Maynard's officers began recruiting Russian irregulars to fight the Bolsheviks.

In London, as the war ended, Cabinet ministers began focusing on Soviet Russia. The unanimity which Lenin imagined was uniting ministers and their military advisers to order a direct attack on Moscow did not materialise. At their first critical discussion on 13 November, two days after the armistice, to decide whether Britain intended to crush the revolution, a small group of ministers gathered with Rear-Admiral 'Blinker' Hall at the Foreign Office to consider the options presented by General Sir Henry Wilson, the Chief of the General Imperial Staff. Wilson was forthright. Either Britain should 'grasp the nettle firmly' and dispatch several divisions to Russia, which might be difficult in the same week as the greatest blood-bath in the world's history had come to an end; or Britain should 'do all we can in the way of material to give our friends a fair start, and then withdraw'.

Churchill, on the eve of his appointment as Secretary of State for War, led the hawks against the 'poison peril'. His banner had been raised two weeks earlier by Lord Robert Cecil, the Parliamentary Under-Secretary at the Foreign Office, who suggested that the contingent based in Russia should spearhead a Western 'crusade against Bolshevism'. Churchill's sensational language, for what became dubbed 'Mr Churchill's Private War', identified the politician ever after as a sworn enemy of Bolshevism: 'Russia,' he said, 'is being rapidly reduced by the Bolsheviks to an animal form of barbarism . . . The Bolsheviks maintain themselves by bloody and wholesale butcheries and murders . . . Civilisation is being completely extinguished over gigantic areas.' He urged the Cabinet to 'break up their power', using a massive multinational intervention army, because otherwise the Allies would 'come away from the Peace Conference rejoicing in a victory which was no victory'. Although by the end of 1918 there were 180,000 foreign troops on Russian soil and the area held by the Bolsheviks was still comparatively small, none of the senior Cabinet members supported Churchill's aggressive proposals. Lloyd George led the condemnation of the 'mad enterprise' which in his view 'would cause a revolution' in Britain. But Churchill was adamant. Hearing that the Prime Minister was even considering negotiating with the new regime, he rushed to Downing Street and told his leader, 'one might as well legalise sodomy as recognise the Bolsheviks'. He vehemently denounced Lenin's atrocities and pogroms as the consequence of 'a phial containing a culture of typhoid or of cholera to be poured into the water supply of a great city'. But the

Prime Minister was as equivocal as his minister was critical.

Faced with a dilemma, the politicians opted to fudge. Some extra British troops would be sent to Archangel; troops, advisers and supplies would be dispatched to General Anton Deniken who was leading the anti-Bolshevik armies in the south; and a detachment of soldiers would be posted to guard the rail line between the Black Sea and Caspian Sea. In the ensuing weeks, 4,000 British troops were sent to Archangel, bringing the total to 6,300 (as opposed to 5,200 Americans), and their numbers would soon increase to 18,400. That compromise was subject to very different interpretations. While the Foreign Office believed that Britain should not interfere in the internal affairs of Russia but nevertheless feared that a withdrawal of British troops would send the wrong signals, others believed that the decision was a commitment to destroy the Bolsheviks.

Among those who arrived at Murmansk in 1919 was 19-year-old Harry Carr, who had managed to find a route back to Russia and a chance to serve in the army. Recruited by the War Office as an interpreter, he was attached to General Maynard's staff and within days was introduced to the inner sanctum of British machinations. Six weeks after his arrival, his father approached the Expedition's new commander, General Edmund Ironside, and secured his son's transfer to the headquarters at Archangel and reunion with his family.

Interpreters were members of the army's Intelligence Section and Ironside's headquarters relied more than usual upon spies and purveyors of information. The general's ADC was Colin Gubbins who, twenty years later, would become a founder of the Special Operations Executive, SOE. Travelling daily with Ironside, Carr was initiated into the profession of secrecy.

Russia at that moment still seemed to be on the verge of disintegration. The Red Army was besieged on three fronts and the majority of non-Russian races from Siberia to the Baltic had proclaimed their independence. In the

12

Crimea and Ukraine, the Cossacks, Georgians, Armenians and Azerbaijanis had all staked claims for statehood; while the Lithuanians, Latvians and Estonians had taken advantage of the Brest-Litovsk Treaty to appeal to the West for recognition of their nationhood, a request which was promptly satisfied by Britain and America.

Amid vivid reports of communist atrocities and the gruesome threats of worse to come from the revolutionary leaders, Carr witnessed the fabric of his adopted homeland disintegrate. Scornful of Ironside's condemnation of the White Russians as 'the riff-raff of Tsarism . . . who want other people to save Russia for them', he cast his fate with Churchill's forebodings of the communist menace.

In London, the new Secretary for War, ignoring the Prime Minister's equivocations, had launched his crusade to destroy the Bolsheviks. Churchill's directive to Major General H.G. Holman, Commander of the British Mission to Deniken's army in the Don, had been specific that the purpose of intervention was to destroy the revolution. Churchill ordered that an RAF squadron, two tank corps and howitzers be shipped to the Crimea to support Deniken's forces.

As they arrived, a naval squadron under Admiral Sir Walter Cowan sailed into the Baltic. In Cabinet, Arthur Balfour, the Foreign Secretary, argued resolutely that Britain's moral obligation prevented the nation from abandoning those Russians who had been 'loyal' to the Allied cause and were now fighting for their lives. 'I have been pressing the Admiralty for some time to put on a show of force in the Baltic,' said Balfour, 'to strengthen the populations of that part of the world against Bolshevism.'

Admiral Cowan's orders, which effectively placed Britain at war with Russia, were to blockade the Russian fleet in Kronstadt. In the discharge of his duty, Cowan intercepted a Soviet naval attack on the Estonian port of Tallinn, sinking several Russian ships; covered Estonian and Finnish soldiers as they infiltrated behind the

13

Bolshevik lines; landed British troops in Latvia to secure that nation's independence; and protected General Sir Hubert Gough's Allied Military Mission in Finland which was seeking to organise the White Russians under the command of General Nikolai Yudenitch, who were planning to cross the Gulf of Finland and capture St Petersburg.

Before leaving London, Gough had been briefed at the Foreign Office not to interfere in Russian affairs. That stricture was contradicted at the War Office by Churchill who, pacing in front of a huge map showing the White Russian armies converging on Moscow, urged the soldier to hasten their victory. Gough followed Churchill's orders but on his arrival was confronted with stark limitations. The new Baltic governments refused to support the Allied crusade against Bolshevism, fearing that it would jeopardise winning Lenin's recognition of their independence, and dealing with Yudenitch proved gruelling. Like most Czarists, the general was reactionary and too willing to co-operate with the German armies, led by prototype Nazis, who still occupied the Baltic States.

In the winter of 1919, the battle for Russia was in stalemate but political attitudes had hardened. Those in the Kremlin harboured no doubts that the British government and SIS were intent on their forcible removal, a realistic view considering a speech delivered by Admiral Hall to his senior staff on the eve of his retirement as Director of Naval Intelligence: 'I want to give you a word of warning. Hard and bitter as the battle has been, we now have to face a far, far more ruthless foe. A foe that is hydra-headed and whose evil power will spread over the whole world. That foe is Soviet Russia.'

Churchill's Russophobia and his conviction that special operations was a method of military and political warfare particularly suited to the British, encouraged Sir Mansfield Cummings to take bold risks to accomplish Lenin's demise.

In 1919, Paul Dukes, one of Reilly's replacements in Russia, who had infiltrated into Bolshevik Russia from Murmansk in 1918, was anxious to escape. For the

14

previous ten months, posing often as a Red Army soldier or even as a Cheka agent, and in liaison with the Czarist White Army, Dukes had passed information to London through Helsinki. But Dukes' cover had been blown and he had become the target of a particularly widespread Cheka manhunt. To extricate his agent, Cumming organised a rendezvous on the Baltic coast with Captain Augustus Agar, who was waiting with two specially converted speedboats.

In the weeks while he was moored in a Finnish inlet opposite the Kronstadt naval base, Agar had obtained a torpedo from Cowan's squadron and successfully sank the *Oleg*, a Russian cruiser. Impressed by his bravery and the audacity of the operation, Cowan launched a combined operation of British bombers and a flotilla of coastal motorboats against the Russian fleet in the port. The Russian losses – two battleships sunk and the submarine depot in ruins – provoked an anti-Bolshevik mutiny, causing renewed fears in Moscow and earning Churchill's praise.

On their separate return to Britain, both Agar and Dukes were fêted as heroes. Both received an audience with King George V; Dukes dined with Churchill and was subsequently knighted, while Agar was awarded the VC. But theirs was a pyhrric victory. In summer 1919, the counter-revolution began to sour.

Suffering from gross mismanagement and inadequate British support, Yudenitch's attack from Finland, which had penetrated the suburbs of Petrograd, ended in a bloody rout. In Siberia, the White Russian advance towards Moscow, despite American, Japanese and Czech support, barely progressed before it, too, ended in disaster. 'A not very creditable enterprise,' wrote Lord Hardinge in the Foreign Office minutes as the last British and American troops withdrew. In the south, the advance by General Deniken's army to within 200 miles of Moscow halted abruptly. Ineptness and corruption among his own staff, combined with widespread pogroms against Jews in the towns which were captured, sapped his army of

15

self-confidence and credibility among the accompanying British and French officers. His army began an irretrievable retreat towards the Crimea.

In the north, Ironside's armies mutinied and many Russians deserted to the Bolsheviks. Carr interpreted for the commission investigating the murder of British officers. The general's order for withdrawal was completed by 27 September and all the Allies' impulsive and half-hearted plans for toppling the Bolshevik regime ended ignominiously. Britain had spent more on the anti-Bolshevik crusade than all the other Allies put together. In the post mortem, Lloyd George would claim credit for securing the independence of the Baltic States and Finland, and the chance of independence for the Russian nationalities. Churchill philosophised that the powers would regret their failure 'to crush the Bolshevist peril at its centre before it had grown too strong'. Both Foreign Office officials and the generals who returned from Russia agreed that the brutality and totalitarian traits of White Russian generals with whom they had fought 'were no different from the Bolsheviks'. In autumn 1920, 150,000 White Russians, the remnants of Deniken's army, plagued by disease and chaos, were evacuated with British help to Gallipoli. They dispersed around the world, where they would be sought by Western intelligence agencies to become agents in the continuing battle to undermine the communist regime.

Among those Britons evacuated with Ironside were Carr and his family. In common with so many admirers of the Russian people, Carr's fastidious character and conservatism were offended by the anarchy introduced by the Red revolution. By the time Ironside's army had destroyed its equipment and abandoned its mission, Carr was imbued with an impassioned fear and loathing of the bloodshed and chaos caused by the Bolsheviks. And Carr harboured an additional personal grievance: his family's entire savings, deposited in a Russian bank, had been lost for ever; his father was unemployed and comparatively impoverished. Not unnaturally, the younger Carr was attracted to any course of action that offered the chance to settle accounts and escape unemployment.

On demobilisation, Carr had started a course to learn typing and shorthand, an accurate indication of his intelligence and abilities. His prospects seemed limited until his father coincidentally met at a club George Wiskeman, the former British Vice-Consul in Archangel. Wiskeman inquired about the young Carr's employment and suggested that he might be interested in becoming a translator at the British Consulate in Helsinki.

Carr was summoned for an interview in Charing Cross. The venue was a shop with sacks of coal in the window. He was met by Riley Le May who introduced him to Commander Ernest Boyce. Their conversation at the rear of the shop concentrated on his background and languages. Carr left the interview without any notion that Boyce had been SIS's representative in Russia during the war. His ignorance was not cured when he was introduced to Mansfield Cumming in 'C's' flat in Whitehall Court, near the War Office. The Chief of the Secret Intelligence Service's offer of limited job security and the low income of £500 per year, rising to £750, did not deter the 21-year-old from joining. Carr would confess sixty-seven years later that it was only after some days, translating agents' reports in the back room of the Passport Control Office in Helsinki, that he realised the real nature of his duties.

Carr, like most early SIS officers, considered earnings unimportant. While some enjoyed a private income sufficient to render immaterial the monthly remittance, Carr and others were motivated by a sense of service which would make them, albeit briefly, legends in their own lifetimes. A few months after his appointment, however, the precariousness of his status was revealed when he witnessed Cumming, in the midst of a row with Vernon Kell, the head of MI5, swipe at Kell's head with his detached wooden leg. It was symbolic of SIS's struggle to survive with a fifty per cent reduction in its budget.

With Reilly, Bruce Lockhart and Dukes out of Russia, gathering intelligence about the Bolsheviks became especially perilous. Foreigners were under constant surveillance and even the diplomats' opportunities were restricted after the consulates in Leningrad and Odessa were closed by the Soviet government. Accordingly, Cumming sought allies in neighbouring countries, from the Baltic down to the Black Sea, to establish bases for his agents. Placing those employees depended upon agreement with the Foreign Office whose traditionalists were adamantly hostile to the misuse of diplomatic cover. Spies, they complained, would compromise the diplomats' integrity. The solution was the creation of a Passport Control Office (PCO) within the Foreign Office whose officials would enjoy neither diplomatic status nor the benefits of government pay and pensions. Members of the SIS would be attached to the PCO and were to be paid in cash to avoid any trace of their employment, even by the Inland Revenue – a fiction which was unlikely to deceive those who were intended to be misled. They would be tolerated by the Ambassador as long as they confined their activities exclusively to events in neighbouring countries.

Although Whitehall's rivalries barely affected Carr, there was among the officers who were recruited in 1919–20 a batch of like-minded young men who had all grown up in Russia and possessed an understanding of that nation and its people which bolstered confidence in their own professionalism. Following Churchill's example, they were committed to the view that the British empire was in peril unless communism was defeated. Spurred on to attack the Bolsheviks, their only potential allies were the White Russians, now exiled but who claimed to have established lines of communication to stay-behind networks of their own agents inside Russia. The most important of these émigré groups whom Cumming would agree to finance, on Reilly's advice, was led by Boris Savinkov, a passionate anti-communist, militarist, assassin and professional conspirator whom Churchill described in emotional terms after a meeting arranged by Reilly in 1922: 'His being was organised upon a theme: the freedom

18

of the Russian people. In that cause, there was nothing he would not dare or endure.' According to Reilly, Savinkov was among the 'two or three people during whose lifetime the Bolsheviki [sic] will never sleep in peace'. Perpetually dressed in a formal black frock coat and patent leather boots, and displaying a frigidly polite manner, Savinkov dispatched agents across the Polish and Finnish frontiers into Soviet Russia to organise intelligence cells and return with information. SIS's liaison officer with Savinkov was Commander Boyce, who had recruited Carr. After the debacle of 1920, Boyce had divided his time between Tallinn and Paris to maintain contacts with the White Russians, but in 1921, as the importance of Finland as a base for operations inside the Soviet Union grew, he had transferred to Helsinki.

Finland had only been an independent nation since 1917, when it took advantage of the October revolution and ended one century of Russian occupation. The Finnish proclamation of independence provoked a brief but fierce civil war ending in the defeat of the pro-Bolsheviks by Marshal Carl von Mannerheim who immediately permitted other anti-Bolsheviks to use the country to launch raids against the revolutionaries. Despite the sharp reduction in SIS's budget, the Helsinki station had been allocated £20,000 per year for operations, and the formal appointment of an Assistant Passport Officer – Harry Carr. In March 1921 Carr was at the heart of Britain's attempts to topple the Bolsheviks and was about to be exposed to the most salutary lesson which any aspiring intelligence officer could hope to receive.

Carr's appointment coincided with the signing of a trade agreement between the British and Soviet governments, the first formal British recognition of the Bolshevik state. Although the agreement included an undertaking by both governments to cease hostile intelligence activities, the provision was ignored. Both the War Office and the Admiralty identified Russian aggression as Britain's most serious threat and 'The most probable [cause of] war in the near future in which the British Empire might be engaged'. In these circumstances, SIS was unlikely to abide by the agreement, but the service was handicapped both by a lack of informants and an embarrassing exposé of two SIS operations against the Soviets.

Soon after the Baltic States had signed peace treaties with Lenin's representatives in 1920 which recognised their sovereignty, SIS obtained premises in Riga not far from the huge Embassy on Rainis Boulevard. In an atmosphere of relative security, a succession of passport officers and military attachés working with White Russian refugees could operate, with the eager help of the Latvian police and military, against the communists across the border. The British Embassy became a well-known hub for collecting information and a base for British officers to learn Russian. Leslie Nicholson, who became SIS station chief in Riga in the thirties, recalled that the town was 'a hotbed of intrigue . . . the venue of dozens of unscrupulous agents of all nationalities who would sell their services to the highest bidder – with little compunction, at a later date, in passing the same information to the opposition, though at an increased price'.

A similar potentially fruitful network was established in Tallinn by Colonel Robert F. Meiklejohn, a former Royal Warwickshire Regiment officer who had served in the intervention army. In 1921, Meiklejohn recruited as an agent a Volga German called 'Gregory' who claimed to have access to the secret codes at the Soviet Embassy which was under the control of Maxim Litvinov. With glowing satisfaction, Meiklejohn sent London nearly 200 'paraphrases' of Litvinov's cables which seemed to suggest that, contrary to the trade agreement, the Soviets were financing Sinn Fein in Ireland and anti-colonialist agitators in India. For the British government, then faced with unrest in both countries, the reports confirmed their suspicions. But before a protest could be delivered, SIS's search for corroboration among decoded intercepts of other cables proved Meiklejohn's purchase to be forgeries.

The discovery intensified the pressure upon Cumming

to produce intelligence, which the government was convinced existed, to prove that the Soviets were in fact organising and financing an increasing number of anti-British agitators, particularly in India. Evidently with some relief, Cumming received from the SIS agent in Berlin a copy of a document purportedly stolen from the office of the Soviet representative which confirmed a Soviet plot to destabilise British rule in the sub-continent. Promptly, on the orders of the Foreign Office, the British representative in Moscow handed over the incriminating evidence with a strong protest. The reply was delivered with equally impressive speed. The document, the Russians proved, was merely a copy of a White Russian propaganda sheet distributed in Germany.

At precisely that moment a potential new source of information for SIS presented himself. Aleksandr Yakushev, a canal engineer, arrived in Tallinn from Moscow. Yakushev was known to the White Russians as an executive member of a monarchist underground group. Travelling from Tallinn to Berlin and Paris, Yakushev cautiously approached the leaders of the important White Russian émigrés and explained that across the border in Russia the foundations had been laid for a powerful anti-communist organisation to destroy the 'Forces of Darkness'. The Moscow Municipal Credit Association, explained Yakushev, was a new bank, established by the communists for international business. But unknown to the Bolsheviks, monarchists using the cover name the 'Trust' had already infiltrated the bank. Although some émigré leaders were suspicious of Yakushev, others were encouraged by his reports of resistance. Their admiration for their informant increased as they witnessed the ease with which he could travel across the frontier, bringing information and messages that Bolshevism was struggling to survive. As the flow of information continued, the émigrés also realised the virtue of exploiting their new asset to establish a stronger political position. The products of their network were offered to SIS and other Western intelligence agencies. It was a fortuitous moment.

21

With SIS's own sources discredited, Cumming was easily attracted by the enticing prospects offered by Yakushev. Those who urged caution were assured that the Polish, French and Finnish intelligence services had all accepted the Trust's credibility. As presented by the White Russians and confirmed by Boyce, the Trust was the West's exclusive source of reliable intelligence about conditions inside Russia.

However, unknown to the exiles, Yakushev had, just months before his first arrival in Tallinn, been arrested, incarcerated in the Lubyanka and released only after Dzerzhinsky had skilfully persuaded the engineer to become a Bolshevik agent. Dzerzhinsky's quest was to penetrate the White Russian organisations which were plotting a counter-revolution in the West.

For the Soviet Politburo, the one million Russian exiles and especially the organised remnants of Deniken's army still seemed a potent threat. The Bolsheviks had good reason to recall the Czar's fears that those beyond his borders were inspiring sabotage and chaos inside Russia. 'We are watching this second Russia,' wrote V. Triandafilov, a senior Cheka official in 1922. The Cheka's tactics were the same as those of the Czar's Okhrana. The bank and the 'Trust' were especially created by Feliks Dzerzhinsky to penetrate the exiles' groups.

Yakushev's principal target was Boris Savinkov who had cultivated Baron Piotr Wrangel, a ruthless but effective general who, out of the rump of Deniken's army, had fashioned a paramilitary combat organisation based in Paris, numbering 15,000–20,000 men, which was led by General Aleksandr Kutyepov. With singular dedication, Kutyepov was training young émigrés for military action against the communists and clandestine activities inside Russia. His activities simultaneously stimulated the hopes of the exiles and the attention of the Cheka. During 1923, Yakushev regularly met Kutyepov, convinced the émigré of the Trust's resources, and gradually developed a close relationship with Boris Savinkov.

By 1924, when the Trust had become Savinkov's and

SIS's prime source of information, Savinkov received a series of messages from his contacts inside Russia that the conditions were ideal for a counter-coup and that the Trust had assembled an armed and influential anti-Bolshevik network which he should lead. Although wary, Savinkov, after conferring with Boyce, accepted the invitation and travelled with Yakushev to the Soviet border. Soon after crossing, he was arrested. News of his fate, with reports of his confessions of guilt at a show trial, soon reached the West. Savinkov was even made available for interviews by Western journalists but the circumstances of his arrest were not revealed. Six months after his trial, the Soviets announced his suicide in the Lubyanka prison.

Sidney Reilly was devastated by the news. The year before he had successfully sold to SIS a letter allegedly written by Grigori Zinoviev, the president of the Communist International in Moscow, to the British Communist Party. The letter instructed the party's members to prepare for the revolution against the British government. Endorsed as authentic by Cumming, the Foreign Office and even the Labour Prime Minister, the letter's publication in the *Daily Mail* had swept the Tories to power on a wave of anti-Red sentiment. In Helsinki, Carr assured the Finnish government of its authenticity. In fact, the letter was a forgery and reconfirmed the Soviet conviction of SIS's perfidy. Reilly's euphoria was crushed by Savinkov's arrest and confessions. For seven years, the Ace of Spies had fought a dangerous but apparently futile war against the communists, seriously depleting his fortune.

When in early 1925 Boyce wrote suggesting that he undertake another operation inside Russia, Reilly was uncharacteristically hesitant to reply. Eventually, after several entreaties, he travelled to Paris to meet Boyce. The SIS officer revealed that representatives of the Trust had provided some tantalising information which was worth pursuing, especially concerning the existence of a blood feud in the Kremlin in the wake of Lenin's death.

23

Despite Savinkov's capture, Boyce told Reilly of his conviction that the Trust was 'a movement of considerable power within Russia'. He needed, however, to ascertain whether the organisation was still reliable. Boyce urged Reilly to make his initial contacts with the Trust's representatives in Helsinki using the good offices of his new assistant, Harry Carr. On 21 September 1925 Reilly arrived in Helsinki and met the 'very intelligent youngster, keen as mustard' who introduced him to Nikolai Bunakov, representing the Trust.

Four days later, any suspicions Reilly might have harboured had clearly been allayed. In a letter to his wife, the spy wrote that 'something really entirely new, powerful and worthwhile' was happening in Russia and ended, 'I am leaving tonight . . . there is absolutely no risk to it.' After bidding Carr farewell, he travelled to the Soviet border to meet a group who introduced themselves as White Russians. Led by Yakushev, the group described the power and success of the Trust and suggested that Reilly travel for three days to Moscow to discuss plans with the Trust's leaders. Accompanied by guides, Reilly waded across the River Sestry into Russia. One week later, *Izvestia* reported the interception and death of three agents on the Russo-Finnish border. Three months later, *The Times* announced Reilly's death. For 'C' and SIS, Reilly's death drew to a close a halcyon era and, worse, discredited them in both the Foreign and War Offices. On the assumption that OGPU (the new version of the Cheka) had extracted from Reilly enough to compromise all of SIS's operations in Russia, Boyce was hastily transferred to Tallinn and then retired, without thanks. His successor in Helsinki, appointed by the new 'C', Hugh 'Quex' Sinclair, was Harry Carr.

Carr had been initiated into the world of espionage by the most potent display of Soviet deception. For although Western intelligence agencies and émigré leaders had been suspicious of the Trust, no one had ever suspected how completely they had been duped. Through the Trust, OGPU had penetrated SIS's operations not only inside

Russia, but also in the Baltic States, Finland and France. Dzerzhinsky's rewards were not only intelligence but also money. The Western intelligence agencies' payments to the Trust had financed many of OGPU's other operations. The indelible lesson for Carr was to place his faith in no one. The Soviets evoked fear and even loathing but their intelligence service demanded respect. For Carr, security implied secrecy, and his pursuit of secrecy would provoke in later years a litany of derision from his colleagues. The man, they would crack at headquarters in Broadway, even suspected his own shadow. Carr remained impervious to their ribaldry. They had not been touched directly by the Trust. Relying upon the émigrés had been costly. Motivated by self-interest and eager to hear information which confirmed their desires, the émigrés, and consequently SIS, had become foolish victims of self-delusion. Security had been compromised and the lessons needed to be drawn. Within Whitehall, SIS was tarnished as amateur and incoherent, lacking the ability properly to analyse the intelligence which it received or critically to question its sources. It was the new generation's task to build entirely new networks free of any connection with tainted sources. Carr and like-minded SIS officers harboured no doubts about their own importance.

Among the cell of young SIS officers recruited with Carr and who became his closest friends were Harold and Archie Gibson. Harold would become head of station in Bucharest and Prague and be credited with managing the most successful spy inside the Soviet Union in the pre-war period. Archie worked at SIS's headquarters, first in Whitehall Court and later when it transferred to Broadway in St James's. A second group were the Sillem brothers who owned a brewery in Estonia, on the border with Russia and Finland, and operated in Riga. A third was Commander Wilfred 'Biffy' Dunderdale, born in 1899 who, based first in Constantinople and then in Paris, managed, in association with the French intelligence service, Kutyepov's group. The batch was nurtured by Quex Sinclair, who was known throughout London as a 'terrific anti-Bolshevik'. Sinclair's conviction about the importance of the battle ahead was inspirational. In a speech on 9 May 1925, Stalin had explicitly identified Britain, the inspiration of the intervention and whose empire still encompassed a quarter of the globe, as Russia's foremost enemy. But Sinclair suffered a handicap. Despite the dedication of his recruits, SIS was consistently outmatched by the opposition.

In 1927 a new crisis erupted in Anglo-Soviet relations. The issue was the renewal of the trade treaty which many Conservative politicians demanded should be cancelled. The Parliamentary debate revealed a legacy of deep suspicion. In the wake of the Zinoviev letter, whose authenticity was still unscathed, politicians clamoured for a cessation of relations as punishment for communist subversion. In the Kremlin, Stalin and his advisers were convinced that the rise in tension could only be the prelude to another Allied intervention and even war. Their anxiety intensified as in the first months of that year they uncovered a sudden increase in SIS-inspired activities.

On 12 May 1927, Scotland Yard raided Arcos House in London, the headquarters of the Soviet Trade Delegation which was suspected of being the centre of OGPU's subversion. Russian officials later claimed that they had been subjected to humiliating personal searches; the British government responded that their operation had unearthed incriminating evidence that the Comintern was conspiring to cause mayhem throughout the empire. Nineteen days later, the British government formally severed relations, which encouraged SIS to return to the offensive.

That same week, six men and women, members of Kutyepov's Combat Corps, probably with Carr's help, crossed the border from Finland into Russia. Armed and equipped with explosives, the team divided into two groups and made their way towards Moscow and Leningrad. Their intention was to kill OGPU officials in the veined optimism which had inspired earlier SIS operations: that a small spark might trigger a widespread revolt. After planting bombs which claimed several

OGPU lives and civilian casualties, three of the agents were killed in ambushes but the remainder returned. Shortly afterwards, the Soviet Ambassador to Poland, Pavel Voikov, a Bolshevik allegedly involved in the murder of the Czar and his family, was assassinated while walking in a Warsaw street. OGPU was convinced that the British were masterminding another anti-Soviet conspiracy and launched a dragnet to capture what was condemned as a fifth column. Soviet newspapers reported that nearly 200 British and Polish agents had been arrested and that a British intelligence team was inspecting military installations in the Baltic States in anticipation of an invasion. In the first weeks of June 1927, the Kremlin's suspicions again seemed justified.

Encouraged by their first successes, Kutyepov dispatched four more teams of guerrillas across the Finnish border to assassinate communist officials. By August, most of the raiders had been either killed or captured. In a series of trials in Moscow, the prosecutors emphasised that the guerrillas had been helped by the British and Polish intelligence services. 'This was obviously not a conspiracy with roots in the USSR,' announced G.G. Yagoda, OGPU's deputy chief, in an unusual press conference, 'but rather the execution of a task directly assigned by British intelligence and the monarchists living abroad linked with it.' Yagoda's was not the voice of unreasoned paranoia, but a sensible assessment of the communists' foes. To remove the threat, the Kremlin persuaded the Finnish government to expel the Combat Corps' representatives from Helsinki and mounted a second penetration operation modelled upon the Trust. Two years later, General Kutyepov was kidnapped in Paris and disappeared for ever. His successor, General Yevgeny Miller, would meet the same fate a decade later.

Kutyepov's kidnapping once again exposed SIS's failure to obtain from sources inside the Kremlin and the Red Army the quality of information which the British government expected. Instead, SIS's exclusive sources were on the periphery. The British Embassy in Riga had effectively suborned the Latvian secret service to serve SIS. John Lawrence, a First Secretary, received regular reports from Latvia's senior military chiefs, but in their totality the reports forwarded to anxious politicians in London failed to explain Stalin's intentions. The cause of the failure was as much the forlorn notion that gathering intelligence depended simply upon proximity to the target or, as in wartime, upon dispatching agents across a border. Being close to Russia might have reassured Leslie Nicholson's SIS sources in Riga, but it provided few clues to events inside the Kremlin. Indeed, although Nicholson later mocked the peddlers of intelligence, he remained a steady customer of their offerings.

Little changed during the following decade. In 1937, the British Ambassador in Moscow, who had forbidden SIS to appoint a representative in the Embassy because it would compromise his mission, expressed his frustration to the Foreign Office that since Russians dared not visit the Embassy, he received 'no information and the condition of the country is a mystery'. In October 1938 the Ambassador again reported that 'it is impossible to gain even an inkling of what is discussed within [the Kremlin's] walls'. The SIS station in Riga fared little better. In 1938, Nicholson was joined by a new Assistant Passport Control Officer, Kenneth Benton, who had just narrowly escaped arrest by the Gestapo for spying in Vienna. Benton assessed that his superior's reports to London, which both he and his wife enciphered, were valueless repetitions of gossip and newspaper articles. Benton, a former teacher, blamed inadequate training.

Benton and Carr, like other recruits, had received perfunctory instruction in communications, codes and ciphers, and a briefing on handling a budget. But most would confess that they took up their posts still ignorant of their trade. 'Nobody gave me any tips on how to be a spy, how to make contact with, and worm vital information out of, unsuspecting experts,' wrote Leslie Nicholson after his return from Riga. The truth was that those who expected to be taught an instinct were predestined to be unsuitable. But even elementary precautions were ignored. When the British Embassy in Riga was evacuated in 1940, the Latvian caretaker known as 'Toni' revealed that his real employers had been German intelligence.

Helsinki, however, was an exceptional base for SIS and offered Carr the opportunity to build his reputation. Its historic relationship with Russia and its 1,000-mile common border allowed any intelligence service based in Finland a unique chance to penetrate its neighbour. Carr's foremost source was the Finnish military services, whose officers had been trained for more than one century by the Russians, providing a special insight into Russian strategy. It was in the very nature of the British intelligence operation that much depended upon borrowing and purchasing information from the host country whose interest in the neighbouring state would be paramount and whose ability to 'read' events might be more acute than an outsider's. Carr endeavoured to develop an understanding with every possible source of intelligence in Helsinki by ingratiating himself with those Finns serving in the military and intelligence services who were inclined to be helpful. Socially, his great advantages were fluency in Russian and Swedish, an outstanding game of tennis, and particularly his display of old-fashioned English courtesy. Politically, he was among the like-minded. The Finns were zealous anti-Soviets and sympathetic towards the Germans.

Carr's assistant was Rex Bosley. He spoke fluent Finnish, one of the world's most difficult languages, and became a friend of most government ministers and a member of the same Freemasons' lodge as the chiefs of the Finnish military staff. Bosley was Carr's antithesis – a garrulous bon viveur, whose indiscretions went hand in hand with his clowning. Bosley also cultivated the timber merchants and lumberjacks who travelled regularly into Russia. At drunken weekend parties, he entertained them with bawdy folk songs, occasionally slipping in a special request, if a trader was travelling to an area of particular interest, to bring back information or guide a White

29

Russian agent. Among these agents were a succession of Ukrainian nationalists led by Stefan Bandera with whom Carr built a strong relationship which he would draw upon after 1945.

Unlike Carr, Bosley barely hid his intent. On introducing himself at parties, the SIS agent would lift his collar, dart his eyes, lower his voice, and growl *sotto voce*, 'Don't tell anyone, but I'm a spy.' It was a beloved act whose repetition he found irresistible even in 1964 when Khrushchev visited Norway. On his introduction to the Soviet leader at a gala dinner, Bosley presented himself as 'a member of the British secret service'. Together with their secretary Eileen Daggett, Carr and Bosley prided themselves on being SIS's most potent source of intelligence about the Soviet Union. Yet other than sending a succession of unreliable agents across the border and collecting second-hand information from the Finns, Helsinki was as unsuccessful as all the other SIS stations during the years leading to the outbreak of war.

In 1939, SIS failed to predict many crises, not least the conclusion of the Molotov-Ribbentrop Pact in Moscow on 23 August. But while SIS's failure in Russia was not for lack of trying, the breakdown in Germany, attributed by critics to the service's Russophobia, was blamed by SIS's Chief, Quex Sinclair, on the Prime Minister's personal prejudices against the communists.

The Anglo-French agreement with Hitler at Munich in September 1938 to surrender Czechoslovakia proved to many that Chamberlain would in certain circumstances consider an unwritten alliance with Hitler against the Bolsheviks. In his diary, Chamberlain noted, 'I must confess to the most profound distrust of Russia . . . I distrust her motives which seem to me to have little connection with our ideas of liberty.'

In the weeks after the British Prime Minister returned to London praising his own efforts to secure 'peace in our time', the Soviet government had suggested to the British and French the possibility of a mutual support agreement against the Germans. Distrust of Russian intentions had evoked an unenthusiastic answer. Chamberlain clearly believed that an agreement with Hitler was preferable to one with Stalin. Nevertheless, the pressure from Moscow for discussions leading to an agreement required a response and Chamberlain dispatched to Russia, at the Soviets' urgent request, a military team to conduct the negotiations. Chamberlain, convinced that Stalin hoped for a war between Britain and Germany from which the Soviets by default would alone emerge unscathed, sent an unimpressive low-level delegation which travelled by the slowest sea journey without any authority on arrival to undertake proper discussions. Considering the context of Anglo-Soviet relations over the previous twenty years, Stalin concluded that the British had still not forsaken their yearning to topple the Bolsheviks. As confirmation, there were accurate reports from Europe describing the Duke of Windsor's convivial visit to Hitler and a succession of high-level contacts between Goering and British personalities to formalise an anti-Comintern agreement. For SIS officers, most of whom shared the views of the establishment that Britain's foremost enemies were the communists and not the Nazis, Stalin's judgment was accurate. SIS's misunderstanding, however, was to ignore Stalin's ability to outwit his foes and conclude an insurance policy with Hitler.

In the course of the charged Russo-German nego-tiations in the Kremlin, Joachim von Ribbentrop, the German Foreign Minister, assumed that the temptation for Stalin to conclude a pact with his other sworn enemies, the Nazis, was the unexpected opportunity to recapture those territories along Russia's western borders which Lenin had relinquished in the Brest-Litovsk peace treaty in 1918: Byelorussia, the Ukraine and the Baltic States. Von Ribbentrop suggested that Russia could re-annex the bulk of those areas in the event of a German war with Poland.

Von Ribbentrop had gone considerably further than the Anglo-French team's offer during the recent explora-tory talks in Moscow. The British negotiators, mindful of

31

Britain's pledge just twenty years earlier to protect the Baltic States' new independence, had offered only the possibility of Soviet influence, not sovereignty.

Stalin grabbed the German offer, drank a toast in champagne and bade the jubilant Germans farewell on their return to Berlin. Ten days later, Hitler invaded Poland and after the unprecedented Blitzkrieg, Russia and Germany shared a common border. Britain and France had in the meantime declared war against Germany.

SIS's station in Helsinki assumed a new importance in September 1939. Stalin, distrusting his new German allies, began secret negotiations in Helsinki to forestall a German advance through Finland and to prevent the mining of the Baltic Sea which would paralyse Russia's fleet in Kronstadt. But the Russian offer of military aid and the fortification of key islands in the Baltic approaches was rejected by the Finns who claimed that any agreement would compromise their neutrality. Stalin was unimpressed. When the occasion presented itself, he judged, Hitler would not respect Finland's neutrality.

On 30 November 1939, after negotiations had ended in impasse, Stalin ordered a limited bombardment of Finland's coastal areas, air raids on the capital and the dispatch of the Seventh Army to capture Helsinki. The Soviet leader expected victory within one week. His optimism was shared by Lieutenant Colonel Vale, the British Military Attaché in Helsinki who, while providing little information about the Red Army, dismissed the possibility of the Finns surviving the invasion for more than a few days. Carr took an opposite view. Probably inspired more by his emotional attachment to the Finns rather than a fine understanding of military tactics, he reported that Vale had misjudged the realities of fighting in temperatures of minus forty where quality counts for more than quantity. There would not, Carr reported, be a swift victory. Monitoring the fighting, Carr dispatched hitherto unobtainable information about the Red Army's tactics, weaponry, leadership and abilities, for open warfare is nothing less than a public display of military details which in peacetime are closely guarded secrets. Combined with Marshal Mannerheim's estimate that the Red Army's casualties were mounting towards 200,000 Carr's correct judgment won the officer high praise in Broadway and the Foreign Office.

As the Soviet advance collapsed, Chamberlain's government began changing its attitude. Hitherto, wrote Sir Orme Sargent, Deputy Under-Secretary at the Foreign Office, Britain had not attached 'any real importance to the continued existence of Finland' but that had changed. Britain now wanted to exploit the opportunities of Finland's fight against Russia. This was an important moment for Carr. Although Britain was at war with Germany, he was operating in a country fighting for its existence against Russia. He was not alone in sensing the revival of a crusade against communism. Sir Paul Dukes arrived in Helsinki on SIS's behalf to gauge the opportunities for anti-Soviet propaganda and even the possibility that the Finns might rout the Red Army and occupy Leningrad. The Finnish military and intelligence officers listening to Dukes and Carr believed that SIS and even the British government were eager allies since both officers described, with much exaggeration, the vital war material which Britain had dispatched. For Carr's career, the Winter War was a blessing. The closer relationship which it triggered between the SIS officer and the Finnish intelligence services was the key to his promotion.

Isolated both geographically and politically, Finland's intelligence network and in particular its decryption agency directed by Reino Hallamaa were important assets. In the early 1930s, Hallamaa had bought from the Japanese the key to a Soviet five-digit code used in the Far East. In 1937, the Soviets began using the same code in the West; consequently, during the war, the Finns could read Russian land and marine messages. That was of particular interest to SIS because in 1927, after the Baldwin government had presented to the Soviet government decrypts of Soviet messages, proving that the communists were engaged in anti-British activities as the pretext for breaking off diplomatic relations, the Soviets changed their ciphers. Inevitably, British cryptologists had been unable to read any further Russian cables. In 1940, Hallamaa's secret was revealed to Carr who began supplying a steady stream of information about the Soviets to London. Carr, however, was unaware that the Finns regularly sold their product not just to the highest but to any bidder, and that Hallamaa's codebreakers had also broken SIS's ciphers. Carr's messages to London were decrypted and sold to the Germans.

Carr prided himself on the flow of information which he was sending to Broadway. Colonel Seamus McGill, however, the new British Military Attaché who arrived in Helsinki in 1940, was sceptical of SIS's confidence in Finland's long-term resistance. Carr was prone, he reported, to believe unquestioningly the Finns' intelligence about Russia, which he believed 'was often wrong'. There is little reason to doubt McGill's assessment. In February, despite gallant fighting, Finland was overwhelmed by massive Soviet bombardments. And subsequent analysis of the intelligence gathered by the military and naval attachés in Europe before 1939 has shown that, despite their own grave mistakes, they were more accurate than SIS's estimates.

Finland and Russia agreed to a ceasefire on 13 March 1940. Over the following year, Carr and Bosley were the focus of intense attention from a host of anti-Soviet Finnish officials. The Finns' information about Soviet intentions was generally worthless but one Finnish army officer presented Carr in December 1940 with the single item of intelligence which guaranteed its recipient a place in SIS's history. Germany, he had heard, would attack Russia in spring 1941. Combined with reports from the German Balts in Riga, Carr forwarded the report to Broadway and could justly claim in later years to have won for SIS a modicum of the respect which the agency

34

so desperately sought, and for himself the right to promotion.

In June 1941, when Carr's prediction proved correct and Germany invaded Russia, Finland allied itself with the aggressor against the communists. The British Embassy closed and the staff transferred to neutral Sweden.

Two

WARTIME NETWORKS

Carr, Bosley and Eileen Daggett arrived in Stockholm in June 1941 to a mixed reception. As an SIS officer with twenty years' solid service in Scandinavia, Carr displayed the self-confidence of one who demanded respect of his peers. But the resident head of SIS's Stockholm Station, John 'Pincher' Martin, was less than effusive towards his colleague. Martin's staff, based in the Birger Jarlsgatan, was already five strong and would now increase by a further three officers. The Swedish capital had become one of SIS's strategic locations for monitoring German diplomatic and espionage activities, gathering intelligence, and infiltrating and exfiltrating Allied agents into and out of occupied Europe. Martin did not welcome any incursion on his authority, especially from the likes of Carr, whose reputation within SIS was as an expert on Soviet Russia and as a passionate anti-commuist. His expertise, Martin reasoned, did not suit the new reality that SIS's exclusive target was Germany. He suspected that Carr would find the acceptance of Soviet Russia as Britain's ally difficult. In the event, it was decided that Carr could move into the British Embassy as a First Secretary, under cover of which he would continue to act as head of the Finland Station and gather information about Britain's newest enemy.

The British Ambassador Victor Mallet belonged to the school of diplomats who regarded espionage with extreme caution and viewed Martin in particular with disdain.

Since 1940, Mallet had been at pains to restrict all British intelligence operations in Sweden, especially those conducted by the newly created Special Operations Executive. Churchill's personal enthusiasm for SOE reflected his old passion for covert activities in Bolshevik Russia but Mallet's dislike mirrored a major feud within Whitehall between the new agency and SIS. Blunders, indiscretions and crimes had already led to the arrest of SOE's agents in Sweden, which had prompted Mallet to block all attempts to rebuild the organisation of 'bunglers' in his jurisdiction. The Embassy, said the Ambassador, was not to be used as a base for subversive activities. To enforce his stricture, he insisted on notification of every contact between any British agency and any Swede who might be inclined to help the Allied war effort. Towards the gentlemanly Carr, however, the Ambassador showed a marked tolerance, not least because his new tenant was an excellent tennis player and the ideal fourth in what Mallet believed was a diplomatically important regular doubles match with senior politicians and the head of Swedish intelligence.

To diplomats at the American mission, Mallet personified a peculiar conundrum. The British tolerated Sweden's wholehearted military collaboration with Germany to a degree which prompted some to believe that Mallet was 'more pro-Swedish than the Swedes themselves'. Sweden's uninterrupted annual exports of 100 million tons of steel and millions of ball bearings to sustain the German war machine seemed to the Americans a perverted alliance between the European powers against the communists. Carr, however, found nothing strange in that arrangement.

Compared to London, life for all SIS officers in Stockholm during the war was positively luxurious, but Carr in particular realised the benefits. Besides frequent opportunities for physical exercise, there were no obstacles for indulging his hypochondria, which Eileen Daggett willingly pampered. His only exposure to physical danger was an annual journey to see his family in Britain when

37

he flew across the North Sea in the belly of a Mosquito bomber. To Carr, discomfort equalled peril.

In Stockholm Carr's unsurpassed concern for security, which previously had been known only to those few SIS officers who had passed through Helsinki, soon became a conversation point among a wider circle. His various tips to the wartime recruits – 'If you're carrying secret papers, pin them to your inside pocket' – were a regular source of lampoons over drinks at the end of a day's work for the small coterie of Passport Officers. Their tales were often spiced with colourful accounts of how to recruit agents. 'I told Harry to put a gag in his mouth when he went to bed,' laughed a colleague, 'to prevent himself disclosing secrets in his sleep.'

Among those amused by Carr's obsessive secrecy was Peter Falk, a former schoolmaster at Rugby who had been recruited by the counter-intelligence branch, Section V, and posted as an Assistant Passport Control Officer to Stockholm in March 1943 to identify enemy agents. As a newcomer to the business, Falk was naturally intrigued by the venerable Carr whose tight-lipped reticence never quite concealed his endearing thrill of discovery and delight in his personal success. Falk, an unmalicious and unambitious officer, began independently to check Carr's sources, in the belief that they were impeccable. He was soon disillusioned. Among those upon whom Falk discovered by chance that Carr was relying were a coterie of British and Finnish journalists whose information Carr rewrote and then encoded before transmission to London. Ossian Goulding, the resident correspondent of the *Daily Telegraph*, supplied Carr with information from Swedish sailors whom he regularly met in bars in the port of Göteborg. It was a valid if mundane source of intelligence. More colourful was Carr's use of Goulding's expertise on the German-Russian war. Both the British and Amercian military missions in Moscow were failing to obtain reliable information from the Soviet government about the course of the war and Carr presented Goulding to Broadway as an expert. Falk became intrigued by

Goulding's sources. The journalist, he discovered, regularly listened to the BBC's World Service and then, after consulting a huge map of Russia which hung on his bedroom wall, wrote reports about the movement of the Red Army spiced with the names of Russian generals randomly picked from a pre-war army list. It was harmless but raised questions about Carr's accuracy.

During their regular weekly discussions, Carr also disclosed to Falk that an important source of his information was the former Estonian Director of Military Intelligence, Colonel Villem Saarsen, and an aide, Richard Massing. Both were serving with the German army hunting communist partisans and sent messages from Estonia to Stockholm about the situation in German-occupied Russia. According to Carr, the Estonians were supplying information to the Swedes which was passed on to British intelligence. For two years these reports, encoded and transmitted to London, had been treated with great respect. In 1943, Falk obtained access to the safe of the German Air Attaché in Stockholm, Karl-Heinz Kraemer, after recruiting the German's maid as an agent. To Falk's surprise, it became apparent that Saarsen was supplying the same intelligence to Kraemer and that it was at best unreliable and at worst manufactured. Falk was too unassuming to make any judgment about his genial superior. 'What's nice about Carr,' Falk would confide to his more sceptical colleagues, 'is that he judges people on what they do, not what they are.' It was the sort of homespun affability which had appealed to Colonel Seamus McGill in Helsinki although he had suspected that Carr's obsession with secrecy might distort his judgment about his sources since the SIS officer seemed to believe that security was an end in itself.

Those were the circumstances in 1944 when Carr began to establish what he hoped would be his greatest coup: the effective penetration by British agents of Soviet Russia through the Baltic States. He set about the task with great precision and, faithful to his preoccupation for security, gave no hint of his plans to Falk. Through intermediaries, his accomplices and agents would be Baltic nationalists who before the war had been important sources for SIS in Riga and Tallinn and who in 1944 hoped to re-establish their countries' independence after the conflict. Yet considering the British government's policies towards the Baltic States since 1939, Carr's proposed collaboration rested upon principles which had been secretly abandoned by his masters in London.

Throughout history, the three Baltic States – rural communities each barely larger than Holland or Switzerland – have been victims of repeated invasions and colonisation by Prussian, Danish, Swedish and Russian armies. Like flotsam, squeezed claustrophobically between the major powers, the three nationalities never lost their starky dissimilar languages, religions and cultural identities but were unable individually to resolve their common historical fate.

The first occupation was in the twelfth century by Teutonic knights who were known as Balts. In 1410, with Polish help, Lithuania was liberated and during the following one hundred years gradually became Polonised, resisting the Russians, while Sweden occupied Estonia and Latvia. In 1721, Russia successfully defeated Sweden in war and progressively occupied the three states. Unwittingly, their integration into Russia by the Czars accelerated their emancipation, literacy and national consciousness. Britain's support for their independence in 1918 was motivated purely by self-interest: an opportunity to erect a *cordon sanitaire* against communism and to protect the huge investments accumulated during the Czarist era by British banks and traders. Twenty years later, when the investments had been lost for ever and Britain was more interested in a bulwark against Nazism than against communism, the Foreign Office wavered while considering Russia's demand in 1939 to re-annex the three states. In previous months, British officials had shown scant concern for the plight of persecuted Europeans. Their common reaction to vivid eye-witness accounts from occupied Europe about the fate of trade unionists, clergy and the

Jews was invariably sceptical. The accurate and contemporaneous eye-witness reports from Kiev of over 30,000 individual murders in Babi Yar within two days in September 1941 had been immortalised by Victor Cavendish-Bentinck as 'products of the Slavic imagination'. The same cynical principle of self-interest governed the Foreign Office's consideration of the fate of Britain's pledge to the Baltic States when it was called to the test.

In April 1941, when Britain was fighting the Nazis alone, the British failure to sacrifice the Baltic States in exchange for a pact with Russia, seemed in retrospect to Sir Orme Sargent to have been a missed opportunity. In the wake of the Molotov-Ribbentrop Pact and before the German invasion of Russia, Sargent had written to his colleagues regretting that the concession was not made in 1939: 'We could not bring ourselves to make this sacrifice of principle,' he wrote, 'and we paid the penalty accordingly.' The senior official clearly implied that if the opportunity should in theory be offered again, principles would be forsaken. Four months later, when Churchill and Roosevelt met on HMS *Prince of Wales* at anchor in Placentia Bay, Newfoundland, Sargent's retrospective pragmatism was ignored. Although the American government was still officially neutral, the President insisted that he would not tolerate any territorial exchanges.

Ever since the Soviet annexation, the American administration had condemned the 'predatory activities' which had robbed the Balts of their independence. In October 1940, the President had personally assured the Lithuanian-American Council, which represented one million Lithuanians living in America, that their nation's independence was not lost but 'only temporarily put aside. Time will come and Lithuania will be free again. This will happen much sooner than you expect.' Preoccupied by the actual war, little attention had been paid by the two Western leaders on the *Prince of Wales* to events following the Soviet annexation.

The re-absorption of the three states into Russia began soon after the Molotov-Ribbentrop Pact was signed. The

Kremlin felt little compassion for those who had broken the continuity of 200 years of Czarist rule. The three Balt Prime Ministers had been invited to sign 'mutual defence and assistance agreements' with Stalin which permitted the Soviet Union to place military bases on their territory in order to guarantee their independence. Since the alternative was war, all three reluctantly agreed in the hope of finding an escape later.

Their fragile relationship with Moscow survived until Germany invaded France in May 1940. In that same week, the three leaders were summoned back to Moscow, accused by Molotov of treacherously breaking the 'mutual assistance agreements', and given orders to form governments which were sympathetic to communism. By 18 June, the Red Army and the local Communist Parties were in total control of the region. Sovietisation was rapid and relentless since the Baltic States were, as Molotov eulogised, 'to join the glorious family of the Soviet Union'. Their parliaments disappeared, their currencies were changed to roubles, books which were deemed 'unsuitable' were banned, newspapers shifted their allegiances, factories, restaurants and businesses were seized by the state, and, most drastic of all, farms were collectivised. It was a rapid introduction to Stalinism which was completed throughout the region during the night of 11–12 July 1940. Knocks on the door at night, a brusque order to pack a small bag, and thousands of unfortunates were arrested, never to be seen again. The victims were those who had championed the nationalist cause, but they were soon followed by White Russian exiles and those in the army, Church and middle classes who were suspected opponents of the Soviets.

Eleven months later, on the night of 12–13 June 1941, the full might of Stalinism struck. In a massive dragnet operation, about 100,000 men, women and children were arrested and loaded into railway wagons and shipped to Siberia. In the atmosphere of terror which gripped the region during the following week, thousands of families sat meekly in their homes, packed suitcases by the door, awaiting the arrival of the arrest squads and the second wave of deportations. The lists had been prepared and the trains were again standing in the marshalling yards when, on 22 June, over three million German troops spearheaded Hitler's invasion of Russia. Within days, the Wehrmacht had cut a swath into the Baltic and the Red Army fled eastwards.

The unexpected and sudden release from Stalinist terror triggered a huge wave of gratitude towards the invaders for delivering them from a terrible evil. In Lithuania, the national army revolted against the retreating communists and announced a provisional national government; rebels in Kaunas took control of the city from the Russians before the first German units arrived. In Latvia and Estonia there was no fighting but their leaders hoped and expected that the Germans would restore their independence. Accordingly, German newsreel footage recorded a joyous welcome to the invaders. To the Balts' misfortune, Hitler considered them racially inferior and the German occupation would be markedly similar to the Soviets'. Their nations were to be destroyed and, after mass deportations, the new inhabitants would be Germans. Momentarily, however, the new tyranny seemed a godsend compared to its predecessor, and it was the image of the Baltic welcome to the Nazis which had prompted Sir Orme Sargent to regret further the British failure to sacrifice principle. He was, however, out of step with his master.

In what became the Holy Writ for the nationalists in occupied Europe, Roosevelt and Churchill agreed on 12 August 1941 to issue a declaration which became known as the Atlantic Charter. The justification for the huge sacrifices ahead, they proclaimed, would be the restoration of freedom and independence, the denial of any territorial changes contrary to the wishes of the peoples concerned, and the respect by the two powers of the sovereign rights of people to choose their own government. Even as it was being broadcast on BBC radio, Foreign Office officials, contemptuous of the Balts because of their apparent allegiance to the Nazis against the Russians, were doggedly ignoring the Charter's explicit assurances.

The first opportunity to effect that reverse presented itself on 16 December 1941 when the Foreign Secretary met Stalin in Moscow to discuss the terms of an alliance. During the previous months, while preparing for a new relationship with Moscow, the Balts' apparent collaboration with the Nazis had convinced Eden and his senior officials that an offer to recognise Russia's annexation of the three states would tempt Stalin into a pact. Indeed, once Eden was in Moscow, the Soviet dictator demanded British recognition of the Soviet annexation as the 'acid test' of British intentions. Eden, who was possibly unaware of the mass deportations of Balts to Siberia, reported to Churchill that he considered the proposal reasonable if it was accompanied by a plebiscite which the Russians would be able to organise 'in their favour'. His officials supported his views since, after all, the Balts' independence was 'almost accidental' and worthless compared to an alliance. But to Eden's surprise, Churchill, moved by his own conscience and in anticipation of Roosevelt's outright opposition, vetoed the idea. The American Secretary of State, Cordell Hull, wrote to Eden that acceptance of the Soviet demand 'would destroy the meaning of one of the most important clauses of the Atlantic Charter and would tend to undermine the force of the whole document'.

That piety dissolved one year later. In April 1942, as Molotov was due to arrive in London to negotiate the final terms of a formal twenty-year treaty, the Cabinet prepared themselves to ignore Hull's warning and offer the Soviets the concession. But the moment did not materialise. Molotov, fearing that the demand might impede concluding the treaty, made no mention of the annexation. The Foreign Office was spared the indignity of offering the sacrifice.

Yet, paradoxically, the policy reversal had assumed its own momentum. In the following months, Sumner Welles

44

at the State Department agreed that there was 'no vital interest in opposing their union' with Russia, and Roosevelt became coldly pragmatic. 'The Russian armies,' the President told Eden, 'would be in the Baltic States at the time of the downfall of Germany, and none of us can use force to get them out.' Accordingly, Eden obtained the Cabinet's approval that any European peace settlement should be based on both the principles of the Atlantic Charter and on recognition of Russia's borders on 22 June 1941. The inherent contradiction was ignored for sound reasons. At great sacrifice, the Red Army had won the battle for Stalingrad and the eventual outcome of the war was certain. Recognising the Soviets' power, Roosevelt judged that there was little purpose in clashing with Stalin over the fate of the Baltic States. This sentiment prevailed when the President met the Russian privately in Tehran on 1 December 1943.

Stalin was surprised by the American's candour. 'What I want to explain to you,' said Roosevelt, 'concerns internal American politics. According to our constitution, we must have elections in 1944. I don't want to run but if the war's still going, I'll have no choice.' To the wry amusement of the American officials present, the dictator nodded his understanding of the predicament. 'There are,' continued the President, 'six to seven million Americans of Polish extraction and, as a practical man, I don't want to lose their vote. I understand your position on moving Poland's borders westwards but because of the elections, I can't enter into any public discussion on the subject at present.' Stalin's reply was short but soothing: 'Now you've explained everything, I understand.'

The President moved on. 'I've also got a lot of former Lithuanians, Latvians and Estonians as voters in America. I realise that the three states have been historically part of Russia and . . .' Whatever problems Stalin might have anticipated dissolved as the President smiled and said jokingly, 'When the Soviet armies re-occupy those areas, I don't intend to go to war about their future.' Stalin laughed as Roosevelt continued, 'But the big issue in the

United States will be the question of a referendum and the right to self-determination. World opinion will want some expression of the will of the people. Perhaps not immediately after Soviet occupation but at some stage.' Stalin's face, which momentarily revealed no emotion, brightened as Roosevelt added, 'Although I'm confident that the people there will vote to join the Soviet Union.'

Stalin's reply revealed how precisely Roosevelt had judged his partner. The three republics, said Stalin, had not enjoyed autonomy under the Czar, and Russia had nevertheless been an ally of both Great Britain and the United States. For 200 years no one mentioned the question of public opinion: 'I don't quite see why it is being raised now.'

'The truth of the matter is that the public neither knew nor understood,' agreed Roosevelt. 'But it would be helpful for me personally if some public declaration about future elections, to which the Marshal [Stalin] has referred, could be made.'

'There'll be plenty of opportunities,' smiled Stalin, settling the President's electoral dilemma, 'for the will of the people to be expressed.'

With the fate of the Baltic States sealed, the two leaders moved on to discuss the creation of a United Nations organisation which would guarantee the world's future freedom and peace. The first practical result was that the Ambassadors of the Baltic States in London were relegated to a special position at the bottom of the diplomatic list. The Balts never suffered that indignity in Washington.

For the third leader at the conference, the context rather than the content of the discussions assumed over-riding importance. Although the British and American media, cajoled by their governments, had projected a positive image of the Big Three's alliance, the reality was persistent mutual suspicion only occasionally dispelled by displays of genuine goodwill. At Tehran, Churchill was preoccupied in particular with the cavalier treatment inflicted upon him by the other two leaders. Despite the

46

smiles for the photographers, the Prime Minister felt intentionally snubbed by the President in front of Stalin. Roosevelt seemed overly concerned to convince the Russian that the Anglo-Saxons were not 'ganging up', while the Russian did his utmost to precipitate divisions between the Allies. Squeezed between the goliaths, Churchill, in his eagerness to cement an alliance with Moscow, remained suspicious in Soviet eyes. After all, twenty years earlier he had overtly supported attempts to overthrow the Bolsheviks, and that legacy could neither be forgotten nor concealed. Stalin doubted the genuineness of Churchill's conversion despite the Prime Minister's direction to the Chief of SIS, Stewart Menzies, in 1941 that the service was to cease all its anti-Soviet activities and even to break contact with its informants.

Stalin's suspicions were fully justified. Churchill's sentiments oscillated violently. On occasions he cursed the Bolsheviks, but then, elated by Russian victories, he allowed his emotions to overcome his heartfelt and lifelong conviction that the communists could not be trusted. At Tehran and later at Yalta, he pursued friendship because he admired Stalin as a member of the club of leaders. But his fear of Soviet expansionism, aggression and deviousness provoked moody silences or uncontrolled attacks on Russia's historic barbarism.

Aware of Churchill's mixed emotions, Menzies was roused in 1944 to reconsider SIS's cessation of activities against the Soviet Union. The foundations for the initiative, provoked by his own instinctive mistrust of the Bolsheviks, had been laid by the three Chiefs of Staff, Sir Alan Brooke, Sir Charles Portal and Sir Andrew Cunningham. In summer 1943, the Chiefs had invited Foreign Office officials to start discussions, restricted to the top echelons, about Britain's peacetime policy. The forum for their meeting was the Post-Hostilities Planning Committee (PHPC). At their first meetings, the three Chiefs proffered scenarios based on the assumption that after the Nazi defeat, Russia would once again become Britain's primary enemy. Britain, the Chiefs suggested, should forge an agreement with Russia mutually to respect each other's spheres of interest. The Foreign Office representatives disagreed about the inevitability of antagonism but nevertheless the discussions continued. Their amicability began to disappear in early 1944. The Chiefs of Staff were convinced that after the war there would be military confrontations with Russia in Greece, Turkey and central Europe. Surprised, the Foreign Office officials suggested that any disagreements would be settled by negotiation. That panacea was brushed aside by the military's unanimous analysis that the Soviets were 'sinister'. Their disagreement reached its climax just seven weeks after the D-Day landings, at the end of July 1944.

At the regular PHPC meeting, the Chiefs presented a post-war scenario which was a radical departure from Foreign Office policy. America, they suggested, would return to isolationism and Britain's only option to avoid 'losing the peace' was to consider a future alliance with Germany against Russia. Although the prevailing assessment was still that the war would be over by Christmas, the proposal was breathtakingly radical. In the past, individual Foreign Office officials had temporarily succumbed to the gloomy view that a war with Russia was possible if not inevitable, but the military's conclusions were undiscussable. 'A most disastrous heresy which ought to be nipped in the bud at once,' opined Sargent who secured the Foreign Office's immediate withdrawal from the committee. The military 'welcomed' their departure. The Soviets' cynical refusal to support the Polish Home Army's uprising in Warsaw, which had caused thousands of deaths, and the discovery in the Katyn forest of the mass graves of Polish officers killed by the Russians, more than justified, in the Chiefs' opinion, their antagonism and apprehension.

The battle line between the Chiefs and the Foreign Office was formally drawn on the eve of Churchill's visit to Moscow in October 1944 where, with a flick of the pen, the Prime Minister and Stalin divided Europe in a percentage agreement. In a tense meeting with Eden and

Sargent on 4 October, the three Chiefs refused to accept that Germany was Britain's only possible enemy and won the argument that contingency planning for a war with Russia should continue, but confined to 'a very restricted circle'. At Sargent's request, the Chiefs agreed that their discussions and their records would be given 'special security treatment' because of his fear that 'the shadow of the Bear' might fall across the papers. Foreign Office officials already suspected the presence of Soviet spies in Whitehall because early in the war 'government departments had become less inclined to exclude Communists from secret work and, in fact, numbers of the Communist Party [were] known to have been placed in positions where they [had] access to information of great secrecy.'

Since both the military and some Foreign Office officials were once again suggesting that Russia was Britain's most potent threat, it was natural in November 1944 for Sir Stewart Menzies to plan the re-establishment of Section IX, the anti-Soviet division. His anticipated appointment as head of the section was Felix Cowgill who had successfully run Section V, the counter-intelligence branch, against the Abwehr and was already sifting through SIS's records of abandoned Soviet sources. But by deft exploitation of office politics, Menzies was persuaded to appoint the head of SIS's Iberian section, Harold 'Kim' Philby.

Menzies' brief to Philby was to rebuild SIS's counter-espionage capability to search out Soviet agents who were operating abroad. But in the course of their first meetings, Philby sought Menzies' approval to broaden Section IX's responsibilities to encompass British espionage inside the Soviet Union. In the light of the Foreign Office's discussions with the Chiefs of Staff, Menzies felt amenable to Philby's suggestion. SIS, he concluded, needed to resurrect its ability to gather information from inside the Soviet Union. Philby received formal approval in February 1945 and began contacting those officers whose activities would contribute to his new responsibilities.

Among those whom Philby approached was Harry Carr

49

in Stockholm whose reports seemed particularly encouraging. Since the beginning of the year, Carr told Philby, he and Bosley had successfully gathered reliable intelligence from the Baltic States and had established a radio link with the resistance in Latvia. Sweden, reported Carr, had developed into an ideal location for monitoring the Soviet Union because of the increasing flow of refugees from the Baltic States. Until 1944, only a trickle of Balt refugees had arrived to an unwelcome reception in Stockholm, fleeing first from the Russians and then from the Germans. In 1942, the Balts were no longer confused about whether the Germans had come as liberators or conquerors. Their property, which had been confiscated by the Russians, was not returned; their currency was further devalued; and the arrests and deportations had recommenced. While some Balts were sent to German factories and work battalions, nearly a quarter of a million Jews were ensnared on the Nazis' production line to be murdered. But those massacres barely featured in the nationalists' protests about the fate of their homeland which were passed to Carr and other Allied intelligence agents in Stockholm. Their overriding concern in 1944 was the imminence of the Russian reoccupation of the Baltic States. That wariness was shared by the Swedish government which rapidly relaxed its restrictions and during the following eighteen months admitted about 30,000 refugees who arrived either overland from Finland or by boat.

The Swedish government's shift of allegiance away from the Germans towards the Allies reflected its self-interest once the seemingly indisputable German supremacy had paled. Although publicly there was no comment, the volte-face was expected by the two Western allies; they did not anticipate that the switch reflected a real change of attitude by the Swedes themselves. Generally, the Swedes were pro-Aryan and anti-communist although that did not always mask the sharp division between those who sympathised with the Allies and the pro-Nazis. This split, as British and American intelligence officers discovered, was very evident among the personnel of the two Swedish intelligence services: the military section, the Svenska Mileter Tgänst, and the civil agency, the Allmanr Säckeraetst. The split had not disappeared in 1944 but the priority of Swedish intelligence became closer to that pursued by SIS and OSS agents: to discover the progress of the war across the Baltic Sea. The Swedes feared above all that the Russians intended to liberate Denmark and Norway and possibly invade Sweden. The ideal source of information would be agents infiltrated into the Baltic States. In 1944, Carr heard that both Swedish intelligence agencies were preparing infiltration operations and naturally he hoped that SIS would receive some of the benefits.

SIS's continued existence in Sweden depended upon the Swedes agreeing that any operation proposed by the British agency was not an infringement of the host nation's neutrality. Hence it became incumbent upon Carr to ingratiate himself with Swedish intelligence just as he had done in Finland. Among his best contacts was Ake Eek of the military intelligence service SMT.

Eek had already developed a natural cover story for the infiltrations. With Swedish government permission, a flotilla of small boats had begun to cross the Baltic on 'lifeline missions' to collect refugees. Most of the arrivals were innocent civilians who had fled for their own safety, but others came to Sweden to seek aid for groups of partisans who they said were living in the forests to escape deportation. Although politically they described themselves as nationalists, their resistance seemed confused since they acknowledged that hastening the demise of the Nazis would only speed the arrival of the Soviets. But they consoled themselves that under the Atlantic Charter the Western Allies guaranteed their nations' independence. A third category, whose numbers increased towards the end of the war, were German and Baltic SS and police officers who had enforced German laws or worked in the concentration camps and feared Soviet retribution.

Ake Eek, suspected by most of being a Nazi sympathiser, favoured in particular the latter as his best sources of information. Their credentials as anti-communists were irreproachable and their expertise was invaluable. Despite the knowledge that their recent duties had included torture, deportations and executions, the Swedish authorities deemed these officers to have worked for 'patriotic purposes' and to have authorised murders to 'liquidate traitors' because their victims were often 'communists'. On arrival in Sweden, some were employed as government 'archivists' and eventually would be granted citizenship or money to emigrate to South America. Drawing on all three groups, Eek organised in summer 1944 the first of over sixty operations, transporting his agents in the rescue boats to undertake short-term reconnaissance missions. The responsibility for liaising on SIS's behalf with Eek was entrusted to an important addition to Carr's team: Alexander 'Sandy' McKibbin.

Born in Moscow in 1891, McKibbin was the son of a wealthy market owner whose family had lived for two generations in Russia. Like Carr, McKibbin spoke fluent Russian, loved his adopted homeland, and was appalled by the Bolshevik revolution. In later years, when he was immersed in sending agents into Russia, he would jocularly retell the story of how in 1917 he had made a bomb which he intended to throw at a Communist Party building, only to be stopped by his father. 'Don't forget,' he was told, 'you're Scottish and what the Russians do is none of your business.'

During the inter-war years, McKibbin had established himself as a well-known and popular timber dealer in Tallinn. Although he was not a full-time SIS agent, he was a trusted informant who spoke Estonian, Russian and German and, with the help of Helmi, his Finnish wife, built a wide network of informants among the Estonian military, political and intelligence services. At Carr's request, he travelled regularly to Vilnius, in Lithuania, especially after the full-time SIS agent there had been withdrawn as an economy measure. But the two men had little in common other than their cause, if only because, unlike the ascetic Carr, McKibbin daily consumed considerable quantities of whisky and vodka.

In 1939 McKibbin fled to Helsinki, abandoning his business, home and possessions. He arrived loathing the Bolsheviks more passionately than ever. For a time he continued to supply Carr with information obtained from his Estonian contacts and especially a network of seamen established by a former diplomat and SIS informer Alexander Warma, but in 1940 he finally returned to Britain. In late 1943 he arrived in Stockholm as a full-time SIS officer with a brief to build a network of Balt informants which would be expanded into Russia itself.

McKibbin's Lithuanian contact in Stockholm was Walter Zilinskas, a 31-year-old former junior diplomat whom he had met before the war at the Lithuanian Embassy in Tallinn. Zilinskas and his chief, Vytautas Gylys, had no direct line of communication with Lithuania but were receiving a trickle of information from Colonel Kazys Skirpa, the Lithuanian representative in Berlin, which they passed on to McKibbin.

Skirpa's reliability might have seemed questionable to McKibbin but Zilinskas, voicing an explanation which would constantly be repeated about all dubious Balts over the following years, assured the Briton that Skirpa was not pro-Nazi, merely anti-Russian. McKibbin received and passed on to London Skirpa's colourful account of Lithuania's non-violent resistance to the Germans which was restricted to underground newspapers and non-cooperation. The Lithuanians prided themselves on the German failure to create an SS battalion but omitted to mention that approximately 20,000 Lithuanians had joined the 'police battalions', which were effectively murder squads implementing the Final Solution, while others fought with regular Wehrmacht groups against communist partisans. Instead, they extolled the virtues of General Povilas Plechavicius who, in agreement with the Germans, had recruited 30,000 soldiers to fight the Soviets, only to order their desertion when the Germans reneged on their promise that it would remain a national Lithuanian army rather than be incorporated into the German army. In autumn 1944, this trained force, McKibbin was told, was the buttress of a growing anti-communist partisan army attracting hundreds of Lithuanians to flee into the forests, prepared to fight to the death.

Zilinskas suggested to McKibbin that the West's most reliable ally in the area was an organisation called VLIK, the Supreme Committee for the Liberation of Lithuania. The former diplomat explained that although VLIK was collaborating with the Germans, its leadership was committedly anti-communist and nationalist. SIS should establish contact with VLIK which could co-ordinate and lead the resistance when the Red Army arrived. Zilinskas' candidate for the mission was Algirdas Voketitis, an anti-German nationalist. McKibbin was eager to help but lacked the finance. It was therefore agreed that Zilinska would approach representatives of the American Office of Strategic Services (OSS).

The American Ambassaor to Stockholm, Hershel Johnson, viewed intelligence activity as a 'satanic practice' and, like his British counterpart, hindered OSS officers whenever possible. Among the sufferers was Iver Olsen, officially a Financial Secretary at the Embassy, who in 1944 was also seconded as a special attaché to the War Refugee Board.

The Board was established by Roosevelt to save the victims of Nazi persecution who still survived in Europe. The Board's methods were either to exert diplomatic pressure or to take direct action. With a quarter of a million dollar budget, a large sum at the time, and with the Swedish government's agreement, Olsen hired boats to cross the Baltic to rescue the persecuted. Among his notable successes was the dispatch of Raoul Wallenberg to Hungary where the Swede saved thousands of Jews. Olsen's efforts, on his own assessment, saved 1,200 people but his attempts to use those same boats to infiltrate agents came up against the US President's strictures forbidding any activity which Stalin could construe as hostile.

In 1942, William Donovan, the founder and director of the OSS, had been told by the President that the Soviet Union should not be an intelligence target for the agency and all operations must cease. The following year, Donovan tried to reverse that ban but, although he might have received oral approval from the Joint Chiefs, the President's policy was to forge close co-operation. By December 1943 this had culminated in a high-level agreement between the OSS and the Soviet secret police, NKVD, to exchange information and representatives. An internal OSS memorandum dated 4 February 1944, entitled 'Intelligence to be Furnished to the USSR', stated that Russia 'may be given intelligence which is of distinctive OSS origin and which may be of aid to that country in prosecuting the war against Germany.' Edgar Hoover, the Director of the FBI, blocked the exchange of personnel, but Donovan obeyed the President and handed over 1,500 pages of Soviet codes which the OSS station in Stockholm had obtained from Reino Hallamaa, the former head of Finnish intelligence who was exiled in Sweden. Another gift, which Roosevelt personally presented to Stalin in 1944, was an intelligence dossier on the resistance in Latvia which the OSS in Stockholm had compiled from interviews with refugees. Throughout 1944 the flow of intelligence was exclusively one way, from West to East; Soviet imperviousness blocked any dialogue to effect an improvement and it therefore fell to individual officers to obtain what intelligence they could. In Sweden the best sources were the Baltic refugees.

At the request of the two Lithuanian diplomats, Zilinskas and Gylys, Olsen agreed to finance the infiltration of Algirdas Voketitis into German-occupied Soviet Union. Olsen secured from the Swedish government the provision of 'technical facilities': a boat to drop the agent on the Lithuanian coast and a radio channel for him to use to communicate from Lithuania. After training, in spring 1944 Voketitis was landed on the beach near Palanga with orders to contact a trained radio operator who would put the Lithuanian partisans in direct communication with

Sweden. Just one week later, Voketitis was arrested and sent to Stutthof concentration camp. For the remainder of the war, there were no further operations into Lithuania.

SIS's prospects in Latvia were more encouraging. The service's Latvian contact was Dr Valdemars Ginters who had been an important SIS source in pre-war Riga and had fled in 1943 to Sweden to escape from the Germans. Ginters claimed that a major nationalist underground group, the Latvian Central Council (LCC), had been created in Latvia at the end of 1942 and was offering its services to SIS. The LCC's members included Verners Tepfers and Bruno Kalnins who were both known anti-Nazis, an important consideration since over 30,000 Latvians had volunteered to join two Latvian SS legions and others had been conscripted to serve. Reliable informants had confirmed that Himmler's officers had tapped a willing reservoir of Latvian volunteers to massacre tens of thousands in the forests outside Riga and that several Latvian execution squads were roaming through eastern Europe murdering countless innocent civilians every day. Ginters was clearly not associated with these atrocities. He could offer his old SIS contacts an unblemished record and, more important, a radio link with Latvia which was sending reports about the German occupation.

The radio was under the care of Valdemars Salnais, a former deputy foreign minister who had first helped SIS in 1922 and had fled to Sweden at the outbreak of war. Salnais offered both the British and Americans a deal. In return for prime intelligence from inside German-occupied Russia, the Allies should agree that the Salnais nationalists would be recognised as the post-war government of Latvia.

The British accepted his offer and passed him 50,000 Swedish kronor which, for reasons of propriety, was paid indirectly through a Swedish naval officer, Captain Johannson. From the Swede, Salnais would in future obtain his documents and permits.

The key to Salnais' offer was an agent, Peter Klibitis, who had crossed the Baltic to Sweden in a small fishing boat bringing one nugget of vital information: a new resistance network of 1,000 men had been established in the Courland woods under General Janis Kurelis. Initially, Carr did not quite understand Kurelis' politics other than that he was against both the Germans and the Soviets. With British help, Klibitis returned by boat to Latvia. Travelling on the same boat was a stranger, Erwin Haselmann, codenamed 'Lilia', who had been tasked both with organising a British network in Latvia which could report on Soviet activities after the Germans withdrew and with leading a ten-man band across the front into Soviet-held territory.

Delighted by his success, Salnais sent the details of the agreement to Riga and began regular monthly meetings with SIS and OSS representatives who forwarded their reports to London and Washington where they were incorporated in the summaries for the chain of command into Downing Street and the Oval Office.

But unknown to Allied intelligence officers and Salnais, both the LCC and the Kurelis group had been monitored by the Sicherheitsdienst in Riga. The German security service had a particular and growing interest in the resistance as a conduit for monitoring British intentions. In summer 1944, as the Red Army advanced into the Baltic States and the Germans retreated back into Poland, that interest increased.

Latvia's Courland, a heavily forested area along the Baltic coast, evolved into a huge, militarised no-man's land. Although ostensibly and gradually falling under Soviet control, the enclave was infested not only with a large group of disciplined but desperate members of the Latvian SS and Wehrmacht soldiers but also with Baltic nationalists – students, factory workers and farmhands – who feared for their lives. Other Balts who had collaborated with the Germans or who feared a communist regime were also preparing to flee. Families bought train tickets for Germany and abandoned their homes for ever. Thousands of teenagers were travelling westwards involuntarily, swooped up from their classrooms by the Wehrmacht to dig anti-tank trenches to protect the retreating army and then to work as forced labour in Germany's factories. The able-bodied who remained at home met a predictable fate during that summer: deportation to Siberia as enemies of Russia or recruitment into the Red Army to continue the war. The communists' latest dragnets drove more into hiding in the forests and countryside.

Among the casualties of the German retreat was the Kurelis group. Judged to have become a nuisance, those members who were easily accessible to the SS were swiftly executed. Others escaped into the Courland forests and hid along the coast, in contact with SIS by radio and fishing boats. Their messages spoke of 10,000 partisans in the Courland promontory living alongside thousands of German troops who were cut off by the Red Army. Combined with Zilinskas' reports of at least 30,000 partisans in the Lithuanian forests and another 10,000 active in Estonia, the possibilities for SIS's activities seemed promising. To describe them as 'partisans' or 'members of the resistance', so equating them with the French underground, was convenient both for themselves and their sponsors, but the description was wildly inaccurate. Nevertheless, all those in the wilderness recalled Britain's support for their nations' independence in 1918 and believed that the past BBC broadcasts about the Atlantic Charter were certain guarantees of their independence and deliverance from the Red Army. None of the intelligence services in Stockholm disillusioned their informers' hopes that the West would use its best efforts to restore their countries' independence. On the contrary, all three agencies began discussions about increasing their support for the partisans, accompanied by misty promises about the future.

Among those in Broadway reading the reports from Carr was Kim Philby, who found three factors of particular interest: the estimated size of the partisan groups; the apparent ease of communications with Sweden; and the replacement of the pretence of gathering information about the Germans by a commitment to plant agents inside Soviet territory. Sentimentally, Philby recalled that one of his first major Russian contacts had been a Latvian. As *The Times* correspondent in Spain in 1937, his contact with the KGB had been Janis Berzins, who was acting as a military adviser to the anti-Franco forces under the cover name 'General Grecien'. Philby's messages had been passed to the Latvian via an intermediary in Portugal but the two had met and become friends. Philby's commitment to communism had not swayed in 1939 when Berzins had been recalled to Moscow with other Latvian KGB officers and executed as traitors in Stalin's purges. Their deaths robbed the Latvian KGB of qualified officers and hampered the agency's mass arrests in 1939. Five years later, when Philby began reporting to Moscow about the Baltic operations under Carr's direction, the KGB had barely restored even a nominal presence in that area. Carr's reports were therefore of particular interest to Section IX and he received encouragement for his work. In March 1945, Carr reciprocated the positive attitude which London had evidently adopted towards gathering intelligence inside the Soviet Union.

SIS was in contact with two networks in Latvia: Haselmann who was based near Riga and Valdemars Ginters who had recruited the remnants of Kurelis' partisans to guard the 'window' at the coast with access to Sweden. To secure better communications, two radio operators, Arturs Arnitis and Rihards Zande, trained by Tepfers with equipment supplied by SIS, were sent individually to Latvia. Arnitis' cover was as a port engineer at Ventspils while Zande hid above a dairy in Krapa. Both were protected by Ginters' group which included among its number Latvians who had served under the Germans. Typical was Roberts Sebris, an officer in the German Jagd Kommando who, in the previous three years, had maimed and killed any Latvians who opposed the German occupation. Some would later allege that Sebris' group, who called themselves the 'Wood Cats', had shot Latvian families at random to prove their efficacy to their German masters. Others in Ginters' group were members of a

59

special commando led by Major Victor Arajs, which had spent the past two years as an execution squad in Eastern Europe. That disparate group, momentarily secure from the Red Army and KGB, waited as the battle for Berlin was fought 1,000 kilometres away, convinced that their real allies were the intelligence services in Sweden.

Three hundred miles southwards, in Lithuania, a full-scale battle was underway between the partisans and the country's new occupiers. Responsibility for bringing Lithuania back under Soviet control was entrusted personally by Stalin to Mikhail Suslov, a rising star in the Party's Central Committee. But by the late summer, Suslov admitted that the countryside at night was unquestionably under the control of '1,067 partisan groups and 839 bandit groups'. Suslov appealed to Moscow to dispatch a specialist who could stem the unacceptable losses which the Red Army was suffering. The troubleshooter who arrived in September was General Sergei Kruglov, Beria's deputy in the Commissariat of Internal Affairs, who had won a reputation which mirrored his agency's during Stalin's purges. Kruglov's principal tactic, which he explained to a conference of all the military, security and political chiefs in Panavescis, 150 kilometres from the capital, was unconditional suppression. He believed that a scorched-earth policy to punish anyone who assisted the partisans was his only available tactic.

The Red Army's return revived memories of the forced collectivisation, seizure of property and the mass deportations which had already claimed the lives of twenty per cent of the population. Many consoled themselves that the Russian occupation would again be temporary. The German military, they speculated, would overthrow Hitler and would be invited to form a coalition with America and Britain to launch a crusade against communism, driving the Red Army from Berlin back into Russia. In a multitude of huddled and secret meetings, the anti-communists spoke about the possibility of a Third World War to impose the Atlantic Charter upon Stalin. The secret diplomacy started by Eden in 1940 and cemented

60

in 1944 by Roosevelt in Tehran was, to its victims, inconceivable. Their fateful misinterpretation of the wartime alliance between the Big Three was not unique. The same scenario was proposed by many senior German officers and politicians to Allied intelligence officers in Sweden and Switzerland. Allen Dulles, the OSS representative in Berne, even transmitted the idea to Washington, but those passionate anti-communists ignored Roosevelt's determination to remain on good terms with Stalin and adhere to the agreed policy of Germany's unconditional surrender.

Kruglov's violence in Lithuania flushed out some thousands of partisans but left untouched a hard core of 20,000 committed to the fight. There were many still hoping that the American President would honour his public pledges. The same sentiment rose in the Latvian Courland, although Ginters, exhausted and fearing capture, boarded a fishing boat and headed for Sweden. Arnitis and Zande, the two radio operators, and Sebris joined him. As the war ended and Soviet control was consolidated, SIS seemed to have lost their contacts inside the Soviet Union just when they were most needed.

Three

FATAL MISTAKE

Carr returned to London at the end of July to the discomfort of British austerity. Overcoming the housing shortage was difficult but eventually he rented a small mews house in De Vere Gardens, Kensington. Life in England had other disadvantages, not least the disappearance of servants and foreign allowances, but there were compensations.

After the early disasters, SIS had enjoyed a relatively good war thanks to the Ultra intercepts, and the agency's future was no longer in question. Menzies could guarantee his officers relief from the indignity of lowly incomes and even lowlier status as Passport Officers except as an agreed cover. In the eyes of the Civil Service, the amateurs were transformed into professionals. Menzies was too conservative and too near retirement fundamentally to reorganise his service but he did initiate a division of intelligence-gathering into two parts: Requirements and Production. There were nine 'R' sections, each responsible for a particular subject – politics, economics, science and the individual military services – which pinpointed what information was required from the five geographical 'P' sections responsible for worldwide agent operations. Although there was an opportunity to introduce new blood into SIS, Menzies naturally looked to his old and trusted colleagues to become the controllers of the Production sections.

Carr's reward for his service in Helsinki and for his

wartime successes in Stockholm was the CMG (Companion of St Michael and St George) and promotion to Controller of SIS's Northern Area. His domain from the sixth floor of Broadway mirrored the responsibilities of the Foreign Office's own Northern Department: Norway, Denmark, Sweden, Finland and the Soviet Union. With twenty-five years' practical experience in these countries, his claim to SIS's most important controllership seemed unrivalled. Under his aegis were the SIS stations in each of the five capitals, whose principal task, now the war was over, was once again to gather intelligence, principally about Russia. He could only reflect that his career had progressed substantially. On demobilisation after his return from Archangel, he had been set to learn shorthand and typing in order to become an office clerk. Twenty-five years later, without any further education or professional qualifications, he was an important channel of intelligence for the Prime Minister and the Foreign Office about the internal affairs of Britain's foremost enemy.

To Carr it seemed good fortune that in the new chain of command he was to report in the first instance to Kenneth Cohen, the Director of Production: his predominant interest was France and the Low Countries and he usually requested unspecific reports about Northern Area's activities. Among Carr's clients was Philby's new section, R5, counter-intelligence, which had replaced Section IX. Philby was still responsible for supervising the worldwide collection of all anti-Soviet and anti-communist material. Carr remained responsible for the security of his own operations, however, since Menzies had not created a parallel counter-intelligence group to monitor SIS's own activities and its agents.

Carr's wartime experience in the calm atmosphere of neutral Sweden contrasted sharply with that of colleagues who had operated under fire in Britain, the Balkans, North Africa, France and Germany. Throughout his career, and until his promotion in 1945, Carr had been insulated from the in-house pressures of Broadway and, significantly, had been aware only at second and third hand of some of the catastrophes which had befallen the service during the war. About those which afflicted SOE, he knew precious little. The early blunders in Scandinavia confirmed SOE in his opinion as an organisation which could command little respect. There was, however, one SOE calamity, an unwitting foretaste of his personal fate, about which Carr was briefed in limited detail: SOE's operations in Holland.

Between 1940 and 1944, in the belief that the flow of radio messages from across the Channel was sent by a genuine resistance network, 140 SOE agents had been parachuted in to fight with the Dutch underground. In reality, SOE was the victim of 'Nordpol', a huge deception operation mounted by the Abwehr. Nearly all SOE's agents were 'received' by the Gestapo and, after London had heard messages reporting their 'safe arrival', were executed. At the time of Carr's appointment, the Dutch governmennt was demanding from markedly reluctant British authorities a proper inquiry into the disaster which was caused by SOE's poor security, bad management and hostile office politics in London. In contrast, SIS was proud that detective work by their officers had uncovered the German deception.

Carr, who in 1925 had experienced the finest example of deception as practised by the Trust, needed no warnings about the perils of poor security and the requirements of absolute compartmentalisation to protect individual agents. His reputation as a stickler for secrecy convinced his chief that operations under Carr's control would be among the Firm's safest. Carr's relationship with Menzies was close, not socially but professionally. The son of an impoverished timber mill manager had little in common with a member of White's and the Beaufort hunt. Yet both shared a loathing for communism, an enduring suspicion of the Bolsheviks and, in common with many in their service, a distrust for the popular view that Stalin's Russia would be a durable peacetime ally.

Menzies brought in one outsider: Air Commodore

James 'Jack' Easton. He had won praise during the war as the RAF's Assistant Director of Intelligence with responsibility for providing facilities for SIS's and SOE's activities, and was appointed 'C's' deputy. A quiet but experienced organiser, Easton was shunned on arrival by the coterie of swashbuckling old Russia hands, who disdained the notion that a man without 'green thumbs', insensitive to the world of spies, should exercise authority. 'A tetchy atmosphere,' Easton commented to his wife after a few days in Broadway. His critics, excited by the anticipated resumption of their cloak and dagger work against the Bolsheviks, should have reported to Easton, but the new deputy quickly realised that they were avoiding his office adjacent to Menzies' on the fourth floor. Carr's group preferred to obtain approval for their activities directly from 'C' or occasionally from his vice-chief, Sir John Sinclair, another member of the old school who, regardless of the pressure and demands of work, habitually left the office at precisely 6 p.m. to catch his commuter train home to Chichester. Their refusal to consult Easton was not sinister but merely a habit of confining secrets to the family circle.

The old Russia circle included Wilfred 'Biffy' Dunderdale who, as the SIS officer in Paris before the war, had supervised the large White Russian group working against the Soviets. In 1945, Dunderdale resumed his links with a 'big crew' of about thirty émigré Russians in London to intercept Soviet communications. Housed in a separate building, 'Biffy' presented his operation as a valuable 'spare knee' against the Bolsheviks and insisted upon direct access to 'C', avoiding Easton, to protect his operation. No one had realised in 1939 that his Paris group was totally penetrated; equally, no one was allowed to become aware in 1945 that his team were 'long in the tooth and had lost everything'. That would only emerge during the 1950s.

Harold Gibson was another who 'played his cards close to his chest'. Before the war, Gibson claimed notable successes in Prague and Bucharest. Now Easton noticed how the officer waited for hours outside 'C's' office for a meeting rather than discuss his operations with the more objective deputy. Whenever circumstances compelled Gibson to explain his activities to Easton, the newcomer felt dissatisfied; there was never any meat, it was like chewing cotton wool.

Similarly, Carr rarely discussed his Soviet operations with Easton. The solitary Controller, who projected an aura of trustworthy professionalism, avoided the deputy's office and chose instead to go direct to Menzies. But between the old colleagues there was no talk of overthrowing the Bolsheviks any more, only about the need for containment. For the first time in history, Russian troops were based at the heart of Europe, and all the Western intelligence agencies were seeking to penetrate the fog of uncertainty about Soviet intentions.

For British and American intelligence, the division of Germany into zones provided a unique opportunity to observe the Red Army and the KGB at work. Unlike in Russia, where they could cocoon themselves from prying eyes, in Germany Western intelligence agencies could monitor their personnel, techniques and targets. For the first time, too, higher authorisation and sufficient personnel were not lacking to SIS*. At their base at Bad Salzuflen, SIS could exploit the huge wartime expansion of manpower and equipment. A mere signature was sufficient to requisition or confiscate any desired object from any German.

But Menzies urged caution upon his staff. Although comfort could be drawn from the scepticism which the new Foreign Minister Ernest Bevin was known to harbour about the communists, the Labour government was expected to continue the friendly wartime relations with Moscow and would condemn any embarrassment caused by SIS. While contact could be cautiously renewed with the anti-Soviet nationalities and agents could be sent into

*Originally SIS, known as MI1(c), was renamed MI6 in 1923. The historical acronym has been kept throughout this account.

the satellite nations, the Soviet Union was still barred to obviously SIS-sponsored operations. That, agreed Menzies, did not exclude renewing, as Carr urged, support for the Ukrainians, Georgians and especially the Balts who would eagerly volunteer for any engagement to liberate their countries. Carr recommended the dispatch of one radio operator from Sweden to the Latvian partisans who, by all accounts, were still engaged in a fierce war with the Russians. Menzies agreed but again urged caution. All support should be channelled strictly through intermediaries. There should also be liaison with the head of R5. Privately, Kim Philby would judge Carr's venture as a renewal of hostilities.

The responsibility for managing and supervising the new operations was handed by Carr to Sandy McKibbin who was attached to the Special Liaison Centre in Ryder Street, near Piccadilly. Although there was little affection between the two men, Carr believed that McKibbin possessed suitable credentials. He spoke the languages, he had long experience of the area, he was dedicated and trustworthy, and he was prepared to remain within the service when so many others were opting out, lured by lucrative prospects in the City. But McKibbin remained an outsider, more foreign than English, and easily irritated by Carr's unflattering pomposity and insistence upon time-wasting procedures. It was nevertheless a price he was prepared to bear for the opportunity to fight the communists and the Russian occupation. His sentiments were encouraged by the three Baltic Ambassadors in London, who no longer had nations to represent and were ignored by the Foreign Office.

Regularly, the three Ambassadors addressed letters to the State Department and Foreign Office pleading that the two governments acknowledge their countries' right to exist. Although in Washington they were treated both officially and unofficially with cordiality, the Foreign Office privately condemned their communications as 'pathetic appeals'. Basil Smedley in the Northern Department spoke for all his colleagues when, after reading a description of the desperate situation in the Baltic States from the Latvian Ambassador, Charles Zarins, he wrote: 'There is nothing that we can do to assist them and no argument drawn from the history of Latvia or Estonia or Lithuania can affect their future . . . No acknowledgement to be made.' The same attitude prevailed after T.C. Sharman, a First Secretary from the British Embassy in Moscow, was allowed in October 1945 to travel to Riga for the first time and confirmed Zarins' allegations of terror and mass deportations to Siberia which, in the local euphemism, 'render the opponents harmless'. Significantly, Sharman reported that there was no resistance movement against the Soviets. Probably Carr and McKibbin read Sharman's report but correctly dismissed his observations as the blinkered view of a lowly and inexperienced officer who was travelling under tight supervision. For, at that very moment, the KGB were suffering serious losses in their bloody campaign to suppress the partisans.

The three Ambassadors realised that the balance of power had shifted across the Atlantic and that their nations' liberation depended upon Washington since so many East Europeans lived in America. In the years before the First World War, no fewer than 100,000 Russians and Eastern Europeans annually had migrated to America, and in some years the total reached nearly 300,000. Thirty years later, the majority were still alive and had passed on their devout nationalism and suspicions about communism to the next generation. Throughout the Second World War, the migrants had lobbied Roosevelt on behalf of their countrymen, bombarding Congress and the White House with petitions demanding the implementation of the Atlantic Charter.

In February 1945, the League for the Liberation of Lithuania had written to Roosevelt complaining that there was no mention at Yalta of the Baltic question and predicting that 'the ever growing appetite of the communists will not be satiated with the Baltic States. If we divert justice and cease to guard moral principles then we will lose the very thing for which our sons are dying in this war and will sow the first seeds for a Third World War. If we sacrifice small nations today, then the larger ones will have to be offered tomorrow.' There had also been a flood of appeals in the weeks before the Potsdam conference, many delivered in person by delegations to the State Department, which bore the hallmarks of an organised lobby. All mentioned the inherent contradiction of Yalta and the Atlantic Charter. Surely, the petitioners urged, the Baltic States had the same rights to independence and self-government as other nations. The government officials reacted with bland self-effacement. None wanted to reveal Roosevelt's jocular remark to Stalin when he dismissed the Soviet occupation of the Baltic States and Poland: 'I don't intend to go to war on this point.'

Their pressure upon Roosevelt's successor proved more fruitful. In a speech on 27 October 1945 in New York's Central Park, Truman reaffirmed his support for the dispossessed and his commitment to the Atlantic Charter. The President's audience was gratified and expectant. After all, America, the only nation to possess the atomic bomb, was sufficiently powerful to extract concessions from the Soviets. Even if Truman was unwilling to break the friendship with Stalin which Roosevelt had bequeathed, the Baltic leaders in America believed that the British government would certainly aid their cause, since they had heard from the Ambassadors, unofficially, that SIS had not forsaken its traditional interest.

Carr's brief to his subordinates was to re-establish a presence throughout the Soviet Union. SIS needed émigré leaders from each of the areas who could represent a credible nationalist organisation to gather information and recruit agents. Carr instructed his officers to seek out and resume relationships with those who were SIS's friends before or during the war, usually regardless of their wartime collaboration with the Germans. Among these was Stefan Bandera, the Ukrainian nationalist with whom Carr had worked during the thirties in Finland. In 1945, he was a refugee in West Germany. Another was General Wladyslaw Anders, the leader of the Polish

Home Army, who was urged by SIS to re-establish relations with his officers in Soviet-occupied Poland. Operations in both these areas were Carr's overall responsibility. The re-establishment of SIS's relations with the Balts was McKibbin's direct responsibility.

In early July 1945, McKibbin returned to Stockholm to meet Walter Zilinskas, the former diplomat. The Lithuanian was struggling to survive. Soon after the war ended, the Swedish government, fearing reprisals from Moscow, had given the Lithuanian Embassy two days' notice of closure and an order to transfer all their files to the Soviet Embassy. By the expiry of the deadline, most of the files had either been destroyed or transferred to a small flat in Odengarten. Although SIS's wartime operations into Lithuania had been unsuccessful, McKibbin spoke optimistically about the future and told Zilinskas he would be given whatever financial support he needed to gather information for SIS. The Swedes had agreed that operations could continue, McKibbin informed the Lithuanian. Temporarily, Zilinskas' contact in the British Embassy remained George Berger, a Passport Officer, but a new SIS officer was due to arrive, Maclachlan Silverwood-Cope, who would work in the Embassy under the cover of Second Commercial Secretary. Zilinskas was to report regularly to Silverwood-Cope.

Days later, Algirdas Voketitis, the SIS/OSS-sponsored agent who had been sent to Lithuania in 1943, returned to Sweden, having survived incarceration in a concentration camp. At a hurriedly arranged meeting, he told McKibbin that the leaders of VLIK, the Supreme Committee for the Liberation of Lithuania, had survived German imprisonment. They were SIS's best hope, said Voketitis, because VLIK was a mature political and military organisation which had links with the thousands of armed anticommunists fighting in the forests. It was a purpose-built resistance movement, added Zilinskas.

At that precise moment an American intelligence officer was also seeking the VLIK leaders, and the wartime co-operation between the two Allied intelligence services was, as one cynical American officer grunted, 'disappearing as fast as butter melts in the sun'.

The war had barely ended before Second Lieutenant Anthony Vaivada, a very junior intelligence officer at General Patton's Third Army headquarters in Munich, began pondering how to undermine the Soviet grip on Eastern Europe, and especially Lithuania. A short, thoughtful 34-year-old, Vaivada had been nurtured by his Lithuanian parents from birth to hate the Russians. Although he was born in Philadelphia on the east coast of the United States, Vaivada and his family, like so many who had found sanctuary in America from Russian totalitarianism, had never forsaken their roots. In 1920, excited by their country's independence, they returned to Lithuania, only to succumb to destitution and disillusion. Six years later, they re-emigrated to America to rekindle, with one million others of Lithuanian extraction, their irredentism from a distance.

At Patton's Munich headquarters, there was much talk about the threat of communism – a strange paradox considering that for nearly four years the Soviets had been America's allies. Some of Vaivada's fellow officers seemed more concerned about the Reds than about the Nazis, whose entrenched power and influence was still so pervasive around Bavaria. Many would say that their prejudice stemmed from the episode in May 1945 when the Third Army came face to face with the Red Army in Czechoslovakia. Unlike the joyous scenes recorded by an American army cameraman when the two victorious armies met on the banks of the River Elbe, the encounter near Pilsen was tense and unfriendly, inducing American officers to turn a blind eye as their subordinates helped trapped Wehrmacht units and fugitive SS officers escape westwards. Others would say that the Third Army took their lead from their commander, George Patton, who quipped that the Russians were 'a scurvy race, Mongolian and permanently drunk'.

During those early days of victory in Germany, as Third Army units scoured Bavaria dispatching thousands of reports to Patton's headquarters about sightings of war criminals, discoveries of loot, the location of arms dumps, and every conceivable aspect of German conditions, Vaivada noticed that the reports included accounts of the millions of non-Germans who, as the flotsam and casualties of war, were wandering around the countryside in search of survival and a new existence. Most were the victims of the SS, who had been kidnapped from their homes in Eastern Europe either to work in German factories and mines or for incarceration in one of the many concentration camps strewn around the Reich. Although the largest group by far were Poles, Vaivada noted that many others were Ukrainian, Cossack, Azerbaijani, Byelorussian or Armenian, whose territories, according to the Yalta Agreement, irrefutably belonged to Russia. Some were the victims of Nazism, some had fought with the Germans against the Soviets; others were refugees who had fled westwards in fear of communism, and among these were nationals of the three Baltic States.

It was the listing of the Lithuanians which struck Vaivada. Letters from his parents enclosed messages from the large Lithuanian community in Chicago asking for news of relatives and requests that he help his countrymen. During those early days of May, Vaivada began driving hundreds of miles around Bavaria seeking out Lithuanian refugees, speaking with them in their native tongue. They told him of the horrors perpetrated by the Russians; of how, fearing communism, they had abandoned everything; of their fear that the Americans would forcibly transport them back to live under the Soviets like other Eastern Europeans; and, worst of all, of their belief that the Red Army would soon be marching westwards to occupy more of Europe. Their tales fuelled Vaivada's hatred of the Soviets. He was also irritated that so many of his fellow American officers addressed the Lithuanians as if they, in common with other Russian refugees, had collaborated with the Nazis. The Lithuanians told another story which Vaivada believed: that they had opposed both the communists and the Nazis and that their underground

72

organisation, VLIK, had organised passive resistance against the Germans for which they had been punished in the last months of the war by imprisonment.

On his own initiative, but with the authority bequeathed by his uniform, Vaivada began to seek out surviving VLIK leaders. Criss-crossing Bavaria in his army jeep, Vaivada was convinced that his search was both making a humane contribution to the Lithuanian cause and adding to American knowledge about the situation in Russia. His quest was rewarded. He found some VLIK members still held in Coburg prison and ordered their release; others, who had fled with the Germans in late 1944, had settled in camps for displaced persons. All were former politicians, army officers, academics or clerics. Their accounts of suffering under the Nazis and how they had smuggled information about wartime conditions to British intelligence in Stockholm were too similar, Vaivada felt, to be contrived. But, above all, he was impressed by their fear and loathing of the Russians. On his direction, they headed for Würzburg to create, as Vaivada explained to his superiors, a reservoir of fresh information about the Soviet Union and a centre where the trickle of refugees still arriving from Lithuania could be debriefed. Although they were a shaky coalition of very disparate opinions, they shared a conviction that a Third World War was imminent. The Soviets, Monsignor Mykolas Krupavicius, a crude and forceful clergyman who was VLIK's leader, told Vaivada, would not be content with restoring the old imperial empire but would, any day, move westwards. Although mounds of corpses still lay unburied across the continent, Krupavicius' predictions were not uncommon among the dispossessed of Europe.

In the first days of June 1945, Vaivada typed out a three-page memorandum, addressed to his superior, called, 'Report on Underground Lithuanian Government'. Using temperate language, he outlined the plight of VLIK who 'stated an earnest plea that they be given an opportunity to present their case to authorised American representatives' on behalf of 300,000 displaced Lithuanians.

In an added comment, Vaivada noted that 'all entertain violently anti-Soviet feelings and state categorically that neither they, nor Lithuanians in general, will return to Lithuania. To some "that would mean certain death, to others Siberian exile". They appeared bitter that "American D.P. authorities" accused them of pro-Nazism because of their anti-Russian attitude. Fear of the Soviet regime appears to be a dominating motive in the thinking of the entire group.' Vaivada deliberately omitted Krupavicius' dire predictions of war despite his own conviction about Soviet intentions.

In Patton's headquarters, the Second Lieutenant's report was read and registered. By July, it had wended its way higher through military channels to Robert Murphy, the political adviser to General Lucius Clay, commander of the military government in the American Zone. Few officers in Clay's headquarters sympathised with the fears and suspicions of Russia which the Germans and refugees unceasingly urged upon them. They dismissed as ridiculous the complaints that the American army should not have halted at the River Elbe but advanced to Berlin and then headed even further east. They voiced General George Marshall's support for Eisenhower's words: 'I would be loath to hazard American lives for purely political purposes'. The Germans, it seemed to Clay's staff, still did not understand the realities of the wartime alliance or the fact that it would continue. There had of course been irritations, especially the excuses which the Soviets contrived to delay the Allied arrival in Berlin until some weeks after the German surrender. But the Soviets were still allies. Accordingly, Vaivada's report was not considered worth pursuing, although it was forwarded by Murphy to the State Department in Washington where it arrived in September, a full month after the four powers had signed an agreement at Potsdam resolving the governance of Germany and concreting the national borders of Europe. Vaivada's report was therefore considered irrelevant in Washington, too. After registration, it was filed.

By then, Vaivada was already sailing from Europe to return to civilian life, and his work was unravelling. The divisions among the exiled Lithuanians were much deeper than he had understood. Monsignor Krupavicius, the aggressive priest, argued that VLIK should constitute itself as a government-in-exile with a military council to lead the partisans; Stasys Lozoritis, the senior Lithuanian diplomat in the West, insisted that he personally represented the nationalist government and would not tolerate usurpation of his authority.

It was in the midst of this bitter, irreconcilable and utterly futile feud that General Raymond Schmittlein of the French Deuxième Bureau arrived in Würzburg in September. Schmittlein had been based in Lithuania before the war and knew all the personalities gathered in Würzburg. He made them an enticing offer. VLIK was invited to transfer its headquarters to Tübingen in the French Zone where it would be financed and trained to foster a resistance army for operations in the very near future. His offer was immediately accepted but there were dissenters who argued with conviction that the partisans fighting in Lithuania would never take orders from an exiled group which had terminated its collaboration with the Germans only once the end of the war was in sight. It was a discomfiting argument for those who preferred to forget their wartime affiliations and were as unprepared to risk their lives in peace as in wartime. But their bogus claims to have actively resisted the Germans were of little interest to either Schmittlein or the other intelligence agencies.

Among the minority dissenters was Stasys Zakevicius, a likeable 33-year-old historian who had studied in Oxford and was a passionate nationalist. During the war he had been an adviser to the German government of occupation. Zakevicius had fled with the Germans in autumn 1944 but in May 1945 had considered returning home to Lithuania from Denmark to join the partisans. Just before he boarded a boat, he was warned that on arrival he faced immediate arrest by the KGB. Unknown to the VLIK council, on his return to Germany in July 1945, he had been contacted by McKibbin and another SIS representative, Major John Liudzius, whose parents had emigrated from Lithuania to Britain many years earlier and spoke the language fluently. When the political disagreements erupted, McKibbin tempted Zakevicius to work for SIS rather than the Deuxième Bureau. Zakevicius arrived in Tübingen later in 1945 with new, well-cut clothes, a motor car and ample funds. He also bore a new name, Stasys Zymantas.

Zymantas was the nucleus of SIS's new Lithuania operation. He was joined by the diplomat Stasys Lozoritis and by a well-known 31-year-old journalist who had escaped to the West in early 1945, Jonas Deksnys. In autumn 1945 Deksnys volunteered to return to Lithuania to assess whether VLIK was representative of the fighting partisans and to assess the scale of the uprising against the Soviets. In October, travelling with false Polish papers, Deksnys and a colleague, Klemensas Brunius, crossed into Eastern Europe.

SIS's leverage to start clandestine operations in Latvia was more realisable, despite the political splits among the nationalists and competition with the other intelligence agencies in Stockholm. The SMT, the Swedish military intelligence service, had given sanctuary to approximately 150 Balts, former SS and police officers who were wanted by the Allies as war criminals, and was using their expertise and contacts to infiltrate long-term agents into the Baltic to warn of any Soviet preparations to invade Scandinavia. Robert Anderson, a senior intelligence officer at the American Embassy, offered money, radios and weapons to any serious applicant who could set up an information network in Latvia. He employed two Latvians to liaise with his most important source, Hugo Ginters, a representative of the quasi-fascist Ulmanist party. On the other side of the city, the British stuck to their long-term relationship with the democratic LCC, the Latvian Central Council, led by Dr Valdemars Ginters and Verners Tepfers.

In August 1945 Valdemars Ginters was asked by an SIS representative to sound out Arturs Arnitis about the possibility of his returning to Russia and reopening radio contact. Two days later Ginters reported that Arnitis needed little persuasion. He welcomed an opportunity to serve the nationalist cause. Arnitis' mission was to return to Latvia, retrieve his radio set and code books which had been carefully hidden there three months earlier and establish contact with Sweden. Further instructions would follow but he could be assured that the British would send a boat for his return journey.

Two weeks later, three more agents had been recruited: Janis Smits, a former German army lieutenant who had been recruited to guard the radio operator, and Laimonis Petersons and Eduards Andersons who would form a second team.

On the night of 15 October, the four men neared the Courland coast in an expensively equipped speedboat. About one hundred yards from the shore gusts of wind overturned the boat. Drenched and dispirited, the four men struggled onto the beach and, abandoning any attempt to recover their weapons, equipment, food supplies and money, headed into the forest. At daybreak, a border patrol found the incriminating debris washed up on the sand and launched a massive manhunt. Two days later, Petersons and Andersons were discovered. Under interrogation their resistance broke and they disclosed the presence of Arnitis. The agent was arrested by the KGB three weeks after arriving in the port of Ventspils. By then, he had recovered his hidden radio and acknowledged his arrival.

Major Janis Lukasevics, number five in the Latvian KGB's counter-intelligence section, the Second Chief Directorate, was assigned to the interrogation. Lukasevics, a short, dapper and ambitious police officer, had been born in Riga in 1920 and had joined the illegal Latvian Communist Party in 1937. During the war, Lukasevics had been trained as a radio operator for clandestine operations behind the German lines but had never been sent into action. Instead, he was recruited by the KGB. Although the exiles in Sweden would claim that torture was used to extract a confession from Arnitis, Lukasevics always boasted that the hidden threat was sufficient for his purposes. Since SIS had not provided Arnitis with either a cover story or valid identity cards, only the limits of his physical endurance could delay the emergence of the truth. The KGB showed little mercy. Lukasevics passed his preliminary conclusions to his superiors. The British, he reported, had resumed their pre-war anti-Soviet activities. The evidence was irrefutable although four men with radios did not suggest a major operation. Nevertheless it was an omen and further action was required.

The report passed up the channels, first to Alberts Bundulis, of counter-intelligence, and eventually to Victor Kozins, one of the four deputies of the KGB chief in Latvia who reported to Alphons Novics, the Minister of the Interior. Few important decisions were taken by the minister without consulting his senior staff and, accordingly, Novics summoned Kozins and another of the four deputies, General Janis Vevers, to discuss Lukasevics' report. Of the three officers, Vevers could claim the best pedigree as a Chekist. He had joined the security police in Moscow in 1919 and had worked with the famed Feliks Dzerzhinsky. Vevers had been fostered on the details of the Trust deception and suggested to the minister that approval be sought from Moscow to mount a classic counter-operation: pretending to the British that they did indeed have a loyal radio operator *in situ* and then awaiting events. Vevers' recommendation and Lukasevics' report were forwarded to General Sergei Kruglov, Beria's deputy, who was supervising the suppression of the Lithuanian partisans. Kruglov was probably one of the few KGB officers who was not surprised by the arrival of the British-sponsored agents. A top-secret summary which he had been allowed to read on a strictly 'eyes only' basis some weeks earlier had reported that SIS had resumed its efforts to penetrate the Soviet Union. The origin was described as a reliable and well-placed KGB agent in London. A priority message was dispatched to Riga: proceed with the counter-operation. Supervision of the task was assigned to Vevers while the operational officers were Bundulis and Lukasevics.

Throughout the war, the KGB, in common with MI5 and SIS, had used captured German agents to transmit radio messages back to their headquarters, giving the appearance that they were operating freely and sending genuine intelligence. Just as Hitler was deceived that the Allied landings in continental Europe in June 1944 would be in the Calais area and not Normandy, the Red Army had confused the Wehrmacht during its westward advance. Lukasevics, however, had lost the possibility of using Arnitis or the others for a similar deception. One of the less salutary aspects of General Janis Vevers' past was his reputation for sadism at the Lubyanka prison in Moscow during Stalin's purges. Torture had become his regular work practice by the time he returned to Riga. In the case of Arnitis and the three agents, Vevers had ordered that no mercy was to be shown. His henchmen had obeyed and the four's physical condition rendered them unreliable as collaborators. Moreover, it had to be assumed that their capture was known to the British. All that survived was Arnitis' radio and his code books. It was thin material but sufficient for an ambitious officer like Lukasevics.

The prerequisite was to find a radio operator who had communicated with Sweden during the war. Lukasevics recalled meeting a possible candidate, Augusts Bergmanis, in a POW cage in mid-May. Bergmanis had served in the German army and had operated a radio for the Kurelis group. The first hurdle was to persuade Bergmanis to serve his former enemies. In late 1945, Bergmanis was transferred from the POW camp to a cell in the KGB headquarters on the corner of the newly named Lenin and Engels Streets in Riga. Soon after his arrival, Lukasevics walked into the cell with a cup of steaming coffee. 'You haven't been brought here for punishment,' he told the nervous anti-communist. 'I need your help and I want to make an offer.' As Bergmanis' tension slipped away, Lukasevics spoke about the KGB's interest in punishing only those who were the real enemies of the Soviet people, not those like himself who were mobilised. Bergmanis nodded his agreement that his future was in Russia. To his amazement the KGB major then handed him his passport and other papers, and a permit to leave KGB headquarters. The only condition attached to his release was that he remain in a house provided by the KGB.

In the following weeks, Lukasevics cultivated the friendship. There were long conversations about their respective wars, their youth, their families and the future. At the end of three months, Lukasevics mentioned to this grateful friend that he needed someone to establish radio contact with the British in Sweden. Bergmanis' story would be that Arnitis had given him the radio and codes shortly before his capture and, in view of his wartime allegiance to Kurelis, he was willing and eager to resume contact. Bergmanis nodded his agreement.

In March 1946, Bergmanis, with Lukasevics sitting alongside him, began tapping out Arnitis' call sign, precisely timed to match Arnitis' agreed schedule. Twice and sometimes three times every week for the next three months the two men transmitted their short signal without evoking any response. At last, in mid-June, there was a reply to Bergmanis' message. The KGB officer disconnected the radio without acknowledging his signal: 'Let them wonder why we are suddenly missing our scheduled calls. Their quandary will turn into anxiety and their anxiety will eventually turn to relief and then belief.' For three weeks, at Moscow's command, Lukasevics kept his silence as the SIS radio operator in Stockholm regularly transmitted his own call sign precisely according to the timetable.

Bergmanis' calls had been heard in Sweden but deliberately ignored at first because there were genuine suspicions that it was Arnitis calling under KGB control. When, after some deliberation, the SIS officer had finally acknowledged the call, a swift response might have confirmed those suspicions. Instead, when Bergmanis eventually broke his silence, his explanation was convincing: 'Operating is so dangerous here that I was forced to go underground. What follows is my background.'

Over the next weeks, the radio operator in Sweden tapped out a series of questions which London hoped would provide conclusive evidence of Bergmanis' identity and trustworthiness. 'No,' replied Bergmanis, 'I did not meet Arnitis but I was able to find his radio set. I discovered its whereabouts from a message passed on to me by others in the Kurelis organisation.' The suspicions of the professionals at Broadway relaxed slightly. But they remained sufficiently sceptical to refrain from any mention to Bergmanis of a new mission that had been implemented to establish Arnitis' fate.

The political mood in the Foreign Office had changed substantially since Arnitis had set out on his ill-fated voyage. In the summer of 1945, the US administration's warmth towards Stalin had appalled Ernest Bevin, the Foreign Secretary. Bevin, a renowned Somerset-born trade union leader whose opinions and policies would shape so much of SIS's and even the CIA's operations inside Russia for the remainder of the decade, had suffered the conspiracies and double-dealing which the communists had perpetrated during the pre-war years: 'You can never . . . deal with the Russians if you lie down and let them walk over you,' he advised.

Bevin's display of self-restraint towards Molotov and Stalin, whom he blamed personally for the deaths of countless Soviet peasants, lasted barely two months. When the four Allied foreign ministers met for the first time in London in September 1945, Bevin's antagonism was soon evident. 'We never asked where the Germans got their oil with which to bomb London,' he said sarcastically to Molotov, referring to Soviet oil supplies to Hitler. 'They just bombed us.' Molotov, who had been christened 'smiling granite' by a British diplomat, remained po-faced. After all, it was the same Molotov who had personally congratulated Ribbentrop on victory in France. As the disagreements increased and the tension rose, Bevin snarled at the Russian: 'You're behaving like a Nazi.' As the translation was completed, Molotov stormed from the conference room. The following day Bevin apologised but his fears about Soviet encroachment on Britain's traditional spheres of interest were confirmed by Molotov's demands for Soviet bases in Libya and elsewhere in the Mediterranean. These demands were matched by broken agreements and unrest in Eastern Europe and Greece, and new agitation in India which seemed to be Russian-inspired. Bevin, who insisted that his unease should receive absolutely no publicity, admitted to his aides, 'The depressing thing is the utterly realistic and selfish approach of the Russians and the complete absence of any wider consideration of the interest of peace for the benefit of all.' The following month, October, Bevin agreed with Attlee that 'the time had come where there must be a showdown [with] the ideological imperialists'. But the British were negotiating from weakness and their sentiments were not shared in the White House.

Since becoming President, Truman had, like Churchill, swung between praising Stalin as 'honest, but smart as hell' and warning that the Russians were 'planning world conquest'. Like his Anglophobe Secretary of State, James Byrnes, Truman believed that negotiating with Stalin and Molotov was akin to horse-trading with party power brokers in Chicago or a cabal of rebellious senators in Congress, where much acrimonious give and take was the necessary precursor of an ultimately firm and honourable deal. But during the autumn of 1945, the President sensed that he was being outmanoeuvred by the Kremlin. Just after Christmas, in a letter to his Secretary of State, Truman complained about Russia's seizures of territory in Poland and Persia and of new threats to Turkey. Soon after, the two men met on the presidential yacht, the *Williamsburg*, moored on the Potomac. Truman was irate: 'Unless Russia is faced with an iron fist and strong language,' he told Byrnes, 'another war is in the making. There's only one language they understand: "How many divisions have you got?" I do not think that we should compromise any longer . . . I'm tired of babying the Soviets.' Truman's frustration and uncertainty were reflected by American and British diplomats in Moscow who knew about Bevin's apprehension, although it was still politically impossible to publicise any suspicions about their wartime ally.

From the British Embassy in Moscow, Frank Roberts, the young Minister, sent evidence of increasingly virulent attacks in Russian newspapers against Britain and especially its policies in Germany. The Soviet propaganda machine, reported Roberts to credulous colleagues in early 1946, suggested that the Kremlin's intention was to exploit Britain's weakness and destroy the Empire. There was, he wrote, 'a tremendous revival of orthodox Marxist ideology, which left the impression that the Soviet people were the chosen people, and that they were surrounded by a hostile world'. His interpretation was dire: Russia was in a war-mongering mood which could possibly lead to 'a military adventure in the spring'.

One incident which particularly provoked Roberts' alarm was Molotov's accusation that America and Britain were preserving 'hundreds of thousands of German troops' in formation and were collaborating with anti-communist Polish and White Russian generals in Germany, Austria and Italy. They were preparing, Molotov claimed, a future war. A similar accusation was uttered at the same time by Andrei Vyshinsky, a prosecutor during the trials of the great Stalinist purges, to Sir Stafford Cripps. White Russians, Vyshinsky insisted, were being harboured in Britain and the only conclusion he could draw was that the British were repeating the same tactics as they had used after the Bolshevik revolution. Cripps' denial was brushed aside.

Among those in the Foreign Office who read Roberts' warnings was another young diplomat, Thomas Brimelow, who had served in the British Consulate in Riga in

1939 and had become very friendly with many Latvians, including Charles Zarins. Steeped in the frontier-town atmosphere of pre-war Riga, Brimelow's antagonism towards the Russians had surged after the war on hearing about the disappearance of his many Latvian friends during the first Russian occupation. After reading Roberts' report that the Soviet leaders were 'addicted to the study of history' and that the nineteenth century's rivalry with Britain was being repeated, Brimelow predicted that West Germany might well go communist, followed by Greece, Italy and France, not to mention Eastern Europe, where the Soviet promises of free elections seemed increasingly uncertain.

Brimelow's opinion was passed to Christopher Warner, the head of the Foreign Office's Northern Department. Aware that the War Office was formulating contingency plans for a conflict with Russia and that SIS was supporting anti-communist groups, Warner wrote a long memorandum entitled 'The Soviet Campaign against this Country and our Response to it', analysing the Soviets' 'most vicious power politics'.

'We should be unwise,' Warner wrote, 'not to take the Russians at their word, just as we should have been wise to take *Mein Kampf* at its face value. All Russia's activities in the past months confirm this picture. In eastern Europe, in the Balkans, in Persia, in Manchuria, in Korea, in her zone of Germany, and in the Security Council; in her support of Communist parties and Communist efforts to infiltrate Socialist parties and to combine left wing parties under Communist leadership; in the Soviet Union's foreign economic policy . . . in every word on foreign affairs that appears in the Soviet press and broadcasts.' Warner warned that there would be dangers if Stalin interpreted Britain's response as weakness and appeasement.

Warner recommended that wherever Britain's natural allies were fighting the communists, Britain should offer 'all such moral and material support as is possible' to the anti-communist forces. His opinions were amplified by analysts in SIS, some of whom had for long argued that the Kremlin was still committed to world domination. Echoing the similar creation after 1918 of a 'vigilance committee' on Bolshevism, a new Russia Committee was established to co-ordinate Britain's response to Russia's 'long-term attack' against the West. Although the committee's existence won the approval of both Attlee and Bevin, who were convinced of the existence of a Soviet masterplan to strike at Western interests, Bevin insisted that he would persevere to persuade the Russians of his goodwill. For the moment the Foreign Office hawks were to be denied the opportunity to launch a 'full-dress anti-communist campaign'.

The Russia Committee's first meeting on 2 April 1946 coincided with the first shift of policy in Washington. The American Joint Chiefs of Staff agreed formally to recognise that Russia was 'the greatest threat to the United States in the foreseeable future'. New bases were to be commissioned surrounding the Soviet Union from Greenland and Iceland across the polar cap to Okinawa.

The following day, George Kennan, a senior official in the American Embassy in Moscow, dispatched an 8,000-word telegram to State Department officials who had requested an explanation of Soviet hostility in the face of Washington's desire for friendly relations. Like Roberts, Kennan had become disillusioned with the Soviet leadership, especially after a speech by Stalin on 6 February in the Bolshoi Theatre, which he judged to be warlike. 'The Soviet leaders,' he reported, 'believed that they were encircled by hostile capitalists whom they would soon have to fight.' Kennan warned that 'a concealed Comintern tightly coordinated and directed by Moscow' was conspiring through front organisations to destabilise the West in the belief that the 'internal harmony of our society [should] be disrupted, our traditional way of life destroyed, the international authority of our state broken, if Soviet power is to be secure'. Facing the Soviets, wrote Kennan, needed the same thorough strategy as fighting a war, since 'the Soviets were suspicious and dangerous and quite unlike us or anything we have ever tried to deal with . . .'

Kennan's reflections were printed and circulated among hundreds of top American officials and policy makers. Although the White House still insisted on maintaining its friendly stance towards Stalin, many date Washington's conversion to anti-Stalinism to the receipt of Kennan's telegram. But there were limits. Truman and his officials rejected Bevin's opinion that Molotov was 'madly offensive, even crazy' and ignored Kennan's later intelligence summary that the Soviets expected both France and the whole of Germany to become communist.

The evidence of Soviet espionage could not be ignored, however. In February, Truman was told that Harry White, the Assistant Secretary of the Treasury, was a Soviet spy and that Alger Hiss in the State Department was also under suspicion. Another investigation underway in Canada suggested that a Soviet spy ring had been operating there since 1924. On 15 February, Canadian police arrested and charged sixteen people with seeking to discover America's atomic secrets. Four days later, the British atomic scientist Dr Alan Nunn May was arrested and charged with passing samples of uranium 235 to a Soviet agent. The evidence was overwhelming and he confessed.

Publicly, the governments in Washington and London remained silent. The politicians nervously withheld criticism but privately Christopher Warner and other senior officials feared that the world communist movement, like a 'fifth column', afforded the Soviets a huge spy network to 'undermine British and American influence in all parts of the world, and where possible to supplant it'. Formal discussions began between the British and American Chiefs of Staff to prepare plans in case the war of nerves escalated into a real conflict, and the intelligence agencies reassessed their operations.

But not every politician remained silent. On 5 March, at Fulton, Missouri, Churchill finally abandoned his wartime sentimentality and returned to his principles. 'An iron

Harry Lambton Carr, Controller of SIS's Northern Area, shortly before his retirement from SIS in 1961.

Carr (seated, second from left) was an interpreter for General Ironside, the commander of the British Intervention Army.

Top left: Alexander 'Sandy' McKibbin, born in Moscow, and his Finnish wife Helmi worked for SIS in Estonia until 1939.

Above: In 1945 McKibbin (second from left) became head of SIS's operations in the Soviet Baltic States. On his right, Stasys Lozoritis, the diplomatic representative of the Lithuanian resistance movement; on his left, Stasys Zymantas (*also top right*) who organised the recruitment of SIS agents to Lithuania.

Top left: Rudolph Silarajs was SIS's organiser for Latvia.

Above: Charles Zarins (centre), the Latvian Ambassador in London, was a focus in the recruitment of agents for SIS.

Top right: Former SS Colonel Alfons Rebane from Estonia recruited his old SS comrades to become SIS agents in their homeland.

Top: Eriks Tomsons at the harbour wall where he landed on an SIS mission in 1947. Tomsons came with the radio operator Rihards Zande. Both fell into the KGB's web.

Bottom: The Ujava lighthouse on the Latvian coast – the reference point for the drop of SIS agents.

Walter Zilinskas
(far right), SIS's
representative in
Stockholm, sitting with
four Lithuanian agents
just prior to SIS's first
major operation in May
1949. Left to right,
Jonas Deksnys, Juozas
Luksha, Justas Bredis
and Kazimieras Piplys.

Unknown to SIS,
Deksnys was already
under KGB control.

Left: At the last moment Fred Launags withdrew from SIS's first clandestine infiltration of six agents in May 1949 because he suspected that Vidvuds Sveics (*bottom left*) might be a KGB infiltrator.

Below: Vitolds Berkis led SIS's second batch of agents for 'Operation Jungle'.

Opposite page, top left: Major Alberts Lukasevics of the KGB's Second Chief Directorate masterminded the deception operation.

Top right: Major Janis Bundulis posed as the leader of the 'Maxis' partisan group.

Bottom left: Kazimirs Kipurs, now retired from the KGB, in the Kurzeme forest where he lived as a 'partisan'.

Bottom right: KGB General Janis Vevers vetted the intelligence reports sent to SIS.

Top: A small part of the KGB's booty.

Left: Hans Helmut Klose, a wartime German E-boat commander, was recruited by SIS to drop the agents on the Baltic coast using the reconditioned S208 (*middle*).

curtain,' he told his audience, which included President Truman, 'has descended across Europe from Stettin in the Baltic to Trieste in the Adriatic', and beyond the curtain Soviet influence and control dominated. Russia's aggression, he warned, had to be curtailed to prevent a slide into a new darkness. Churchill would later claim that he had ordered Montgomery, when collecting German arms, 'to stack them so that they could be easily issued again to the German soldiers whom we should have to work with if the Soviet advance continued'. Montgomery confirmed that he had obeyed his orders and Moscow interpreted Churchill's peroration as the preamble to a new clandestine offensive.

SIS's obstacle to mounting a serious counter-attack was Britain's bankruptcy and Bevin's caution, but there was sufficient political uncertainty to allow SIS officers to follow their own instincts. To the KGB, the evidence from Western Europe suggested that the British were once again, as after the Bolshevik revolution, collecting and recruiting dissident anti-communists for future operations.

During the last weeks of the war, the British and American armies in Germany and Austria had come across thousands of Russian-speaking soldiers dressed in German uniforms. From the Baltic to the Black Sea, the Germans had recruited Cossacks, Georgians, Ukrainians, Caucasians and Balts to fight against their historic enemy, the Russians. In the last days of the war, thousands of survivors of those divisions fled westwards, beyond the reach of the Red Army, to surrender to the Americans and British. They were a fraction of the approximately two million Russian nationals who would end the war in the West mingling with liberated POWs. According to the Soviet government, all of them were bound under the Yalta Agreement to be returned.

The agreement between the three Allied leaders at Yalta in 1945 had in many respects been a milestone in their wartime relationship. On the very site of the last major stand by the White Russian armies against the

Bolsheviks in 1921, Churchill, the great crusader against communism, had agreed that after the German surrender anyone who was a Soviet national at the outbreak of war in 1939 would be classified as Russian, regardless of their wishes, and would be handed over to Red Army officers.

Theoretically it seemed an unemotional task. British and American soldiers could have little sympathy for Russians who, for reasons they could not understand, had volunteered or agreed to fight alongside the Nazis. Those Russians naturally had cause to fear their treatment on return since they would be viewed as traitors. But their sentiments were irrelevant to those Allied officers who in early May 1945, burdened by inadequate food and facilities, were keen to speed up the repatriation of liberated POWs in the Russian Zone and wanted to remove any cause which might aggravate Stalin. 'We pushed them onto trucks and trains without asking questions,' recalls Bill Coffin, then twenty-one years old, who became haunted by the experience. Like many young Americans, Coffin had contemptuously rejected the pleas which both the Russians and Germans so energetically propounded as they were being hustled into oblivion: that the communists were their enemies and the Americans should unite with them in that common cause. As penance for his brutal scepticism, Coffin would return to Germany in 1950 as a CIA case officer to fight with the dissident Russians against the communists.

By mid-May, many British officers despaired of their task, especially in Austria where approximately 35,000 Cossacks had gathered. In impromptu history lessons during the first days of peace, the Cossack leaders had explained to the bewildered British soldiers that they were not Russian nationals but victims of Soviet imperialism. They had hated the Czars, loathed the Bolsheviks and had turned to the Germans, ignorant of the politics and crimes of Hitler, because they were offered the opportunity of liberation and independent nationhood. Similar explanations were offered by the Balts and others who had fought under the Russian general Andrei Vlasov. All had fought with the Germans on the eastern front and pledged their respect for the Western, anti-communist Allies.

But many of the non-Russian groups who had fought with the Germans had, in liaison with SS units, committed the most horrendous brutalities. War crimes investigators were discovering that few groups were more feared in Eastern Europe than the Latvian SS, the Lithuanian 'Police Battalions', the Ukrainian SS Galizien Division, or the Cossacks. According to Nikolai Krasnov, the grandson of a famous Cossack general, 'They robbed like bandits. They raped women and set fire to settlements. Their disgraceful behaviour cast a stain on those who came to fight against communism and carried out their duty in an honourable and soldierly manner.'

The British soldiers in southern Austria were either ignorant of these war crimes or knew at least that the Cossacks' victims were not British. Certainly they were affected by their prisoners' painfully translated accounts.

The issue came to a climax at the end of May when the commander of V Corps, Lieutenant General Charles Keightley, was asked by the Soviet commander across the zonal line for the Cossacks' return. Keightley was prepared to comply until Major General Robert Arbuthnott, the commander of the 78th Division, announced that he flatly refused to carry out the order because the Cossacks were 'old émigrés', who had fought with the British twenty-five years earlier and were not covered by the Yalta Agreement. Once persuaded, Keightley agreed to lobby Field Marshal Sir Harold Alexander, the Commander-in-Chief. As a major serving under Gough in Riga in 1919, Alexander had become a local hero as the commander of the British Baltic Volunteers, protecting the new state's independence against the Russians. 'These were people,' an observer later recalled, 'who had fought with us at Archangel and the Far East of Russia in the Civil War. Many of them had British decorations.'

This was the very reason the Soviets demanded their return. Stalin was set on eradicating the danger of a 'second Russia' of exiles who, if allowed to remain in the West, would never cease to plot a counter-revolution.

Alexander rejected Keightley's humanitarian arguments. Quoting personal instructions from Churchill and Eden, Alexander insisted that his orders be obeyed. Amid scenes of great emotion and even suicides, on 29 May, at Judenburg, 2,000 Cossack officers were handed over to the Russians and certain death. On 1 June, the first of the remaining 33,000 soldiers, wives and children were ordered by British soldiers to board trains for the transit journey. Panic erupted and many Cossacks, rather than return to Russia, threw their children and themselves into the swirling River Drau to drown. By mid-June, when the operation was judged complete, about 4,000 had escaped forceful repatriation. But the consequences were far-reaching. Quietly, 10,000 Ukrainians, members of the 1st Ukrainian Division who had fought with the Germans in Poland as the SS Galizien Division and had taken part in horrendous massacres, were transferred across the Alps to a British POW camp in Rimini. Soon after their arrival, most destroyed their wartime identity documents and claimed to be Polish, not Russian, Ukrainians to forestall their repatriation. Their false claims would be knowingly endorsed by British military and government officials. Another group of beneficiaries were the remnants of the Nazis' Baltic SS units who were also transported by British troops to Italy and Belgium.

Others, however, still remained in Germany. On their behalf, Dr Alfreds Valdmanis, a former Latvian finance minister, sent a plea to Alexander, reminding the field marshal of his glorious heroism twenty-five years earlier. Ever since, he wrote, Alexander had been 'an ideal who was looked upon as a friend of the Latvians'. After mentioning the names of Latvian generals whom Alexander met during his service, all of whom had perished either in Soviet prisons or in Siberia, Valdmanis complained that Latvian Legion officers in Germany had been wrongly placed 'into special SS cages of the prisoners' camps'. The Latvian soldiers, he claimed, placed their faith 'in the great British Fieldmarchal [*sic*]' as their only hope of salvation from this injustice since they were not volunteers but conscripts. Alexander felt sympathetic: 'I was their commander and they were my soldiers, so I want to do all I can for them,' he wrote to the Foreign Office. Brimelow agreed that the Latvians 'did not deserve the fate which had befallen them' of being grouped with the SS. Nevertheless, the diplomat decided, they were not to be separated from the German POWs since 'It is impossible to distinguish between those who enlisted and those who joined up under duress.' The British military were convinced that most had volunteered to join the SS.

A similar plea on behalf of 10,000 imprisoned members of the Estonian SS was sent to Bevin by the Ambassador, August Torma. 'The majority were forced to join the German-controlled Legion,' he wrote, or joined to avenge the Russians' 'brutal terror'. His request for their release from the SS POW camps was rejected by Brimelow.

These pleas coincided with an approach in Berlin from Marshal Grigori Zhukov to Montgomery requesting that the thousands of Balts who had been captured in German uniforms should be repatriated as agreed at Yalta. Asked for guidance, officials at the Foreign Office barely hesitated. The Balts, they told the military, were unofficially deemed 'not to be Russians as defined under the Yalta Agreement' although it was accepted that among the 90,000 Balts was a 'very high percentage of former collaborationists'. Unless the Russians could provide proof that an individual had been a member of an SS execution squad, they were not to be repatriated.

Under the Moscow Declaration of 1943, the Allies agreed that alleged war criminals should be returned for trial to the place where they committed their crimes. Since most Nazi war crimes were committed in Eastern Europe, it was inevitable that there would be a major imbalance in the trade of wanted men. Yet during 1945, only a fraction of those culpable and interned in the West were handed over. The majority remained in displaced persons (DP) camps where they concocted alibis and sanitised their war records. The few exceptions proved to the Russians that there existed a Western conspiracy with Nazi sympathisers.

On 28 November 1945, a Red Army officer arrived at the Zedelghem POW camp in Belgium, a collecting centre for Latvians, with a demand for transfer to Russia of Colonel Arvids Kripens to stand trial as a war criminal. Kripens, a former Chief of Staff and a regimental commander of the Latvian SS Division, had fought voluntarily with the Germans throughout the war. Major Thomson, a British army lawyer who read the Russian evidence, agreed that there was a prima-facie case and authorised his transfer. Even Brimelow considered that Kripens' SS command made the soldier's activities 'look pretty black', but Charles Zarins, the Latvian Ambassador, in a revealing plea to the Foreign Office insisted that Kripens was 'an honest and good man'. Zarins' bias was ignored on that occasion but, to forestall his transfer, Kripens made an unsuccessful suicide attempt and was declared too sick to travel.

And while the murderers were protected, 70,000 East European DPs had been recruited by the British army as uniformed members of labour battalions. The British claimed that the East Europeans were cheap labour to clear the debris of war and undertake menial tasks but the Soviets insisted that they were paramilitaries for use in a future war against Russia. There were good grounds for Soviet suspicions since Colonel Arvids Kripens would, on his recovery, be employed by the British army. Although Bevin personally told Molotov at the conference of foreign ministers in Paris in April 1946 that his accusations of a British conspiracy were untrue, in reality SIS was already planning to draw upon those Balts living in the DP camps.

In early 1946, McKibbin and Zymantas decided to hold a series of meetings for the pro-British Lithuanian group to discuss covert operations. Since SIS's operations were still based in Sweden and Captain Ore Liljenberg, the new Swedish intelligence chief, was naturally curious about all Allied operations, the discussions were held in West Germany. The first in Hamburg in January 1946, which Walter Zilinskas attended, agreed that agents should be sent as soon as possible to establish radio contact with the partisans. In March, a second conference was summoned in Lübeck to consider reports brought back by Jonas Deksnys who had smuggled himself out of Lithuania overland. His accomplice, Deksnys explained, had been arrested. Significantly, no one queried the circumstances in detail. McKibbin and Zymantas were more concerned to hear that the 30,000 active partisans who were giving the Soviets grave cause for concern distrusted VLIK because its leaders had collaborated with the Germans. McKibbin and Zymantas accepted Deksnys' verdict and were delighted that the Lithuanian agreed to return once again with radio sets and money to establish direct contact between SIS and the partisans. Accompanied by another volunteer, Vytautas Stanevicius, he again travelled overland using false passports and bribes.

When the news that SIS had accepted Deksnys' denunciation reached the VLIK council in Germany, the split in the resistance movement became unbridgeable. Deksnys in turn was accused by VLIK of collaborating with the Nazis. Zymantas, who was equally culpable, ignored the riposte. For their part, SIS officers were only concerned to infiltrate reliable agents into the area. Their wartime activities were irrelevant history. Having established contact with the Lithuanians, McKibbin sought to discover the fate of Arnitis, his three colleagues and the Latvian network.

During the night of 6 August 1946, a well-equipped fishing boat quietly slipped along the harbour wall of Zvejniekciems in the Latvian district of Skulte. As it reached the shadows, two men carrying large bags jumped ashore and hurried into the darkness. Rihards Zande and Eriks Tomsons, the unnoticed arrivals, were the latest agents to be recruited by SIS in Stockholm and sent into Russia. Tomsons had made the crossing eleven times during the war and was tempted to undertake this latest journey by the promise of cash rewards on his return. Zande, who had worked with Valdemars Ginters and the Kurelis group until May 1945, was a well-known nationalist. His detailed instructions, contained in a hollowed-out compartment of his hairbrush, revealed that SIS wanted not merely radio operators inside Latvia but a network of informants.

The preparations for the operation had deliberately obfuscated the connection with SIS. Janis Lukins, a young nationalist who organised the actual trip, was certainly unaware of the connection. Lukins was in contact with Hugo Ginters, the quasi-fascist who was associated with Robert Anderson at the American Embassy. It was during a conversation between Ginters and Lukins that the idea emerged of raising money from Latvian exiles and a Swedish pastor to obtain a boat and equipment. The two Latvians' objective, Lukins believed, was simply to locate about thirty partisans in Riga who would be collected by a second boat sent four months later. Unknown to Lukins, the pastor was acting on SIS's behalf and the 'innocent' rescue mission was a carefully planned ploy for Zande to discover, for SIS, the fate of the Arnitis group and to establish a new radio link.

After jumping from the boat onto the quayside, the two men made their way out of the fishing village to the home of Zande's father. Once inside, Zande went to the attic from where he transmitted confirmation of safe arrival while Tomsons unpacked the sub-machine-guns, pistols and ammunition to check that everything was dry. According to their plan, Tomsons would remain in the house while Zande travelled to Riga, found a flat, and contacted sympathisers. In return for information, they were to be promised a safe passage to Sweden.

Zande returned to his father's home in early September, enthusiastic about his achievements, but soon he was having problems with the radio. He was receiving SIS messages from Sweden but their replies suggested that his transmissions were garbled, and he could not repair the fault. The remedy suggested from Sweden was that Zande contact Augusts Bergmanis, the operator whose coded messages were being transmitted under Lukasevics' control.

SIS had maintained contact with Bergmanis despite grave suspicions. Although his explanations seemed plausible, his messages in the course of the past months were strangely propagandistic and occasionally even hysterical. Yet, since Zande's situation was desperate, the risk was worth taking.

In early November 1946, Bergmanis received a message from Sweden which was also sent to Zande, advising the recipients to proceed to a meeting, a *Treff*, at the home of an old woman in Jelgava, near Riga. If Zande was cautiously relieved, Lukasevics was ecstatic. One year's patience had been rewarded. Until that message had arrived, the KGB major had been unaware that any other SIS agents were operating in Latvia. A technical hitch and faulty professional judgment had delivered a rich prize.

Bergmanis was well rehearsed when he arrived at the *Treff*. Zande's questions were easily answered and the existence of a working radio seemed to calm the agent's fears. Zande agreed that his messages should be transmitted by Bergmanis and also ordered him to collect intelligence for London. On his return to Zvejniekciems, Zande told Tomsons: 'The meeting was successful. I am satisfied that Bergmanis is not under KGB control.'

Over the following weeks, Lukasevics became in turn impressed and then concerned about Zande's success. Over twenty people, many in key positions, had been recruited to report on sensitive Soviet activities. Their motives for co-operation were identical. Zande had promised that in return for their help they would be taken on the return boat to Sweden. In the midst of all the wild rumours then circulating in the Baltic States about the activities of a horde of British agents arriving in boats from Sweden, it was not hard for Zande to convince his informants of SIS's strength.

In Stockholm, meanwhile, Janis Lukins raised the

money to procure a larger boat to cross the Baltic. He selected a similarly minded Lavian, Elmars Skobe, to captain this latest mission.

Skobe was seemingly an ideal choice. As an officer in the Latvian Legion's pioneer corps during the war, he proved himself to be an exemplary anti-communist, killing in the last days of 1944 as many Russians as his accurate aim could achieve. For most of 1945, he and his wife and his thirty subordinates lived in the Courland forests, armed with German weapons, harassing farmers to obtain sufficient food for their survival. By late summer, however, Skobe's diminished band of fighters was destitute and increasingly endangered. One night they had been surprised by a Red Army patrol and Skobe had survived only by shooting dead a Russian officer at point-blank range. 'We can't just sit in the bush waiting for the war to start,' Skobe announced, suggesting that they seize a boat and sail to Sweden.

In the midst of planning their escape, on 4 October, Skobe's wife was caught by the KGB. Over the following days, the naked woman was tied to a chair and tortured to extract the location of the partisan group. Delirious and in pain, she conceived a plot to escape. 'I'll take you to the place in the forest,' she told the anonymous KGB interrogator, 'but you'll have to let me walk alone so that my comrades are not suspicious.' It was agreed that the injured woman would walk along a forest road towards a KGB detachment, concealed in the undergrowth. According to plan, she was left on a desolate path and began walking. Once sufficiently distant from her guards, she bolted and disappeared into the darkness. Hours later she was reunited with her husband. It would be weeks before she could walk properly again; forty years later the mental scars still festered.

While she lay recovering in a forest hide-out, Elmars Skobe and another partisan, Fred Launags, searched for a craft. On 22 October, late at night, Skobe, dressed in the uniform of a KGB officer who had been killed by Launags, ordered a fisherman in the village of Jurkalne to launch his boat to search for suspected 'bandits'. Outside the harbour, the hapless fisherman was arrested and the boat, with the remainder of Skobe's band, sailed for Gotland and asylum.

'The Swedes don't know what to do with us,' Skobe confided to his wife at Christmas 1945 when they were still incarcerated in a refugee camp. His visit with Launags to the British Embassy offering their services had been politely rejected. Skobe had told the British official that his ambition was to obtain a boat and return to continue the struggle in Latvia. The longing for a boat became an obsession which only deepened when the Swedes dispatched Skobe to work as a forester in northern Sweden, a 26-hour journey from his wife. In summer 1946, his ordeal was relieved. Janis Lukins wrote that he needed help to prepare a boat for a special journey.

Lukins was unaware of Zande's radio problems. In the compartmentalisation which SIS had imposed, the Latvian radio operator in Stockholm, Karlis Arins, handed Lukins only certain messages and these confirmed that the mission was proceeding according to plan. In conversation with Ginters and the Swedish pastor, Lukins was 'advised' that he would need 3,000 kronor for a boat, which would require a captain and a crew of four. The cash which Lukins received from the clergyman, who was an SIS intermediary, was the precise cost of a shabby, former German naval speedboat which was for sale in Helsingborg. To protect Lukins, Skobe signed the contract and the ship sailed unobtrusively to Stockholm for repairs. Throughout the autumn, the engines of the newly named *Hagbard* were overhauled, larger fuel tanks were fitted and mufflers were installed on the exhausts. The shipyard's costs of 14,000 kronor were obtained by Lukins from the same sources.

By the end of October 1946, Lukins had recruited four other Latvians as crew. A fifth, appointed by Ginters, was to stay behind in Latvia as SIS's new radio operator.

On 17 December, as Skobe made his final preparations, an unknown intermediary whom Skobe would later describe as 'the Colonel' arrived on the quayside and unloaded two brown suitcases. Their contents were self-explanatory: two new American walkie-talkie sets, a new crystal radio transmitter; two American 9mm sten guns, three pistols; ammunition; and a box of medicine. Carefully, Skobe and the crew hid the cases in pre-arranged places. The supplier, Skobe told the crew, was an Estonian. Despite his request to test the boat, Lukins insisted that there was no time: 'Our people in Latvia are getting very anxious.'

Skobe was given two more packets by the Colonel. One contained 11,500 roubles and in the second were radio codes and transmission schedules. 'Let no one else get their hands on this,' the Colonel told Skobe, who tucked the envelope into a bag and stuffed another 3,000 roubles, which had been handed to him, into his pocket. He had never seen so much money in his life. 'Here's one more thing,' said the Colonel, handing over two small packages. 'Eight spare crystals for radio sets. Give them to the radio operator when you arrive.' They were replacements for Zande's impotent transmitter. Skobe hid the packages beneath the navigation equipment. There was one more detail to cover. 'Whatever happens,' said the Colonel, 'you mustn't let the boat and the equipment fall into Russian hands. If you're caught at sea, you'll have to set the boat's petrol tanks alight and perish with the vessel. If for any reason you have to stay in Latvia and you get caught, you must say that you were infiltrated from Germany. Under no circumstances reveal that you came with American help from Sweden.' Skobe agreed and that night passed the message on to his crew.

Two days later, the *Hagbard* quietly put to sea. On board was a Swedish naval officer who navigated the helmsman through the rock-strewn Stockholm archipelago towards Gotland before transferring to another boat waiting on the high seas. Skobe set sail but he was soon spotted by a Swedish naval patrol. In panic, Skobe ordered the *Hagbard* to full speed. The reconditioned engines outpaced the patrol but on arrival in Gotland the boat was impounded. Within hours, despite the discovery of the radios and weapons, a telephone call from the mainland to Bertil Bonde, the island's head of counter-intelligence, secured the ship's release. Once more, on 19 December, the *Hagbard* was en route. Its destination was the bay of Skulte deep inside Russian territorial waters where Soviet patrols would not expect foreign ships to venture. Zande and about twenty Latvians were silently waiting near the beach for their salvation, unaware that Lukasevics and a large KGB detachment were hidden nearby.

The *Hagbard* was well inside Soviet waters and heading towards the rendezvous when Skobe lost his nerve. Although he would later claim that the compass was swinging wildly, in truth he feared that the boat was lost and would be exposed in the coming daylight. He ordered a 180-degree turn and full speed out to sea. In the afternoon, the craft was once again nearing Gotland where it was picked up by the local police. Bertil Bonde had no authority over that police force.

The police interrogator in the fishing port of Tjelders made little headway. 'We raised the money for the boat and weapons ourselves and had no contacts with any governments,' said Skobe. 'All we wanted to do was rescue our relatives and leave some supplies for the partisans.' No one provided any contradictory evidence and Skobe was transferred to Stockholm to the care of Kommissar Otto Danielsson of the civil intelligence agency.

Danielsson prided himself as a professional who disapproved of the activities of competing services. 'Your story is ridiculous,' he shouted at Skobe. 'You're not leaving here until I get the truth.' The misery and loneliness of spending Christmas alone plunged Skobe into depression. When Danielsson returned from his holiday, Skobe signalled that his resistance had broken. On 2 January he began to dictate his confession.

The operation, he claimed, had been organised by one Arturs Plume whom Skobe knew as a partisan. Plume's instructions to Skobe were: 'Go to the Kjellsons

Konditori, the coffee shop in Birger Jarlsgatan, and place on the table a menu card which is torn down the middle. Be there tomorrow evening.'

At the arranged time, Skobe told Danielsson, an American intelligence officer, about thirty years old, 1 metre 78 tall, with light brown hair and of slender build, whom he called 'the Colonel', arrived and offered 3,000 kronor for a boat. The 'American' officer, said Skobe, outlined his requirements: 'We want you to make contact with your partisan group and give them radios which we will provide to establish contact with us. We need information. Especially about the Russian rocket tests. We want to know where their bases are located, their test flight paths and the technical details about the rockets. We need as much as possible about the state of the Red Army and what is happening politically and economically in the region.' It was the Colonel, explained Skobe, who provided the equipment and made the arrangements with the Swedish navy and counter-intelligence in Gotland.

Since the radio equipment was American, Danielsson had no cause to doubt the explanation. The following day, 3 January 1947, Skobe was shown a selection of photographs. Among them were Robert Anderson, the intelligence chief in Stockholm, Colonel Leonard Johnson, the American Military Attaché, and other Embassy officials whom Danielsson suspected might be involved. Skobe looked blank and shook his head. In the long silence, the interrogator was baffled.

Danielsson's staff produced a new clue. One of the sten guns was wrapped in paper on which someone had scribbled 'K 65 IV'. Investigators deduced that 'K 65 IV' referred to the French Embassy which was situated on the fourth floor of Karlav'gen 65. Round-the-clock surveillance had also revealed that a one-armed French diplomat was visiting the Russian Embassy. For nearly two weeks, Danielsson worked diligently towards the conclusion that Skobe's venture was a 'Soviet provocation' using the French diplomat as an unwitting front man. The perpetual obstacle was Skobe's own account. By

10 January, it had become clear that the French diplomat was running a black market in currency. That left only one other nation who could have been responsible: Britain.

Inquiries revealed that Maclachlan Silverwood-Cope, officially designated as a Third Secretary at the British Embassy in Stockholm since summer 1945, had unexpectedly left Sweden and flown to England. The 31-year-old diplomat was known to be the Embassy's senior SIS officer who during the war had developed close contacts with Finnish and Norwegian intelligence. Despite Skobe's denials that he knew Silverwood-Cope, Danielsson concluded: 'It is clear that Skobe's mission was just the beginning of a British plan to recruit agents in Russia and supply them by parachute . . . They had deliberately left "US Army" labels on the radio sets to shift the heat onto the Americans if they were seized by the enemy.' Skobe denied the British connection. 'You're expelled from our country,' said the Swede in frustration.

In the weeks after Silverwood-Cope's hasty flight to London, Lukasevics became anxious about his own deception operation. The KGB was unaware of the reasons for Skobe's non-arrival and had received another message from Sweden that the boat, delayed by a storm, would arrive on 5 January – two days after Skobe failed to identify 'the Colonel' for Danielsson. McKibbin had hoped to arrange an alternative vessel but had failed. Zande and his large group, still under KGB surveillance, returned to their homes.

Zande and Tomsons were now impatient to leave. Tomsons had found a small boat which, with some minor repairs, was ready to sail. On the night of departure, the motor strangely failed to start. Tomsons was perplexed since previously there had been no problems. He would discover only months later that a KGB mechanic had removed a small but vital part from inside the engine which the agent would not notice.

Despondently, Tomsons sought another boat while Zande continued energetically to gather information for transmission by Bergmanis. But by March 1947 Lukasevics' superiors were concerned about the quality of intelligence which Zande was sending and Tomsons' second boat was ready to sail. 'Arrest them,' ordered Vevers, 'they're becoming too dangerous.'

Karlis Arins, the radio operator in Sweden who noted Bergmanis' last message, could tell that the hand which was tapping the Morse key in Russia was desperate – a ruse which Bergmanis performed at Lukasevics' request: 'Great disaster. Zande and Tomsons arrested. I've escaped but fear Zande's interrogation. All activities have stopped. Will contact you when safe.'

In London, this sudden and unexpected development baffled Carr and McKibbin. There had been no hint of any trouble and now there was only silence. The one expert whose advice they could not call upon was Kim Philby. In January, he had been posted to Istanbul and was excluded from further knowledge of Carr's operations to establish a network inside Russia. Instead Philby revealed to the KGB the infiltration of British agents through Turkey and the Black Sea, which resulted in another successful KGB deception operation against SIS.

One option to solve the Latvian mystery was instantly attractive to SIS. The Soviet government was appealing to Balts who had sought refuge in Sweden to return home. Some Latvians, disillusioned by life in the refugee camps, were attracted by the offer and had applied for repatriation. At McKibbin's behest, Tepfers and Valdemars Ginters began seeking Latvians who could be recruited as agents and inserted into the returning trickle to become legitimate Soviet citizens. Each recruit would be individually groomed to present a different account of their past and their motives for returning so as to escape suspicion during the inevitable KGB interrogation. SIS's go-between in the search for candidates was Roberts Sebris who had escaped from Latvia in May 1945. Sebris found a suitable candidate, Feliks Rumnieks.

Born in 1914 in Riga, Rumnieks had served in the Latvian SS Legion before deserting in January 1945. Arrested soon afterwards, he had met an old acquaintance,

Roberts Osis, a Latvian army officer who before 1939 had been a British intelligence source in Riga. During the German occupation, Osis had been promoted to colonel and was charged initially with guarding the Jewish ghetto in Riga, but later commanded a roving execution squad in Latvia and Poland. These wartime activities were only briefly discussed when Osis and Rumnieks met in January 1945. Osis proposed that Rumnieks should sail to Sweden and inform SIS that Osis, their trusted source from pre-war Riga, was once again offering his services. With German help, Rumnieks arrived in Sweden and, after speaking to a British Embassy official, contacted Tepfers of the Latvian Central Council who was already working for the British. Their meeting was fruitless and Rumnieks was incarcerated in a refugee camp, while Osis, with SIS help, eventually arrived in Britain.

When Sebris found Rumnieks in early 1946 and learned that he intended to return home, he asked him to wait. It was arranged that Osis would travel to Sweden from London, on McKibbin's behalf, to meet Rumnieks and persuade him to return to Latvia as an SIS agent. Rumnieks agreed to the plan. On interrogation by the KGB, he was immediately to admit that he had been recruited by SIS, given the codename 'Melbardis' and that his channel of communication with London would be visiting merchant sailors. Having confessed, he would be well placed to build a relationship with local KGB officers and fulfil the true purpose of his mission, namely, to discover the fate of Zande, Tomsons and Arnitis. He would send his information by letter, using invisible ink, to cover addresses in West Germany and Belgium.

Rumnieks' return ran according to plan. His carefully rehearsed cover story was accepted by the KGB and he was allowed to resume a normal life in Riga. SIS and McKibbin could only await developments.

Four

DUBIOUS ALLIES

Maclachlan Silverwood-Cope returned unobtrusively to Stockholm once the ruffled feathers of Swedish intelligence had been smoothed. Temporarily, Sweden had become impractical as a centre for intelligence operations. Local politicians were anxious to placate the Russians and the SMT once again wanted more control over their agencies' operations. Moreover, Carr and McKibbin needed to re-assess their Baltic strategy and reassure themselves that their networks had not been penetrated.

At the height of the Skobe fiasco, Jonas Deksnys had returned again from Lithuania through Poland. He was accompanied by an associate, Vytautas Stanevicius, who had brought his wife. Deksnys, excited by his second successful return, gave Stasys Zymantas, SIS's Lithuanian expert, graphic eye-witness reports of pitched battles between the partisans and the Soviet army. The country-side at night, he claimed, was a no-go area for the occupiers. The Forest Brotherhood were by all accounts fearless, killing thousands of civil servants and officials who collaborated or sympathised with the Russians and terrorising those Russians who had been assigned to the farms of deported Lithuanians. The KGB, in their frus-tration, were adopting their own terror tactics. They dressed as partisans to discover their enemies' supporters and dumped the corpses of their victims in village squares while observing from a distance the reactions of the inhabi-tants. Those who unsuspectingly revealed themselves to be friends or relatives were arrested, interrogated and deported to Siberia. As a counter-measure, to avoid incriminating their families, the partisans were disfiguring the faces of their fallen comrades while those who preferred death to capture exploded hand grenades at their heads to prevent recognition.

To McKibbin and Zymantas, the most important aspect of Deksnys' account was his meeting with the partisans, in particular Juozas Luksha, the 25-year-old son of a large peasant family which in 1941 had been decimated by the deportations to Siberia. Luksha was an acknowledged partisan leader who had skilfully organised the disparate groups in the countryside as self-contained cells to maximise their efficacy and kill their enemies. Deksnys' tales of bravery naturally impressed his SIS debriefers. Here, just as in Latvia and the Ukraine, was a 'hot' anti-Russian war which could be supported at minimum expense and SIS's agent was evidently in touch with its leaders.

None was more important, in Deksnys' opinion, than Dr Juozas-Albinas Markulis who had introduced himself as a nationalist and was attempting to co-ordinate the partisans. Markulis was born in Pittsburgh, USA and had returned in 1930 to Lithuania where he trained for the priesthood although finally he had refused to take his vows. In 1941, he graduated in medicine. Deksnys, who stayed in Markulis' home, was impressed by his host's enthusiasm and resources, especially the doctor's ability to procure the forged passports which had allowed Deksnys to return to the West. In return, Deksnys handed Markulis the radio codes and schedules to contact SIS in Sweden and a list of addresses in Western Europe for coded letters. On SIS's behalf, Deksnys gave the doctor the codename 'Erelis'.

During that visit, Markulis convinced Deksnys that VLIK, the Lithuanian exiled leadership based in Germany, was not trusted by his countrymen because they were former collaborators who were now out of touch. Markulis recommended that a new organisation should be established linking the partisans and the West, called

105

VLAK. For McKibbin and SIS this was a critical proposition. Since SIS had dismissed any relationship with VLIK, McKibbin had been searching for an alternative organisation. Deksnys' report of an established resistance group inside Russia suited SIS's requirements precisely and needed further exploration.

In February 1947, Zilinskas, Deksnys, Zymantas and several other Lithuanians were given tickets by an SIS representative in Stockholm to travel at different times and by different routes from Sweden to Hamburg. On arrival, they were driven to a castle outside Osnabrück where they remained for two weeks. Their hosts were two uniformed British army officers. Both spoke fluent Russian. Their identities were never revealed but much later some speculated that one of the officers was Carr.

The visitors were overwhelmed by the luxury which they enjoyed while discussing their strategy. While the German population beyond the castle walls was barely surviving on less than 2,000 calories per day and the British were suffering bread rationing to support their former enemies, the SIS hosts provided an apparently endless feast.

The discussions focused upon the recognition of VLAK. Deksnys explained that Markulis was summoning all the partisan leaders to a meeting to co-ordinate the struggle. VLAK would be the organisation they recognised. McKibbin, who was not present, had sent his support: 'We need to give the partisans a political reason to fight. Just killing Russians is too crude. I don't trust the VLIK people. They're unrefined. We should back VLAK under Zymantas.' By the end of the conference, the two SIS officers had agreed to the formation of VLAK and promised finance and resources for the fight. Deksnys and Zymantas were delighted. Their pleasure would have dimmed, however, had they known that Markulis' partisan summit, held two weeks earlier, had not developed in quite the way which Deksnys imagined.

Markulis had summoned the conference for 8 January but Juozas Luksha, the partisan leader, suspicious of the doctor's remarkable ability to provide money, passports and safe houses, had warned as many partisans as possible to stay away. On the day of the meeting, Luksha's spies watched Markulis' rendezvous from a distance and noticed that KGB officers had surrounded the building. Those partisans who had not received Luksha's warning were eventually led away under arrest. Further investigation revealed that Markulis had become a communist in 1944 and was a serving KGB officer whose function was to penetrate the partisan movement. In Osnabrück, Deksnys had become his unwitting tool to divide the Lithuanian resistance movement between VLIK and VLAK and cast SIS into the KGB's web. Since Luksha had no radio or addresses to send a warning to the West, SIS continued in ignorance along its chosen path. Carr, who had been nurtured on the legend of the Trust and the sanctity of security, was on the verge of becoming entrapped in another web.

On the eve of their departure from Osnabrück, SIS's grateful guests were briefed for their diverse return journeys. Their passports were returned containing a host of forged visa stamps suggesting that their two-week absence from Sweden had been non-stop travel. The warm farewells reinforced the Lithuanians' conclusion that the partisans had won the British government's support for their independence. 'We've got the army,' reported one SIS officer to McKibbin, 'we're just waiting for political reality to catch up.' Not for the first or the last time, SIS was pursuing its own vision of history. The SIS hosts had deliberately concealed from their guests the 'realpolitik' espoused by their colleagues 'on the other side of the house' in the Foreign Office. In London at that moment, as Ernest Bevin was preparing to leave for a foreign minister's meeting in Moscow, his advisers were preparing a brief which would finally recognise the legality of the Soviet occupation of the Baltic States.

In the memorandum which he prepared for Bevin in early March, Thomas Brimelow of the Northern Department set out the historical background. Britain had been

107

on the verge of recognising the Soviet occupation in 1942 and again in December 1945. Nothing had changed in 1947 to effect that legality. But in return the Soviets should settle a number of financial debts which the Baltic States had incurred to Britain and to British subjects during the inter-war years. But to Bevin's surprise, throughout his month's stay in Moscow, the issue was barely mentioned. For the Soviets, the re-annexation was a fact and Western recognition was irrelevant. The events in Moscow did not influence Brimelow. On his return, Bevin faced Parliamentary demands that the government should protest about the deportations from the Baltic States to Siberia. Brimelow advised the minister that it would not 'do the slightest good to the deportees' and 'the Soviet Government would certainly consider any such approach to be an unwarrantable interference in the internal affairs of the USSR'.

Bevin undoubtedly appreciated Northern Department's efforts to provide a placatory escape route on the Baltic States question despite his fierce antagonism towards the Soviet Union. The Balts' fate was a sideshow compared to the thriving communist subversion throughout Eastern Europe and the outright battle against the communists in Greece. Convinced that the Russians wanted to keep Europe in a state of disorder for as long as it took to achieve communist domination of Europe, Bevin had repeatedly urged Washington to accept their responsibility to stem the communist advance. His pleas were finally rewarded on 12 March 1947. In a message to Congress, Truman announced that the US would send aid to Greece to fight the communists. The unveiling of what came to be called the Truman Doctrine was interpreted by the American Chiefs of Staff as the launch of an anti-communist crusade, and the British Chiefs were invited to draw up joint plans to resist communism.

One of the by-products of the US administration's new policy was the invitation by the State Department of the three Baltic Ambassadors to official functions. When the Soviet Ambassador protested and threatened to refuse to attend in their presence, he was ignored. 'The result,' wrote Lord Jellicoe at the British Embassy to Brimelow, 'had only been the absence of the Soviet ambassador.' Prompted by Washington, the Foreign Office began to review its own policy and passed on the news to 'the other side of the house'.

In Broadway, Menzies recognised that the political atmosphere in London now favoured more operations and was concerned about Bevin's apparent dissatisfaction. The only man in the Cabinet who was indispensable to Menzies was complaining that, despite the worsening relations between the West and Russia, SIS had failed to obtain reliable information. Compared to the wealth of material about Soviet activities in Germany and Austria from intercepts and agents, there was a dearth of intelligence from inside Russia itself. The remedy until then had been complicated by Bevin's steadfast refusal to approve aggressive operations inside the Soviet Union which would prove embarrassing if exposed. Hence the indirect employment of ragbag émigrés in Sweden and elsewhere. Those restrictions had been lifted but his resources had sharply diminished. Britain was tottering towards bankruptcy and the exercise of its foreign policy depended upon the largesse of Washington. In 1947, SIS shared that unpleasant predicament, but there was hope. George Kennan in the US Embassy in Moscow had, according to the British Embassy, advised the President in July 1947 to adopt a policy of 'firm and vigilant containment of Russian expansive tendencies'. Unwilling as SIS officers were to share anything with other intelligence services, there were some operations which needed Washington's co-operation to succeed. Unfortunately for SIS, the American intelligence service was still struggling to emerge from post-war confusion, which complicated negotiations.

Regardless of the glowing legend, the elitists of the Office of Strategic Services who had staffed 'Wild Bill' Donovan's wartime organisation had, like their boss, created too many enemies, as a reckless and inefficient clique, for the White House to tolerate their survival in peacetime. Donovan's bid to persuade the President to allow OSS to continue failed on three counts: firstly, its target was questionable since both Russia and Britain were allies; secondly, the military opposed a civilian intelligence agency; and thirdly, there was a conviction that OSS was totally penetrated by the British. In autumn 1945 there seemed no urgency to decide upon a replacement, so while the powerbrokers in Washington debated whether the task of co-ordinating the supply of intelligence to the President should be under military or civilian control, OSS's functions were distributed to other agencies. Insiders and outsiders alike were baffled in the midst of the competition for differing and often contradictory goals.

No one was more frustrated than Harry Rositzke, the chief of the Soviet Division in the Central Intelligence Group which had assumed OSS's civilian function in Washington. Rositzke was a former academic whose subject was the *Anglo-Saxon Chronicle* and in particular a speech delivered just before the Norman conquest of Britain in 1066. Until May 1945, Rositzke had been an OSS desk officer in London and thereafter opted to remain in what seemed a more exciting career – as a specialist in Soviet affairs for American intelligence. His prime source was an SIS compendium prepared in 1944 describing the Russian Intelligence Service. By 1947, Rositzke's knowledge and experience of the Soviet Union were still starkly limited to a review of published books and articles and an intensive survey of the Soviet's wartime espionage. In the course of that reading, Rositzke had marvelled at the success of Richard Sorge and Leopold Trepper, two Soviet master agents who had so accurately predicted German activities to Stalin. As he read the flow of unreliable intelligence digests from Europe, Rositzke contemplated placing American-sponsored agents inside the Soviet Union to provide a similar service. He was guided by George Kennan's judgment that the Russians were always 'devious, monstrous, incalculable and inscrutable'.

The first hurdle was the absence of enabling laws; to undertake SIS-type activities, American intelligence needed legal authorisation.

The hiatus was partially ended in July 1947 when the President signed the National Security Bill. The 1,800 civilians in the Central Intelligence Group became the first employees of the Central Intelligence Agency. Over the following months, as America's relations with Russia worsened, Rositzke's agenda was set by the Secretary of Defence, James Forrestal, who had anticipated the Cold War before it started. In autumn 1947, Forrestal asked Roscoe Hillenkoetter, the CIA's founding Director, whether the new agency would have the capability to undertake paramilitary campaigns inside the Soviet Union. That could only occur, he was told, once the agency was given extra legal authorisation.

Directive NSC 4, which was issued by the National Security Council on 19 November, required the Secretary of State to co-ordinate anti-communist propaganda. In a secret annexe, NSC 4A, the Director of Central Intelligence was instructed to supplement the propaganda with covert psychological warfare. To implement that directive, a Special Procedures Group was established in late 1947 inside the CIA under the control of the Office of Special Operations (OSO). Rositzke became chief of OSO's Soviet section and automatically one of the new agency's most important officials for covert operations. He felt 'part of the American crusade against Stalin, the same as against Hitler', although OSO was not yet authorised to conduct clandestine warfare.

These restrictions began to fall soon after Hillenkoetter submitted a review about the world situation to the President on 17 December: 'The communists, under Soviet direction,' he wrote, 'have launched a concerted campaign of disorders, strikes, and sabotage in France and Italy . . . The primary Soviet objective is to defeat the European recovery program.'

In December, acting under Directive NSC 4A, the CIA began secretly to spend $10 million in Italy to prevent the communists from winning the elections. Two months later, the Agency began supporting the anti-communists in the Greek civil war.

Throughout Germany, the communists' belligerency sparked talk of a new war. Reinhard Gehlen, formerly Hitler's chief of intelligence for the Soviet Union, who had become a key adviser to the American military, told General Lucius Clay, the US military governor in Berlin, that 175 divisions of the Red Army across the zonal boundary were 'combat ready' and the indications suggested that mobilisation was being planned. Clay, a wartime engineer with no front-line combat experience, was easily persuaded of the report's accuracy. Two years earlier, the Joint Chiefs in Washington had been presented with an estimate that, fully mobilised, the Red Army's fifteen million soldiers or 650 divisions would reach the English Channel within three weeks and Gibraltar in five months.

On 5 March 1948, one month after the communist coup in Czechoslovakia, Clay cabled an historic message to the Director of Intelligence in the Pentagon: 'I have felt and held that war was unlikely for at least ten years. Within the last few weeks, I have felt a subtle change in the Soviet attitude which I cannot define but which now gives me a feeling that it may come with dramatic suddenness.' Although Clay cautioned that his warning stemmed from a 'gut feeling' and not hard evidence, the cable was leaked to the press. In the ensuing hysteria, which was expertly fanned, CIA analysts repeated the warning that war could break out in less than three months although, compared to some other predictions, the CIA's was a voice of reason. The following day Truman, in an address to a joint session of Congress, called for the restoration of conscription.

Clay's warning, when examined and repeatedly re-examined inside the Pentagon, seemed self-justified. The numbers of Russian troops in Eastern Europe were, according to the experts, considerably more than required for a mere occupation. Their ultimate purpose could only

112

be an invasion. No one paused to consider an alternative interpretation: that the Russians might be less efficient or require additional tasks such as administration and construction from their military. No one bothered to reconsider the opinion given in mid-1946 by G2, the army's intelligence branch, that the consensus of 2,000 US Counter-Intelligence Corps officers in Germany confirmed that the Red Army was under-equipped, over-extended and war weary, and that the East German rail system was unfit for mobilisation because the Russians had stripped and shipped eastwards large segments for repair. Nor did anyone in Washington refer to an intelligence assessment from the British military chiefs that the 'Soviet Union is unlikely to start a war before the end of 1956' unless the Soviet leaders thought the USSR was about to be attacked or were allowed to underestimate any Allied reaction to their own subversion. This view was endorsed by Field Marshal Montgomery after an official visit to Russia.

Harry Rositzke could quite easily believe that war was more than likely. Although his files were bereft of any basic data about railways, roads and bridges in the Soviet Union, the judgments from the Pentagon and White House that 'the Russians are coming' were convincing. The reliability of these conclusions appeared to be confirmed when, twenty-five days after Clay's cable, the Soviets imposed the blockade of Berlin. In the excitement, no one in Washington paused to reflect that if this was the beginning of the war, then why was the CIA in Berlin reporting the absence of any mobilisation or stockpiling in the Soviet Zone, and why were American dependants in Germany not being evacuated?

Rositzke's personal conviction was confirmed as, in conditions of great secrecy, he was continually summoned to meetings with senior officers in the Pentagon for briefings about new and constantly changing requirements. No meeting and no instruction would be more evocative for Rositzke than the order he was given in June 1948 by an army colonel who, jabbing at a huge map

113

hanging in a briefing room, barked: 'I want an agent on every airfield between the Iron Curtain and the Urals. I want to know when the bombers are taking off.' The meeting did not signify an intention by the Pentagon to declare war, but it did mirror the common fear that America was blind to Soviet intentions. Rositzke returned to his office with the injunction ringing loudly in his ears: 'Action, action, action.'

The new authority finally permitting the CIA to undertake covert operations was Directive NSC 10/2 which the President signed on 18 June. A special panel was created within the National Security Council to direct the 10/2 operations under the guideline that the 'overt foreign activities of the US Government must be supplemented by covert operations'. The key to 10/2 operations was secrecy and deniability; they were to be cloaked so that the 'US Government can plausibly disclaim any responsibility for them'.

The range of activities was unrestricted: 'operations shall include any covert activities related to: propaganda, economic warfare; preventive direct action, including sabotage, anti-sabotage, demolition and evacuation measures; subversion against hostile states, including assistance to underground resistance movements, guerrillas and refugee liberation groups, and support of indigenous anti-communist elements in threatened countries of the free world.' For Rositzke and those recruited by the CIA as tension escalated, the emotional phraseology of the directive itself resurrected blanket approval for a return to the derring-do days of the Second World War when OSS agents parachuted into enemy territory.

To some, the directives themselves were the cause of more alarm than the actual events in Europe. None was more explicit about the agency's purpose than a top-secret policy document, drafted under George Kennan's supervision, which was adopted by Truman in August 1948. NSC 20 described American objectives as the 'overthrow of Soviet power'. Although Kennan did not advocate launching hostilities and only referred to an 'eventual

114

war', he did recommend policies which could achieve the result without resort to the ultimate struggle. The American government, he suggested, should support those émigré groups who were dedicated anti-Bolsheviks and who were, in his view, 'preferable . . . as rulers of Russia'. Kennan suggested that rather than the US selecting individual groups as ideal candidates, all the émigrés should be sponsored equally and be allowed to 'establish their bids for power' in the chaos of post-Bolshevik Russia. Any group with proven anti-communist credentials was to be supported regardless of its activities during the Nazi era. The top-secret programme was called Bloodstone. The inter-departmental committee which managed Bloodstone was known among the select few participants in Washington as SANACC 395.

Bloodstone authorised the CIA to support any group, including socialists, trade unionists and intellectuals, who could produce anti-communist propaganda. The SANACC 395 committee had discussed in March the 'utilisation of refugees from the Soviet Union' by encouraging defections of the elite from the Soviet block to 'stifle', 'damage' and 'demoralise' America's enemy. Fifty of the most suitable refugees were to be brought to the United States to form a 'potential nucleus of possible Freedom Committees encouraging resistance movements in the Soviet world and providing contacts with an underground'.

The person to organise the recruitment of these highly motivated and intelligent activists was Frank Wisner, an energetic, Mississippi-born Wall Street lawyer who was appointed to run the Office of Policy Co-ordination. The OPC was created by the State Department and although formally it was part of the CIA, Wisner's independence provoked severe internal conflict, not least in his choice of recruits. Wisner specifically targeted refugees from the 'Soviet world' as ideal servants of America's national interest, to write and broadcast propaganda. SANACC 395 empowered Wisner to recruit foreigners who were 'war criminals, quislings and traitors [or who] have voluntarily assisted the enemy forces since the outbreak

115

of the Second World War'. Such blanket authorisation, which contradicted the government's public pledges to prosecute those same categories, automatically bestowed a licence for illegality upon OPC's clandestine activities.

Among those brought to America under Bloodstone was Gustav Hilger, a former German Foreign Ministry official whose task included liaising with the SS Einstazgruppen about their daily employment of murdering Europe's Jews and with General Andrei Vlasov, the most senior Soviet general to defect to the Germans, who had commanded approximately 300,000 Russian soldiers against Stalin. Soon after the war, Hilger had been brought to America for debriefing and later to give advice to the State Department. Anticipating a public outcry if 'any sour apples show up among the imports', the State Department briefed a select handful of Congressional leaders in September 1948 about the programme – to win their support and guarantee their silence.

But the propaganda programme was a sideshow, to some even a fig leaf, for the 'special operations' which the JCS defined as 'activities against the enemy which are conducted by allied or friendly forces behind enemy lines'. The outstanding hurdle during 1948 was to find agents who would fight these 'special operations' inside Russia. Both the targets and methods chosen mirrored SIS's own conclusions.

Kennan had written to Forrestal on 29 September 1947 suggesting that the army should re-establish a guerrilla warfare school. Ten months later, the military's Joint Strategic Plans Committee also recommended the creation of a guerrilla warfare school as 'the means for supporting foreign resistance movements'. In its favour were cited staff studies of the OSS in Europe and Detachment 101 in Burma where guerrillas won 'spectacular success'. To cloak the proposals with some respectability, there was mention that, in the event of war, the military would need 'escape lines for allied air crews and exfiltration of key personnel' and the 'destruction of all rail heads and equipment'. But the country-by-country survey ignored a crucial distinction: the Second World War guerrillas had operated against a foreign occupier, while the operations under consideration in 1948 would be carried out inside Russia itself.

In the event, the Joint Chiefs rejected the proposal, explaining that 'special operations' had become a CIA responsibility. The army would provide training for agents, declared the Joint Chiefs, but soldiers would not become involved in illegitimate warfare where the definition of 'special operations' included 'covert warfare, sabotage and assassination'. The military's decision indicated their awareness of the government's intentions. Dirty business, in their view, was best left to non-Americans.

Politicians and officials in the White House, State Department and CIA who favoured pursuing 'covert warfare, sabotage and assassination' had by then decided that 'special operations' should therefore be undertaken by 'favourably disposed foreigners' who were actively resisting the Soviet Union. Their model of 'underground resistance movements, guerrillas and refugee liberation groups' was General Andrei Vlasov's army which, they believed, had recruited, with German sponsorship, about one million Russians to fight alongside the Nazis against Stalin. Among those countries where the staff identified the prospects for clandestine warfare as 'excellent' was Lithuania; according to numerous diverse reports, at least 30,000 partisans were actively fighting the Red Army there. Latvia and Estonia were not mentioned because American intelligence, unlike SIS, had no sources of information.

In a contemporary policy statement to the National Security Council describing America's objectives against the USSR, George Kennan's study identified the Baltic States as having 'a special status in our eyes' as the one area in the Soviet Union which should be liberated by American forces. 'We cannot really profess indifference to the further fate of the Baltic peoples . . . It should therefore logically be considered part of US objectives to see these countries restored to something at least approaching a decent state of freedom and independence.' But he stressed the cost: 'It is idle to imagine that this could be brought about by means short of war.' Explicitly, Kennan excluded the Ukraine from 'the opportunity to free themselves fundamentally from Russian domination'. Responsibility for the operations went to Rositzke, deemed to be the prime advocate of 'doing something' against the Soviets. The centre for training agents would be in the American Zone of West Germany. The ideal location was judged to be near Munich. Rositzke codenamed the operations to infiltrate reporting sources into the Soviet Union 'Red Sox'; 'legal' agents who travelled through Russia with legitimate passports and visas operated under the codename 'Red Skin'; while the recruitment of Soviet officials in the West was called Operation 'Red Cap'.

Charlie Katek, a veteran OSS agent who had recently been expelled from Czechoslovakia where he had been working under the guise of a war crimes investigator, was appointed chief of the new training base in Kaufbeuren, a small village surrounded by wooded countryside, about fifty miles west of Munich. Three houses were requisitioned for living accommodation on the village outskirts and sealed off by a high perimeter fence despite the risks of exciting speculation from the very people who were intended to be deceived. Every house and farm in the surrounding countryside was available for requisitioning if the need arose. The anticipation and sense of urgency among the new spymasters suffocated any fear of the risks.

The head of the OSO's Soviet Operations Group on Katek's staff was George Belic who had much in common with Harry Carr and Alexander McKibbin. He had been born in Russia in 1911, and his father had been a colonel in General Deniken's army which had fought the Bolsheviks with British help. In January 1920, Belic was evacuated with his mother from Odessa to Constantinople while his father disappeared for ever into the mayhem of the White Russians' last stand against Trotsky's legions.

Three years later, Belic landed in the United States where in 1936 he graduated from Georgetown Foreign Service School. In 1942, he joined the US Navy, became an intelligence specialist, and in 1945 was posted to the US military mission in Soviet-occupied Bucharest, Rumania.

The small American contingent in Bucharest, which included Frank Wisner, had arrived in the expectation that Stalin would abide by his assurances to Roosevelt and Churchill and allow free elections. Instead, Belic witnessed the KGB's intrigue to impose upon the government Rumanian communists brought in from Moscow, while the Russian-trained security service methodically sought out the 'people's enemies' listed for automatic arrest. The experience confirmed his childhood pledge. As Belic would confide over the years, 'Soviet communism was an enemy of mine since I was eight years old and its spread, like a cancer, had to be prevented. I joined the fight with glee.' In 1947, Belic was recruited by Richard Helms to join the Strategic Services Unit (SSU), the CIA's predecessor, in West Germany.

Belic's boss in Heidelberg was Gordon Stewart, a former OSS officer who, unlike the army's Counter-Intelligence Corps, believed that his priority was not to hunt down Nazi war criminals but to assess the communist threat to American interests. The new officer was thrust into what became his lifetime's career – seeking out in the DP camps dissident émigrés who were prepared and eager to join a secret war against communism. For three months, as an apprentice, he observed other SSU officers before being assigned seventeen DP informants who would supply a constant stream of reports about émigré intrigues and the possibilities of revolution in their abandoned homelands. Although the emphasis was still on gathering information and forging contacts, Belic was impressed that an estimated one million Soviet citizens had fought with the Germans against Stalin. No group was bigger than the Russian Army of Liberation led by General Andrei Vlasov. Although Vlasov had been surrendered by the American army to the Russians in May

1945, his successors were anxious to impress the representative of American intelligence with their knowledge and their networks of dedicated anti-communists who had remained inside Russia. Young Belic felt a kindred interest with these impassioned enemies of communism; only later did he realise that the source of their 'knowledge' was false rumours which were sold to the intelligence community's 'paper mills' as reliable information. The customers were not only each of the four occupying powers but also competing national intelligence agencies.

Anatoli Granovski, a senior KGB officer, completed Belic's education about the nature of his father's enemy. Granovski had negotiated his own defection in Stockholm and was delivered in early 1947 to Belic, as the SSU's only available Russian speaker, for six months' debriefing in Munich. It was not long before Belic felt that he understood more about Soviet intentions and methods than most others in the service. This opinion was shared by his superiors who, in the spring, ordered his transfer to Berlin to run a series of informants working inside the Soviet Zone. Belic's prize source, in a textbook operation, was a Soviet officer responsible for the archives at the KGB's headquarters in Karlshorst. Liaising through the Russian's German girlfriend, Belic negotiated for the information in return for a promise of sanctuary in the United States when the operation was terminated. It was a genuine jewel in a city which was rich in disinformation about plots and counter-plots by and against Soviet generals. When Belic returned to Munich in 1948 to run agents into the Soviet Union itself, he was viewed as an experienced intelligence officer who would be able to execute the covert operations whose framework had been unfolded in the previous months in Washington. His motivation was ideal: 'I'm sympathetic to anyone who's anti-communist,' he told Katek. The reservoir of recruits in West Germany was enormous.

Belic's new area of responsibility at OSO was the three Baltic States, a region about which he knew nothing. He was grateful when an American-born Lithuanian called Anthony Vaivada suggested where he might seek contacts.

Vaivada's humdrum existence in Chicago had thankfully ended in 1946 with an offer of a comparatively well-paid job in SSU as an analyst of Soviet affairs, followed in 1948 by transfer to Rositzke's new Soviet section. In his first contacts with Belic, soon after taking up his post in the CIA, Vaivada suggested that the field officer contact the VLIK group and in particular General Povilas Plechavicius, the former commander of the Lithuanian army. During the intervening three years, the Lithuanians had been unknowingly monitored by CIC agents under 'Operation Whiskey' but had received no American help. When the British favoured Zymantas and Deksnys, the VLIK group had accepted an offer of assistance from Raymond Schmittlein of the Deuxième Bureau and had moved their headquarters to Pfüllingen in the French Zone. Belic discovered that Plechavicius was living in the British Zone and was attached to SIS's new VLAK network. Although unavailable to serve the CIA, Plechavicius convinced Belic during their conversation that the resistance network inside Lithuania was still intact, fighting the Russians, and would be eager to co-operate with the Americans. Plechavicius' news was precisely what Belic wanted to hear. Gingerly, the American asked whether contact could be established with the resistance. Absolutely, replied the Lithuanian who then broadly hinted that operations masterminded by British intelligence were already underway.

To Belic, SIS was an agency to be regarded with respect. Although in the trade the relationship between the two sides was classified as 'cousins', every American knew that it was still more like parent and child. During the war, American agents had been trained by British instructors and OSS had fought a vain struggle to overcome its junior status. If, as Plechavicius suggested, SIS was already sending agents into Russia and the Baltic States, the CIA needed to make up lost ground. Plechavicius gave no details of the British operations – he was

121

either discreet or ignorant – but Belic noticed that the general seemed proud merely to possess the knowledge. It was some time after Belic had noticed a similar attitude in other émigrés that he came to two conclusions: the émigrés enjoyed the power which they suddenly held over the Western intelligence agencies who needed their assistance; and their very expression of that influence risked compromising security. But in late 1948, those were secondary thoughts. He was under pressure to find sources of agents for training. Belic's possible misjudgment of the émigrés' motives was not culpable. The émigrés were interested in politics and not security. Carr and McKibbin were already vulnerable to a similar misconception.

Belic's next calls were to Monsignor Krupavicius, VLIK's political leader, and Colonel Antanas Sova, VLIK's military commander, both of whom were still living in the French Zone. The preliminaries completed, the three men discussed optimistically the prospect of Stalin's regime collapsing because of the nationalist revolt against the Russians. Both Lithuanians assured the American that VLIK was in direct contact with four partisan groups who were actively fighting the Soviets. Exaggerations and flamboyant emotions were the oxygen of the émigré leaders' survival, but once again it was only in retrospect that Belic, and also McKibbin, would recognise their past, personal vulnerability. At the time, the émigrés' convincing claims were supported by dispatches from the US Embassy in Moscow repeating local newspaper articles which described the 'strength of anti-governmental activity in Lithuania'; and, "Robber Bands" . . . are a prevalent feature of contemporary life . . . using sabotage, diversion and murder . . . their activities are doing "more than a little harm." ' The Embassy's report concluded, 'Such frank admission of the strength of anti-Soviet activity is significant as an undeniable confirmation of discontent and militant resistance.'

There was further confirmation of the anti-Soviet revolt in early 1948. Ten months after leaving Lithuania with fifteen bodyguards, Juozas Luksha, the partisan leader, arrived in Germany as a hero. Three bodyguards had been killed en route by Red Army detachments. For the first time, the West saw living proof that Stalin's monolith was being challenged. But the excitement soon paled into dissension. Luksha gave a graphic description of Markulis' treachery at the planned meeting of partisan leaders in January 1947. The doctor, Luksha insisted, was a KGB officer. Contrary to Deksnys' account, VLIK was trusted by the partisans; no one had even heard of VLAK, the SIS-sponsored organisation. Deksnys' defence of Markulis was, suggested Luksha, evidence that Deksnys was also a KGB infiltrator. When the news filtered through to London, the split among the Lithuanians widened and prompted McKibbin to fly to Stockholm in summer 1948 to confront Deksnys.

'We need to establish radio contact with the partisans,' said McKibbin.

'You always talk about radio contact,' snapped Deksnys. 'But what about the struggle?'

'We support it,' said McKibbin although he knew that senior Foreign Office officials doubted the strength of the resistance if only because the Russian press actually reported the fighting.

'You may support it,' said the Lithuanian who was drinking more than one bottle of whisky a day, 'but what have you done so far? How will a radio liberate our country?'

'It's a beginning,' answered McKibbin with sincerity.

Deksnys' attempts to contact Markulis by radio had been unsuccessful for some time. The 'intelligence reports' that SIS's Lithuanian contact, Walter Zilinskas, regularly delivered to Silverwood-Cope's home in a brown envelope contained little more than rumours and speculation. The one hard fact omitted was the fate of Markulis. Unknown to both Zilinskas and Deksnys, the doctor had been the target of an attempted assassination by four partisans. To save his life, the KGB had whisked their infiltrator to safety in Leningrad.

Neither Zilinskas nor Zymantas believed that their

organisation was infiltrated by the KGB. McKibbin was often engaged in heavy but good-humoured drinking bouts with Deksnys, which would inevitably have lowered Deksnys' guard, but even in his most uncontrollable, drunken state neither ever gleaned a hint that he was other than a patriot. On the contrary, their conversations revealed a common hatred of the communists 'whom we will crush', and during McKibbin's visit to Stockholm, events were influencing British politicians towards adopting the more aggressive options offered by SIS. In August 1948, five months into the new battle for Berlin, Ernest Bevin told the Cabinet's Defence Committee: 'In my view a decisive struggle for power will take place in the next six to nine months.' Churchill had already predicted the certainty of war with the communists and French ministers had voiced fears that the 'Russians will be in Paris by August'. The alarm spawned intense but discreet activity which included Bevin's approval of a revitalised 'Russia Committee' to submit proposals for a subversive campaign across Europe against the communists.

That same fear of war persuaded Captain Ore Liljenberg, the Swedish intelligence officer, to approach McKibbin on the eve of the Scotsman's return to London. The Swede asked whether SIS would consider supporting an operation to send a large group of Balts by boat to the Soviet Union to report whether the Soviets were planning an invasion. It would be an SIS operation covered by the Swedes. McKibbin replied promptly and positively. SIS's radio contact with Lithuania had vanished and the fate of the three radio operators in Latvia was still a mystery. Nothing further had been heard from Feliks Rumnieks who had returned under the guise of repatriation. His letters had described his attempts to engage various KGB officers in conversation to discover the fate of the three SIS agents, but his silence in 1948 was ominous. In fact, at the end of 1947, the KGB, aroused by his constant approaches, had placed the returnee under surveillance and retrieved some apparently innocuous letters which

124

were subjected to scientific examination. His arrest was followed by a quick confession.

The evidence of recurrent SIS missions and the crisis in Berlin were two reasons for the Moscow Centre to advise KGB headquarters in all the republics to review their strategy in anticipation of increased Western espionage. In remarkably similar offices from the Baltic to the Black Sea, members of the Communist Party, who proudly wore the label of Chekists, turned to their founder's blueprint for combating enemy intelligence agencies who employed dissident Russian émigrés. General Janis Vevers' address to his subordinates in Riga was similar to many others given in the Soviet republics: 'The SIS,' Vevers told his assembled officers, 'are clearly intent on continuing their activities. We need to discover the extent of their intentions. We need to send our own man into their nest.' The responsibility for weaving the next thread of the web to entrap Silverwood-Cope, Carr and McKibbin was given to Major Lukasevics. The fly chosen to lure SIS into the KGB's web was Vidvuds Sveics.

The choice of Sveics was astute. Before the war, he had led an active social life at Riga university and in the army. His range of contacts and friends was impressive. Everyone believed that he was a nationalist and anti-communist and some suspected, rightly, that he had collaborated with the Abwehr. But none of his friends realised that the Nazis' atrocities and especially the collaboration of Latvians in German war crimes had alienated Sveics from the nationalists. The consequence in 1947 was that after delicate KGB handling, Sveics had been persuaded to go into the forests to identify and betray the partisans who were fighting the Soviets.

On 11 October 1948, Sveics was landed on the coast of Gotland and, as directed, surrendered to the local police. In his possession was a letter from Oswald Bieleskans, a British informer before 1939 who had joined the Latvian Central Council during the war. Sveics obtained Bieleskans' letter after cultivating the venerable anti-communist in the belief that he intended to escape for ever and needed a testimonial for his new life. It was addressed to Verners Tepfers, SIS's Latvian organiser, who lived in Stockholm. Delivery was delayed while Sveics was painstakingly interrogated by Bertil Bonde, Gotland's chief of counter-intelligence. Sveics' reasons for escape were unshakeable, as was his explanation of his route: 'I paid a fisherman to bring me across and he returned immediately.' Bonde agreed to his release and Sveics arrived at Tepfers' home. His presence in the West completely changed SIS's plans.

Four Latvians had already been recruited to travel on Liljenberg's boat but Sveics' arrival, in Tepfers' view, added zest and confidence to that plan. Sveics possessed the most precise information about life inside Russia and it was vital, Tepfers believed, to recruit him for the operation. In the first days, the unsuspecting Tepfers only hinted to his guest about his arrangements with the British and Swedes but by the end of November Sveics knew that, at SIS's request, Tepfers was actively organising a training school for agents who were being prepared for missions into Russia. Effortlessly, Lukasevics' agent had planted himself in the midst of McKibbin's operation. Patiently he observed as arrangements were made for his more permanent accommodation in Hid, a hamlet 400 kilometres south of the capital, where he would live with Fred Launags, one of his best friends from pre-war Riga. Sveics was 'one of the brightest boys of my class', according to Launags, who was 'very pleased' to see his old friend.

Launags had arrived in Sweden in November 1945 on the same boat as Elmars Skobe whom he had met in the Kurzeme forests. His personal battle with the Russians had been just as bitter – he had shot at least one KGB officer in cold blood, for which he was unrepentant. Since arriving in Sweden, he had forlornly sought support for the partisans left behind and he had jumped at the opportunity presented by Tepfers in 1948 to travel on the Swedish boat back to Latvia. Sveics seemed an ideal recruit for that operation and Launags, as an old friend, was best placed to verify Sveics' reliability.

126

In early 1949, after Launags confirmed Sveics' trust-worthiness, Tepfers outlined his plan. A group of Lithu-anian, Estonian and Latvian agents were to be trained by Swedish intelligence and dropped on the Lithuanian coast to set up new networks. 'I would like you to join,' said Tepfers.

'No,' replied Sveics, 'It's too dangerous to return. I'm free here and want to stay.'

Tepfers's attempts to persuade the KGB agent were adamantly rebuffed: 'Absolutely not,' said Sveics with conviction.

'I can promise you that when you return at the end of the mission, you will be paid a handsome reward,' said Tepfers when he saw the first hint of Sveics' retreat. Two days later, Sveics agreed.

In mid-January both Sveics and Launags reported to an anonymous house in Lidingö, east Stockholm, where they found six others already gathered to learn the trade-craft of espionage under the supervision of 'Captain André' of SMT. Besides another Latvian and two Estoni-ans, there were three Lithuanians – Kazimieras Piplys who had arrived in the West with Luksha and was anxious to return to the battle as fast as possible, Justas Bredis and Jonas Deksnys. Over the following three months, the group learnt the art of gathering information, coding messages, operating radios and surviving in forests. 'Everyone is so keen,' Launags told his wife. 'Finally we can do something for our countries.'

Events at that moment in the Baltic States added urgency to the operation. Red Army detachments under KGB command had just started their sixth round-up since the war. Tens of thousands of farmers, middle-class professionals and those who had collaborated with the Germans were being deported to Siberia. In scenes reminiscent of the Jewish Holocaust, an estimated 100,000 tearful and frightened men, women and children with small suitcases were loaded onto trains heading for a very uncertain future. The Soviets were eradicating the last vestiges of opposition. Soviet propaganda even boasted

127

that 'the Lithuanian bourgeois-nationalist underground has been liquidated' to make the country 'free from the terror of bandits'. Similar statements were made about the deportations from Latvia and Estonia.

SIS and CIA analysts read these reports as confirming a memorandum written in mid-1947 called 'Lithuania's Underground', which described the huge, well-armed, disciplined armies which, although living in the forests, wore uniforms and were sustained by farmers and other civilians and caused havoc to the Soviets. Rositzke, Carr, McKibbin and other intelligence officers read the recent Soviet reports of a scorched-earth policy as confirmation that the partisan groups still existed. Neither the SIS nor the CIA officers contemplated the consequences of the reports. Namely, that the KGB's deportations were successfully eradicating the partisans' support in the countryside and the Forest Brotherhood was in retreat.

Unaware of these reverses, the eight SIS agents being trained in Lidingö were briefed that the deportations offered the West an outstanding opportunity. 'We must sabotage their operations,' explained 'Captain André', 'and turn the people against the Russians.' Railway lines could be blown up and important Soviet officials killed but the key was to mobilise the partisans to win the support of the country folk who were suffering forced collectivisation. Launags and the others were excited by the prospect. 'André' continued that the agents' long-term and more important goal was to obtain intelligence about Soviet military bases, the technical specifications of their latest armaments and details of Russia's rocket and atomic power station programmes. To the Balts, tantalised by the daily newspaper reports of continuing confrontation in Berlin, tension in the Middle East and communist agitation throughout Europe, the two tasks seemed eminently compatible.

In early April 1949, Launags suddenly announced his refusal to continue, although the preparations were nearly completed for the group to leave Sweden on the first stage back to Russia: 'My wife is pregnant and our relationship

128

has suffered excessively by all my activities. I can't go through with it.' To save the operation from contamination, the dissenter was swiftly separated from the others but not before he had agreed with Sveics a secret code for personal communications by letter based upon the Latvian book *Straumeni*, and a cover address in Stockholm for the correspondence. It would serve as their private channel of communication, without SIS's knowledge. Since the third Latvian had earlier been deemed unsuitable for the operation, Sveics was now the only Latvian entrusted with the success of the mission, and he was given all the operation's most important secrets. Tepfers read out to him the contact list of sympathisers used by both British and Swedish in Latvia, including Augusts Bergmanis, the only radio operator, and Father Valdis Amols, a priest who during the war was a renowned nationalist and subsequently helped the anti-communist resistance. Since his home was within walking distance of the Latvian coast, he seemed to Launags an ideal haven for any new arrival. But as Launags would later explain to other émigrés and SIS intelligence officers, he began to harbour vague doubts about Sveics. 'Some of his stories seemed odd,' he reported, 'but they were too insubstantial to confide to anyone else.'

On 20 April 1949, Sveics and the five others boarded a Swedish boat for the crossing. After six hours, the attempt was abandoned. Liljenberg claimed that the craft was too slow, increasing the danger of capture. After quick consultations with SIS, it was agreed that the pretence of its being a Swedish operation would be dropped and the British would land the agents. The six were flown to the British military airport at Gütersloh in West Germany and driven to Hamburg in a British army truck. While the final arrangements were checked, their accommodation in the bomb-scarred city was comfortable: a large villa overlooking the River Elbe, requisitioned by the military government. Their minders were a mixture of fresh-faced British officers who were resident in Hamburg and a group who had arrived earlier from London.

The latter were older and included a man who introduced himself as 'Uncle': Sandy McKibbin.

The SIS officer from Ryder Street had monitored the group's training but had otherwise remained firmly in the background, partly as a precaution but also because of the geography. On the eve of departure he wanted personally to vet the vanguard of SIS's Baltic network. He spent some time over the following days with the Estonians, while Stasys Zymantas engaged the Lithuanians in what he confessed were 'pep talks', to give them confidence and a belief in what they were doing. The six were deliberately denied any time to brood on their fate; between meals and physical exercises, they were escorted to the shopping centre to buy cameras and watches which would be carefully stored by SIS until their return, and in the evening there would be drinks in bars along Hamburg's Reeperbahn.

In the meantime, the boat which would take them to the Russian coast was undergoing its last checks. It was a captured German E-boat which had been taken to a small shipyard near Portsmouth and rebuilt. Stripped of armaments and torpedo tubes, its twin Mercedes-Benz 518 diesel engines thoroughly overhauled by the Royal Navy's designers, who assured their customer a guaranteed speed of 45 knots, S208 had been transformed into the fastest craft afloat. It was also the most silent. To perfect its ability to approach the enemy's shore with a minimum of noise, underwater exhausts had been installed. The radio and radar equipment, fitted by the Admiralty's Signal and Radar Establishment, would be operated by a single British officer serving on the craft.

While these alterations were underway, an oblique approach had been made by Commander Antony Courtney, a 'lawless' and colourful British naval intelligence officer, to a former German E-boat captain, Hans Helmut Klose. In May 1949, Courtney invited the German to visit the Flag Officer's headquarters in Minden, West Germany. Although he had posed previously as a minesweeping expert, Courtney on this occasion came straight to the point. Introducing himself as 'Tony', Courtney revealed that Klose's wartime activities had been discovered by the Royal Naval intelligence officers who had been examining the German naval war diaries. It transpired that Klose had, from 1944 until the end of the war, captained an E-boat in the Baltic, dropping German agents behind the Russian lines for sabotage operations. Courtney wanted to know whether Klose might be interested in resuming his wartime career as an E-boat commander, this time in the service of SIS.

Born in Micklenburg in 1916, Klose came from a family of German nationalists whose credo was to serve the Fatherland. During the Third Reich, the German navy had few more dedicated officers than Klose although he was not a Nazi, nor did he sympathise with the regime's extremist policies. In the course of his command of E-boats around the Baltic coast, he did witness mass executions of Jews but tempered those atrocities by personally respecting the laws of naval warfare. As he would proudly tell Lord Mountbatten when he was introduced in the early 1950s as a gesture of SIS's gratitude, 'I always suffered when I saw British sailors drowning and thought of their poor mothers.' The shared sentiments which united the international brotherhood of mariners extended to their common dislike of the Bolsheviks. Klose felt no doubts about returning to sea when the British made their approach. Indeed, it was an exciting assignment for an ambitious naval officer who in 1949 could see no immediate prospects for his career.

The white-painted S208 was attached to the Fishery Protection Service, formed by the British military government in Hamburg to help the West German fishing fleet in the Baltic. Klose was entrusted with recruiting his crew from those who had served under him during the war. On agreement, they were introduced to the secrets of the mission. S208 would sail from either Kiel or Eckenforde under the White Ensign for the first segment of the 500-mile journey to a cove on the Danish island of Bornholm where it would hoist the Swedish flag. There, Klose was

131

to wait with the agents below decks for the short and uncoded message from Hamburg giving clearance to proceed at his discretion. If the weather was acceptable and the wind easterly to minimise the noise, S208 was to dash to its rendezvous and return as fast as possible. There was one question which Klose could always anticipate: 'What happens if we're caught?' His answer was reassuring: 'We're faster than anyone else, and trust me. The British never sank my boat during the war.'

Departure was fixed for the night of 29/30 April. S208's destination was Palanga beach in Lithuania. The landing, it was hoped, would be on 1 May, the communist holiday, when it was deemed to be most likely that the border patrols would be least attentive. At dusk on 29 April three cars and a truck pulled up on the Kiel quayside by the craft. Klose watched silently from the wheelhouse as six men carrying rucksacks and guns uttered muffled farewells and mounted the boat's walkway. The occasion seemed so ordinary as S208 slipped its moorings that only in retrospect was the drama of those moments evident, not least the issue by the British officers just prior to departure of 'L-Tablets' – pure cyanide. Each man pocketed the suicide pill without comment. Their conversation over the previous days had become characterised by talk of revenge. Sveics forced himself to smile agreement as his companions jocularly competed in their accounts of how they would cause mayhem among the communists who occupied their homelands. The KGB infiltrator would claim that this was not a display of bravado but genuine intent. In his view, these were dangerous men and as S208 sailed towards Bornholm he pondered his course of action.

In Bornholm, S208 anchored in a small cove used by the Danish navy while Klose waited for the final weather report. The message from Hamburg, meaningless to any eavesdropper, forecast storms. There was no alternative but to wait for an improvement. While the agents remained below, out of sight, Klose maintained the pretence towards his Danish hosts that his was an innocent mission. On 5 May, the weather cleared and S208 set course at full speed directly towards Palanga. Two kilometres offshore, the radar screen was clear and he ordered the engines to be cut.

At 2 a.m., the six men lowered themselves into rubber boats and were rowed to the shore. Their landing was perfect and unobserved. What followed is somewhat uncertain although it is clear that all six ran into the forest and Sveics soon afterwards contrived to separate himself from the group to seek out the local militia and raise the alarm. In the shooting which followed, the two Estonians and Bredis died. Deksnys and Piplys had already left the area before the militia arrived. Piplys would die fighting the Russians six months later.

In his first message to Tepfers by letter, using invisible ink, Sveics reported that the group had been surprised on the beach; that the others had refused to surrender and had begun shooting. A number were certainly dead. He did not know about survivors since he had fortunately escaped and reached Riga where his radio set was in perfect condition. The news of the disaster was partially mitigated by a further letter which Tepfers received. Soon after his arrival, Sveics had visited Oswald Bieleskans, his original contact. He brought a few gifts from Sweden and a sealed letter from Tepfers, to which Bieleskans had replied, confirming Sveics' safe return to Riga and his continuing willingness to serve the interests of the Free World. In the meantime, Sveics, under Lukasevics' direction, had made contact with Valdis Amols, the priest living near the coast, and written to Tepfers that the safe houses which the rest mentioned were still intact.

Sveics' communication was followed by a letter from Deksnys. He reported to Zymantas that after a harrowing journey he had arrived in Lithuania and that he had lost contact with his radio officer. SIS, Deksnys suggested, should arrange to send an operator as soon as possible while he sought the VLAK leaders.

In London, Carr was relieved that at least the skeleton of the Latvian and Lithuanian network was secure.

Further landings now needed to be considered urgently since the pressure to infiltrate more agents had intensified.

The receipt of both letters coincided with a series of meetings in Washington between a British Foreign Office team led by William Hayter and senior members of the CIA and State Department who were responsible for espionage in the Soviet bloc. Hayter was a member of the Foreign Office's Russia Committee which on 25 November 1948 had discussed a proposal to start 'offensive operations' against Soviet satellites and in particular Albania. Their objective was to loosen 'the Soviet hold on the orbit countries and ultimately enable them to regain their independence'. The tactics which would be used mirrored SOE's operations three years earlier: 'promoting civil discontent, internal confusion and possible strife'.

Although some committee members had been sceptical, the voice of Air Marshal Lord Tedder had been persuasive: 'We should aim at winning the "cold war", by which I mean the overthrow of the Soviet regime, in five years' time.' His timetable reflected the common British and American intelligence prediction that Russia would have built an atomic bomb by 1957 and thereafter would be uncontainable since Britain's military chiefs warned that their resources for a 'hot war' were dwindling fast. The same fear, combined with evidence of Soviet subversion throughout Western Europe, persuaded other committee members to agree that Britain's aim 'should certainly be to liberate the countries within the Soviet orbit by any means short of war'. Nothing, however, could be attempted without American co-operation and on that basis the officials had won Bevin's approval to travel to Washington.

The meeting in March 1949 between Hayter, Gladwyn Jebb and Lord Jellicoe on the British side and the CIA's Robert Joyce and Frank Wisner, the impenitent anticommunist, lasted three days and covered a wide range of possibilities for co-operation between the two nations' intelligence services against the Soviet Union. The British were struck by the Americans' enthusiasm to catch up with SIS and embark on covert operations, but were dismayed by the profusion of discussions which exposed the absence of any co-ordination or confident leadership in the American intelligence organisation.

SIS's plan to topple the communist regime in Albania, as outlined by Hayter, struck Wisner as an ideal covert operation of a type which was currently under discussion. Four years, in Wisner's opinion, had been wasted in Washington while the OSS's experience was denigrated, abandoned, espoused and finally emulated. In that time, much had changed, not least the nature of the enemy and the terrain where the war would be fought. Wisner, unashamedly impressed by SIS's espionage traditions, was grateful that the British were willing to offer their expertise and deferred to British leadership in the operation.

Wisner's judgment was endorsed by Frank Lindsay who in 1947 had prompted Kennan to suggest the creation of a school for guerrilla warfare. Lindsay had won plaudits for his wartime service with the Tito partisans in Yugoslavia and had become Wisner's deputy, responsible for Eastern Europe. In Lindsay's view, Hayter and SIS represented the finest traditions of the Anglo-American world. Lindsay's personal experience of communism was unique in Washington. His conviction that it was America's duty to face the evil empire had been cemented by reports of Tito's cruelty since the war. Although Wisner's enthusiasm for covert warfare was infectious, Lindsay's endorsement of the Albanian operation was critical.

The Americans' agreement effectively to pay for SIS's Albanian venture was greeted with relief in Broadway, not least by Jack Easton, the chairman of the committee overseeing the operation. A group of former British SOE officers had already arrived in the Mediterranean and by August 1949 were training twenty Albanians to probe the possibilities of fomenting an uprising. Early in October, the twenty were put ashore and although by the end of the month four were missing, presumed killed, the remainder returned to report that despite the enormous

135

opposition to the communist regime, the inhabitants were cautious about the possibility of a successful coup. For Easton and the other SIS directors this was sufficient to seek higher approval to expand their ambitions. One single event in early September had dispersed the layers of caution and released a flood of demands for more intelligence.

On 3 September, an American B-29 of the long-range detection system had returned to its Pacific Ocean base with conclusive evidence that the Soviets had exploded an atomic bomb. Overnight, all the intelligence and military and political assessments by Western Chiefs of Staff and politicians were redundant. Russia's vast superiority in conventional forces was no longer balanced by America's nuclear threat.

The failure to predict Russia's possession of the bomb sharply discredited both the CIA and SIS, and led to the removal of CIA Director Hillenkoetter. At the same time, the agencies were given more freedom and resources to pursue their objectives. It was a paradox characteristic of the East–West seesaw. Just as Stalin four months earlier had sought to reduce tension by lifting the blockade of Berlin, Whitehall and the White House now acknowledged that the West was at war with Russia.

SIS's virtually unrestricted remit to direct its energies against communism was nevertheless subject to precise procedures of referral. Subversion, if it remained merely subversion, as in Albania, needed the approval of only the Foreign Office's Permanent Under-Secretary. If sabotage or assassination was contemplated, SIS needed ministerial sanction. Hence the papers which Easton prepared, proposing the destruction of ships in Italian ports which were intended to transport Jewish refugees to Israel, made their way up through the channels for submission to and approval by Clement Attlee, the Prime Minister, personally. Similarly, Bevin had given his approval to proposals for covert operations inside Russia and in the satellite nations. In summer 1949, it was agreed that these plans should be substantially augmented.

136

For the tight-knit coterie of SIS officers born in Russia, who had waited for so long to take their revenge upon the Bolsheviks, the government's approval to counter Soviet subversion was welcomed as long overdue. Harry Carr, at the peak of his career, was fulfilling his life's ambition. Northern Area's activities had been expanded to include the dispatch of agents to Poland and the Ukraine. Subject to budget constraints, he had received approval for an increase in his operations.

While expanding their Baltic operations, Carr and McKibbin agreed to hold an investigation into the disastrous mission from Sweden to Lithuania. Since Sveics' and Deksnys' dispatch, a second team had been sent and had disappeared. Carr suspected that they had been arrested. In fact they had all been killed on the Palanga beach by waiting KGB officers. Both Carr and McKibbin believed that their operations had been betrayed and that the evidence pointed to Launags as a possible (although, it transpired, quite erroneous) culprit. His abrupt withdrawal from the mission was certainly more than curious. The investigation was to be controlled from London and, to deflect any suspicion, the initial contact with Launags was made by Elmars Skobe.

Since his release from the Swedish prison, Skobe had served as a merchant sailor on British cargo ships and then, with SIS's help, had settled in Kensington, London. At McKibbin's request, he wrote to Launags and proposed that his friend meet 'Victor Sanderson', an SIS officer who would travel from London.

Launags was delighted by the news that he would be visited by an SIS officer. Although he was still attempting to reconcile his marriage, Launags remained totally dedicated to the struggle against Stalin and the liberation of Latvia. Since Sveics' departure, he and Ginters had recruited more émigrés who were prepared to return to Russia and both were encouraged by the receipt of a coded letter from Sveics reporting his safe arrival in Riga. However, they needed more help from Western agencies and Skobe's message seemed to promise the necessary relief. Skobe's arrangements for the rendezvous suggested that 'Sanderson' wanted Swedish intelligence to remain unaware of any contact. 'You should go to Göteborg railway station and wait for a man in the main hall carrying the *Daily Telegraph*,' wrote Skobe who added the code words which both sides would use.

'Sanderson' was a well-mannered, slightly built, dark-haired Englishman who was deaf in one ear – 'the result of standing near too many bangs during the war'. He spoke fluent German. Although the Englishman seemed pleased to meet Launags, he was more eager to have information about Sveics and seemed unsurprised about Launags' private channel to the agent in Riga.

'Can you send Sveics these questions?' asked 'Sanderson'. 'And express the urgency for answers.'

'What about further operations into Latvia?' asked Launags.

'It's too dangerous for the moment,' replied 'Sanderson'.

Two further meetings were arranged where Launags introduced other Latvians who were keen to become SIS agents but by the end of 1949, for reasons which he could not fathom, Launags realised that 'Sanderson' did not intend to offer another opportunity for covert operations. Perplexed, because his overriding passion was to strike at the communists, Launags reconsidered Sveics' advice to 'get contacts with the Americans' because, Sveics had written, 'they are really very anti-Russian'. Launags never guessed that he was under investigation as a KGB agent.

Through a friend in Washington, Launags made contact with Harry Rositzke's branch of the CIA in early 1950. The Agency officers were unaware of SIS's suspicions because throughout 1949 Carr's passion for secrecy had frustrated Rositzke's attempts to arrange a meeting. To Rositzke and in turn Belic, who were anxious to find reliable agents, Launags seemed suitable and recruits were anxiously needed. In Kaufbeuren, Steve Tanner was making impressive headway towards parachuting a group of Ukrainians into the Carpathian mountains, despite

138

Kennan's deliberate exclusion in 1948 of the Ukrainians from covert operations because he refused to recognise the ethnic group's claim of nationhood. One year later, that restriction had disappeared because the President had urged the CIA to use every opportunity 'to bring about the elimination of Soviet power from the satellite states'. Effectively, Rositzke was working with a blank cheque.

Launags received a message from Washington for a rendezvous in the port of Helsingborg. On the appointed day, two Americans – the elder called himself 'Robert Armstrong' and the younger 'Johnny Walker' – arrived punctually at the railway station. Launags' first thought when he saw them was flip: 'Both are as handsome as movie stars.' The officers' words could also have been written in Hollywood. 'We want you to work for us as a specialist. To send agents into Russia. We also want to recruit your whole network here in Sweden.' Launags was delighted by his good fortune although he demanded time to consult his team, among whom was Edvins Osolins whose personal file would soon feature in Lukasevics' guarded office in Lenin Street under the codename 'Pilot'.

Five

SPINNING THE WEB

SIS's inquiries in Sweden had not interrupted the expansion of the Special Liaison Centre in Ryder Street. Before the two ill-fated missions to Lithuania, Carr had already agreed that the arrangements in Sweden had become unsatisfactory and that future training should be concentrated in London where SIS could exercise total control. To match the expansion, the Baltic section was to be divided into three divisions, one for each of the states. McKibbin required a Latvian national and an Estonian who, like Zymantas, could recruit agents from their ethnic group and supervise their training. McKibbin's two appointments, approved by Carr, reflected the political predispositions of both SIS officers and those 'on the other side of the house' in the Foreign Office.

Since 1947, under Operation Westward Ho, groups of Baltic men and women had been recruited in the DP camps for work in British mines and textile factories, where production was severely hampered by a shortage of labour. Among the arrivals in Britain in October 1947 was a group of Latvians. During a routine medical check at Harwich port the doctor noticed identical tattoos under their arms. He was in no doubt what the black marks signified: they were the marks used by the SS to alert a doctor to his patient's blood group and to warn that only a purely Aryan source was to be used for transfusions. After the war, the tattoo had become an indelible sign that its bearer was a member of a criminal organisation

140

and clearly ineligible for entry into Britain. Within twenty-four hours of their detention, Charles Zarins, the Latvian Ambassador in London, protested to Thomas Brimelow with a colourful excuse for the incriminating trademark. His countrymen, wrote the diplomat, had been forcibly tattooed when kidnapped by the Germans and indentured as labourers. Brimelow and other Foreign Office officials accepted Zarins' false explanation and agreed that the British doctor would 'be asked to confine his attentions to the sick and *not* to meddle with blood groups' (emphasis as in the original).

The admission of these former SS officers was consistent with Foreign Office policy. The 8,000 Ukrainians camped under British control in Rimini who had been members of the notorious SS Galizien Division were also admitted to Britain in 1947, under a convenient classification – 'prisoners of war'. Ministers had assured irate MPs that all of those arriving were screened to exclude war criminals. Privately, however, officials admitted the contrary. The change of attitude by A.W.H. Wilkinson, a Foreign Office expert on refugees, was typical. In just four days in February 1947, the same Ukrainians condemned by Wilkinson as 'in no way to be regarded as political dissidents' who should get 'all they deserve' were transformed into innocent 'political refugees'. Bevin had personally obtained Attlee's agreement to ship the Ukrainians to Britain despite the accusations of his Parliamentary colleagues that they were 'bloodthirsty cutthroats'. The Foreign Secretary had been swayed by the strong feeling expressed by his officials that the Ukrainians should not be surrendered to the Russians and, like the Balts, would be useful to SIS in the future. Two years later, in 1949, that anticipation was fulfilled.

Among the former SS officers invited to Britain in 1947 was Colonel Alfons Rebane, a 45-year-old Estonian who had ended the war as commander of the 20th SS Estonian Division. In April 1945 the division was fighting the Russians in Czechoslovakia. To avoid certain death from the communists, Rebane had fled westwards to the British

Zone with 1,000 men. Two years later, he arrived in Britain to work in a Bradford mill. In 1949, Rebane's friends were surprised to hear that the ex-colonel had abandoned his job, moved to London, and seemed enviously prosperous. Only later did it transpire that he had been recruited by McKibbin to become a full-time SIS officer responsible for dispatching agents to Estonia. Rebane's two conditions on appointment were that the SS division's former General Inspector, General Johannes Soodla, should be appointed as his adjutant and that SS Captain Väino Partel should also be on his staff. Pärtel, he explained, knew the location of all the former members of the SS division who would be suitable as agents and was therefore an essential go-between. McKibbin agreed.

McKibbin's quest for a Latvian had by then also ended, with Zarins' help. The Ambassador, interpreting the British government's interest as proof of its intent to liberate his country, nominated Rudolph Silarajs, a former Latvian air force officer now interned in the Sebors DP camp in Belgium, as the 'ideal candidate'. When McKibbin met him in Belgium in 1948, he was favourably impressed. Silarajs' military training, zealous nationalism and blind hatred of communism were the precise qualities needed for the task. Silarajs also recommended two other DPs, both former air force officers, who were eager to fight the communists. McKibbin arranged for all three to be transferred from Belgium to Britain.

Zymantas, Rebane and Silarajs were housed in London and worked with McKibbin in Ryder Street. The Baltic operations which were assigned the codename 'Jungle' had assumed a more professional and permanent status. To preserve security, Carr required that they neither meet him nor even know of his existence. Although McKibbin faithfully maintained the compartmentalisation, both his secretary Peggy Cockerton and his assistant, Nora Dashwood, noticed how the inharmonious relations between the easy-going McKibbin and the stickler Carr spilled into the working day. The problems of that relationship were also apparent to the three Balts but they tactfully ignored

142

SIS's office politics. Having secured the support of the prestigious secret service, they were preoccupied with finding agents to send abroad. The two SIS officers were in the meantime planning a new infiltration route.

The apparent success of Sveics and Bergmanis in remaining free convinced Carr and McKibbin that most future agents should be landed in Latvia rather than Lithuania. The first agents for 'Operation Jungle 1' had already been selected: Vitolds Berkis and Andrei Galdins, who had arrived with Silarajs.

Berkis, the 31-year-old son of a former Latvian diplomat, had first served with Silarajs in the air force before recruitment to the SS's Sicherheitsdienst in Riga with responsibilities for political intelligence. In 1944, he fled from Latvia with his SD unit and was interned in Belgium with Silarajs. His SIS codename was 'Kranja'.

Andrei Galdins, a 32-year-old son of peasants, had spent the war as an active member of the Arajs commando, an execution squad which roved through Eastern Europe under the command of the SS. Galdins was assigned by SIS the codename 'Meonis'. The training programme which had been devised for all SIS's émigré agents followed the routine perfected during the war by SOE. The only practical difference was that the trainee agents would all live in London to avoid attracting undue attention.

The 'School' was a four-storey Victorian house at 111 Old Church Street in Chelsea which was rented from a British officer posted abroad. A married couple, Eddie and Mavis Flowers, were hired to cook and perform the household chores. The first arrivals, in May, were Berkis and Galdins. They were given five pounds each per week as pocket money, issued new identity cards with false names and set a rigorous routine. In the basement, George Collier taught the use of Morse code and radio exchange. The two Latvians learnt how to send and receive messages, how to code and decode using one-time pads, how messages would be transmitted on dates strictly according to a coded schedule, and basic radio maintenance. On the second floor, John Crofton, nick-named 'Little John', supervised the agents' instruction in trade-craft. A succession of former SOE trainers passed through the house teaching methods of surveillance, avoidance of surveillance, organisation of dead letter drops, unobserved meetings, acting as cut-out agents, approaching a safe house, and how to process the chemicals used for invisible writing. Careful attention was given to explaining security: how their real identities and back-ground should never be revealed, even to the partisan groups they would meet; how to cope with potentially incriminating situations; what to say in the event of capture; where to place the critical code word in Morse messages which revealed that the sender was transmitting under enemy control. During the training, the case officers and their agents became brothers-in-arms. The glory and the suffering would be shared equally. The trainees were reminded of the KGB's efficiency and ferocity. 'They even cut noses off,' Galdins was heard to mutter. The agents would be issued with cyanide pills for use if required.

Practical lessons were given in the field. Training in the use of small arms and sten guns was at an indoor range in Chelsea itself, while preparation for life as an agent in the Russian countryside took place outside the capital. Officers at Fort Monckton outside Gosport on the south coast, SOE's wartime training school, taught the two Latvians unarmed combat, survival in the wilderness, swimming at night (in Portsmouth harbour) and silent rowing from the shore to waiting motorboats. These courses were followed by trips to Dartmoor, Snowdonia and the Scottish Highlands to practise their new skills. Under Crofton's supervision, the two Latvians marched through Britain's wildest areas, skirting villages to remain unseen by the instructors, leaving letters in agreed places and transmitting coded messages. On their final return to London at the end of September, McKibbin was assured that both were ready for their mission.

Crofton, with Silarajs translating, explained that SIS

required information about the Red Army's installations; about roads, railways and ports; and about living conditions. Most important of all, however, was obtaining evidence of the Russian development of atomic energy and rockets. Confirmation of the test explosion of a Soviet atomic bomb in September had been followed by reports from Sweden of Soviet rocket tests in the Baltic. (The latter proved to be false.)

For Carr, this first mission was a probe to reveal the strength of the resistance movement. Mindful of the Trust, Carr told McKibbin to re-emphasise to both agents the importance of showing caution with their contacts. Their faith should be placed in no one until they were doubly certain that the partisans were not infiltrated by the KGB. They were to regard themselves primarily as radio officers and not freedom fighters.

Silarajs' view of the mission's purpose, which he passed on to the two agents, was markedly different. During the many evenings he spent playing cards and drinking Scotch with his fellow countrymen in Old Church Street, Silarajs spoke about the opportunity of liberating their nation from communism; of striking a blow against their enemies; and of toppling the Stalin regime. 'The communists are brutal,' Silarajs said on more than one occasion, 'and we must respond in kind.'

On the eve of their departure for Hamburg, Silarajs arranged an emotional and ceremonial meeting with Ambassador Zarins. 'His Excellency' bestowed his blessing on the two 'vanguards of our nation's future' and urged them to believe that Britain and America would soon be fighting Russia and their country would be liberated. If some SIS officers would later deny knowledge of these exhortations, there was no doubt that McKibbin and probably Carr were aware of Silarajs' unofficial briefings to the two agents and shared the sentiments. 'Realpolitik' rarely encroached upon their fantasies and McKibbin, the driving force, demonstrated supreme confidence in the operation's success.

In the days before their departure, the agents rechecked

145

their equipment. Each would carry a brown suitcase. One contained a radio; the other, two Schmeisser sub-machine-guns, two Walther pistols and ammunition. In watertight plastic bags were code books, 2,000 roubles and false passports. Hidden compartments in their belts contained gold coins and jewellery. Accompanied by 'Little John', the two were driven by truck with their equipment to Fairford for the flight to Bückeburg in West Germany. A third passenger, a Lithuanian, joined the flight at Fairford for the journey to Russia.

The three agents and their British escort were met at Bückeburg by a young SIS liaison officer, Anthony Cavendish. In the days before their arrival, Cavendish had moved into a large villa in Hamburg's fashionable Blankenese district. As a team of SIS household staff cleaned and prepared the requisitioned property, the loft was converted into a communications centre by SIS experts. Cavendish's task was to care for the three until the naval liaison officer, Commander Antony Courtney, was told by Klose that sailing conditions were suitable. The agents needed to be entertained without risking their security and without allowing them an opportunity to brood on the danger of their mission. Cavendish's solution was physical exercise followed by games. On the last evening, as would become traditional, the agents and 'Little John' were invited by Cavendish to an erotic floor show in the Reeperbahn red light district. After heavy drinking of brandy 'nikolaschkas', Cavendish left, agreeing that the others would make their own way back to Blankenese. In the early hours of the morning, he was roused from his sleep by knocking on the door. It was Berkis and Galdins, who had returned alone. 'Little John' Crofton and the Lithuanian had become involved in a fracas at the bar and were under arrest. Cavendish spent the remainder of the night securing their release and worked through the following day trying to satisfy himself that neither, in their drunkenness, had indiscreetly exposed the mission. Apparently neither had, and the group waited in an uneasy atmosphere until Courtney confirmed that S208 was ready to depart.

At 4 p.m. on 31 October, Berkis and Galdins boarded the Fishery Protection vessel in Kiel and went below decks. Only the boat's commander, Hans Klose, knew precisely where the two agents would be landed in Latvia. On receiving the short message from Hamburg to 'go ahead', he sailed for an isolated beach west of Ventspils. When Berkis and Galdins were rowed to the shore, the KGB was unaware of their arrival.

As instructed by Silarajs, the agents buried the two suitcases in a forest away from the beach and made their way through the night to the home of Father Valdis Amols, the pastor whom Tepfers counted among his most reliable contacts. Silarajs and McKibbin were equally convinced of Amols' reliability. But their trust was misplaced. The cleric had been unwittingly ensnared earlier that year by Sveics into the KGB's web. When Berkis gave the passwords: 'Can I buy some beer here?' the priest instantly ushered the two agents through the door. 'We want to contact the partisans,' explained Berkis. Amols knew of one reliable contact provided by Sveics, Augusts Bergmanis in Riga. The following day, after advising the two agents of their best route, Amols decided that he should also alert Sveics of their arrival. Their security, so carefully constructed in London, disintegrated before they even arrived in Riga.

Augusts Bergmanis was surprised by the unexpected knock on the door of his fifth-floor apartment on 5 November 1949. His surprise was greater when the two visitors explained that they were new arrivals from Sweden who had been dropped by a fast patrol vessel off Kurland five days earlier and were here to contact the partisans in the forests and start a new intelligence network. Bergmanis offered his guests several rounds of Latvian vodka and invited both to stay in his flat while he arranged accommodation in a safe house.

The following day, on the pretext of getting extra food, Bergmanis left the flat and contacted Lukasevics. 'They're

147

comfortable and feel quite at home,' he reported. They could stay temporarily, he explained, but personally he could not maintain the façade for long.

Those in the Second Chief Directorate who watched the KGB major during that day recall the unusual glint in his eye. Patience had been rewarded. At the urgent meeting which was chaired by General Vevers in Lenin Street, it was decided that a safe house be provided where the two Latvians could live and be easily observed. But it was only a matter of days before Bergmanis returned to Lukasevics to complain that his guests were restless. 'Our problem,' the KGB major told Vevers, 'is what to do with two British-sponsored agents who are anxious to start operating.' Lukasevics wanted to mount a deception operation but that required time. Both Bergmanis and later Sveics, who had been introduced to the two, convinced Lukasevics that something had to be done about the agents soon. Berkis had explained that the two were just the first of a wave of agents due to arrive from Britain and even America. Both insisted that they be taken to meet some partisan leaders.

Vevers was faced with both a challenge and a problem. To repeat Dzerzhinsky's blueprint and mount a perfect double-cross operation required formidable organisation and perfect synchronisation by the participants. If Berkis and SIS were to be properly ensnared, the KGB would need to create a group of partisans whose personalities and activities would wholly convince Berkis and Galdins. Success would depend upon selecting agents who could survive physically the arduous life in the forests and simultaneously sustain the deception. The operation would require huge resources but the opportunity to penetrate the heart of SIS could not be passed over. After detailed consultations with Kruglov in Moscow, whose report, it would later be said, was even shown to Stalin, it was agreed that the deception which was later codenamed 'Operation Lursen-S', should be masterminded by Lukasevics and Major Alberts Bundulis.

Bundulis was a physically strong revolutionary

communist who had joined the KGB during the war. Compared to Lukasevics, he was a practical police officer, a womaniser and bon viveur, rather than a strategic planner. Vevers had decided that while Lukasevics should direct the operation from headquarters, Bundulis would become the leader of the illusory partisan group, living in the Kurzeme forests, which would be codenamed 'Maxis'. With considerable speed, Bundulis and Lukasevics selected six KGB officers with experience of fighting the partisans in the woods to become members of the 'Maxis' group.

Throughout the remainder of the winter months, the two senior officers concocted with each 'partisan' a convincing cover story of his life, especially his post-war activities, ironing out the slightest hints of contradiction. In early February, while Berkis and Galdins were receiving constant assurance that the difficulties of establishing contact with the partisans were nearly overcome, each 'partisan' was escorted into a committee room in KGB headquarters to be rigorously tested by Vevers, Lukasevics and Bundulis. Kruglov travelled specially from Moscow to chair the sessions. As the deep snow melted, engineers were sent to Tukum in the Kurzeme forests. The site chosen had been the last front line between the Wehrmacht and the Red Army. In this landscape riddled with deeply dug trenches and surrounded by swamps, the Maxis group could convincingly assert they had spent the past years, hidden from the communists.

In the meantime, Sveics persuaded Berkis, who was housed with a 'widower' in Riga, that he had contacted the leader of the Maxis group but that it was too dangerous for the partisan to leave the forest until the snow melted because the security forces would quickly notice the telltale footprints. Emphasising the dangers – 'the Chekists are everywhere' – was Sveics' favourite way of subduing and controlling the restless SIS agents. Playing on the agents' fears and nerves would become the KGB's cherished tool to restrain all those who came to 'liberate' their country.

149

Reluctantly, Berkis agreed to wait until spring and contented himself with demanding industrial and military information which he could pass on to London either in the occasional message which he dispatched by radio or in letters which were addressed to Belgium, France and Sweden. To everyone's amusement, since Berkis was obliged by Soviet law to write on the envelope the sender's address, he used names which appeared in the divorce announcements of that day's newspaper. He reported to London, using the codename 'Wolf', that he was encountering problems but trusted those whom he had contacted. His major complaint concerned his identity papers: 'They are too primitive for use.' They were just a forged sheet attesting to his employment in an agricultural factory.

On 2 May, Berkis' wait came to an end. The leader of the Maxis group had agreed to a rendezvous in a park, announced Sveics. A strict procedure had been agreed which Berkis was to osberve. Dressed in a blue coat and without a hat, he waited at the agreed time by a tree. Punctually Bundulis approached Berkis, they exchanged passwords and, after a brief discussion, Bundulis agreed to introduce both SIS agents to a partisan band commanded by 'Garis'. Their transport to the forest would need to be handled with the greatest secrecy: 'One of the band will pick you up in a truck near Gorky Street,' said Bundulis. 'The rear will be full of empty fish boxes. Both of you must hide beneath the boxes for the entire trip.'

At lunchtime on 13 May, after walking for nearly two hours, Berkis, Galdins and Bundulis stopped in the middle of the forest. Hiding in the thick undergrowth were four 'partisans', including Arvits Gailitis, 'Garis', who had served in the Latvian Legion against the Russians during the war. The four had already spent three weeks in the forest, becoming acclimatised to their environment. At Gailitis' signal, all four armed men emerged from hiding to greet the new arrivals, whose immediate reaction was to congratulate the 'partisans' on their professional concealment.

Lukasevics' strategy depended upon patience. Berkis

and Galdins were taken across three swamps to the camp in the converted trenches, where they were to remain as long as necessary to be convinced of the partisans' bona fides. That would require time while both sides embarked on a critical assessment of their cohabitants. The undertaking was clearly more difficult for the hosts, who feared that a single slip would expose their plot. Berkis, on the other hand, offered simple proof of his honesty: 'Just give me the name of a popular song you want played by the BBC's World Service and to whom it should be dedicated and it will be arranged.' To his surpise, the offer was spurned: 'We know who you are and trust you,' answered Gailitis. For their part, the KGB agents judged Berkis to be an intelligent and thoughtful nationalist who was principally concerned to begin his intelligence-gathering mission. He appeared trusting and therefore not dangerous, though he probed each of the partisans in detail for his background and had a disconcerting habit of suddenly re-questioning an individual on a specific point – 'With whom did you say you robbed that bank?' he would ask two months after he was first told. Above all, Berkis enjoyed playing chess and 'Performance', a card game, which he taught the whole group.

Galdins was more restless and highly-strung. Since the daily routine was a monotonous one of games, cleaning weapons, eating and sleeping interrupted by an occasional radio transmission, nerves easily became frayed, particularly Galdins'. 'He is always suspicious,' Gailitis reported about him to his controllers in Riga. Galdins would react to the slightest noise from the undergrowth by firing wildly at the hidden source in the fear that it was a KGB spy. The targets were invariably wild animals but it put the real KGB officers in the camp on edge. Repeatedly Galdins warned the company that the Chekists were extremely clever. They must be careful not to leave any traces. There must be constant vigilance. Everyone would nod in agreement and Gailitis stressed that it would therefore be best if the two agents never left the forest and relied upon the partisans to gather intelligence and get supplies.

Galdins agreed, but his dissatisfaction with the lack of action provoked arguments with Berkis, who was more concerned with sending intelligence back to London and training a new radio operator.

Kazimirs Kipurs was selected by Berkis from among the 'partisans' as the ideal trainee. The 24-year-old's aptitude seemed remarkable and cross-examination of his past explained his motives for opposing the communists. 'Before the war, my father was a deputy police chief who was sentenced to twenty years' imprisonment by the KGB,' Kipurs told Berkis, 'and when both my mother and sister were sent to Siberia in the mass deportations last year, I escaped to the forest.'

For three months Berkis taught Kipur the techniques of coding and transmitting, pleased that by the end of that period his pupil's speed was sixty characters per minute. Unknown to Berkis, Kipurs had already perfected the professional rate of 120 characters per minute at the KGB training school in Moscow during the war. In October 1950, Berkis signalled 'Gabriel', Silarajs' codename for radio traffic, to introduce his recommended radio operator. After a series of tests, London's approval – 'Your operator has good prospects' – was accompanied by an offer to Kipurs of becoming a fully-fledged British agent at the rate of £20 per month: 'The money will be regularly deposited in a London bank account awaiting your collection when you return.' SIS assigned Kipurs the codename 'Lauva' – lion. To celebrate, Berkis called for a bottle of vodka. As the alcohol took its effect, Berkis placed his arms round his friend's shoulders and confided that during the first weeks he had suspected that the partisans were KGB officers. Both roared with laughter and drank another toast.

Broadway, however, was unimpressed by the group's results. The British analysts complained that the information was bland. It included information about the types of aircraft stationed at airports; economic conditions and rates of production at strategic factories; personality profiles of government and party officials; and estimates of

152

identifiable troop displacements in the region. Expert scrutiny in London, however, revealed the information to be imprecise, although it must be assumed that the material sent from the Latvian forest was included in SIS's intelligence summary regularly submitted to the Prime Minister and the Foreign Office. Vevers was also concerned about the poor quality of 'intelligence' which he handed to Bundulis but the general was severely constrained by Moscow's guidelines about what information could be released, even to maintain such an important operation. Only material already published in the newspapers could be fed to London on the grounds that even 'secret' disinformation would excite requests for more and eventually provoke disappointment and suspicion. McKibbin and Silarajs, whose ambitions to expand their operations depended upon Berkis sending better intelligence, did not conceal their irritation in their short messages, but Berkis' request to the 'partisans' for more intelligence was greeted with reluctance. 'We want the West to give us help, not the other way round,' Gailitis and Bundulis told him, reflecting the instructions received from Lukasevics via another KGB agent who posed as a local historian and biologist. His remote house was situated four kilometres from the camp and he could often be seen wandering around the forest. 'Aid will only be given to those who help themselves,' replied Berkis. The struggle for survival in the forest was gradually immunising him from reality but that changed sharply in June 1950 when he read in a newspaper provided by Gailitis that war had broken out in Korea. This, he joyously explained, was the world war which they had all expected and would end with the defeat of communism: 'SIS will be sending us a lot more help now.'

While Berkis and Galdins fretted in the Latvian forests, the man who was ultimately responsible for their fate, Harry Carr, was crossing the Atlantic on board the luxury liner, the *Queen Mary*. It was Carr's first visit to the

153

United States. Menzies had decided that SIS should co-ordinate more of its Soviet operations with the CIA, especially since the close co-operation in the Albanian venture was proving profitable. On 14 April 1950 the National Security Council had issued a new directive, NSC 68, which ordered the CIA to launch a non-military, covert counter-offensive against the Soviet Union to encourage unrest and revolt. Once again CIA officers were influenced as much by the emotional phraseology of the directive as by events, especially the war in Korea. And in that emergency, the Agency looked to SIS as a reliable ally. To the CIA, Carr epitomised the tradition and reliability of the service.

Among the first to welcome Carr in Washington was SIS's resident liaison officer, Kim Philby. The two had become well-acquainted between 1945 and 1947 when Carr was building up Northern Area's operations and Philby was responsible for Section IX. During the two years that Philby served in Turkey, their paths had not crossed until the spy's promotion and arrival in Washington in October 1949 when there had been a brief but insubstantial exchange of signals about Carr's operations in Russia. To Philby's disappointment, Carr's passion for secrecy had limited the amount of information which the KGB spy had received from London. Soon after his arrival, Philby accompanied Carr to the 'tempo' building on E Street which housed the CIA and formally introduced the visitor to Harry Rositzke, head of the Soviet section of OSO.

The Englishman's natural reticence weakened slightly when he recognised that his opposite number, a relaxed Anglophile, was equally dedicated to fighting communism. Carr intended to discuss, but only in broad outline, his operations in Poland, the Ukraine and the Baltic States. In the event, their agenda was dominated by the Ukrainian operations. SIS and OSO had each parachuted a team into the Ukraine in 1949 but the agents had disappeared and were assumed to be captured. OSO planned about six drops in 1950 while SIS hoped to send at least two more teams. The requirement for co-ordination concerned not only which groups were receiving Western support but also the intended dates of the missions and the target areas. Carr and Rositzke exchanged this secret and predominantly technical information. Their object was to avoid any dangerous clashes. At their request, Philby took notes for future reference. As he recalled, the discussions were dominated by 'many skirmishes' about the Ukrainian nationalist Stefan Bandera in whose favour the 'British put up a stubborn rearguard action' because of their long association. The British relationship with Bandera had started during the thirties when, as head of the Organisation of Ukrainian Nationalist Revolutionaries (OUNR), he had contacted an SIS officer with an offer to place his network of informants inside the Soviet Union at Britain's disposal. The offer was accepted and OUNR received not only SIS finance but also support. Attempts were made to infiltrate OUNR agents from Finland across the border into the Soviet Union. The SIS officer responsible for these attempts was Carr, who became and remained attracted to Bandera's fervent anti-communism. In 1945, Carr sought no information about Bandera's wartime activities; his single-minded purpose was to continue the interrupted struggle against communism. And even in 1951 it is unlikely that he was aware that Bandera's group had committed atrocities while fighting with the Nazis; nor, according to his subordinates, would he have been in the least sympathetic to any inquiries about Bandera's past. His overriding concern was the current campaign against Stalin.

On reflection, Rositzke later admitted that at the Washington conference with Carr, he was 'het up and thinking with my stomach'. At any rate, his unease on that occasion was brushed aside. Carr clearly had the same trust in the Ukrainians as McKibbin did in his Balts. The émigrés were deemed to be valuable assets. Imbued with the optimism of running agents into Stalin's lair, no one was prepared to consider that they might be wasting assets. The Baltic States were barely mentioned. Carr informed Rositzke that the British were active in the region and intended to increase their activities but refrained from mentioning any details. Since the Americans had no assets in the area, there was no need for coordination.

'We're intending to send people into Lithuania,' announced Rositzke, also without giving any details. 'Could we have an exchange of views at the desk level?' Carr agreed that OSO's Soviet chief in Munich, George Belic, could come to London to consult McKibbin.

There was little socialising between Rositzke and Carr before the SIS officer returned to Britain, pleased with his trip. At home, he showed his family the menu card from the *Queen Mary*. Everyone gasped that compared with the drab austerity of their daily lives, there was such an abundance of food on a British ship.

George Belic flew to London from Munich shortly afterwards to meet McKibbin and 'share experiences'. In Europe there was much speculation that Stalin would take advantage of America's preoccupation with Korea to launch a sudden attack on the West. Belic was feeling pressure from Washington to infiltrate agents into Russia and needed reassurance about his plans. He unashamedly respected SIS's reputation and McKibbin barely concealed his own sentiment that he represented the senior service. Nevertheless, the British officer was a convivial host, inviting the American to his club for lunch and to his home for dinner. Belic was particularly struck by the tiny television set in McKibbin's living room, which had a large magnifying glass attached to make the screen visible. Privately trusting that such British quaintness did not extend to the management of SIS, he eventually broached the topic of 'some new developments' in Lithuania.

'I realise that SIS has run nearly all the operations into the Baltic with some Swedish participation,' said the American. 'And of course there is the Deuxième Bureau which has monopolised the Lithuanian VLIK group. But that has now changed. VLIK has come over to us and there is some unhappiness.'

McKibbin listened as Belic recounted a sensitive issue which had already been raised by Zymantas.

In January 1949, Monsignor Krupavicius, the VLIK leader, had visited Washington where senior State Department and White House officials had, for the first time, promised political support and material assistance for covert operations. Before returning to Europe, Krupavicius met Vaivada who, as the CIA desk officer, reassured the priest that the Agency would provide money and support for VLIK. In June 1949, Colonel Antanas Sova, VLIK's military chief, had moved with his family to Munich, at Belic's invitation. The American's promises had been expansive: 'We'll give you as much help as you want if you come over to us. There's no limit.' Belic had been true to his word. Sova had settled into comfortable accommodation with seemingly unlimited money at his disposal, and introduced to OSO eight potential agents selected by VLIK for training.

In the week that the Korean war had broken out, Belic had been presented with a bonus. Luksha and two other Lithuanians had switched allegiance. After eighteen months' training by the Deuxième Bureau, they had been escorted by General Schmittlein to a military airfield outside Paris on the first stage of their return to Lithuania. At the last moment, Luksha was told that his mission was cancelled. The French agency had just lost a three-man team sent from Sweden to Russia and the French suspected someone in Luksha's team of treachery. It was an unfounded allegation and Luksha had immediately offered himself to the CIA, an offer which Belic accepted. Luksha was well-trained, had the best contacts among the Lithuanian partisans and was, in CIA jargon, 'mission-ready'. That was, explained Belic to McKibbin, the problem.

By any reckoning, Luksha had the makings of a Hollywood hero. Dark, handsome and brave, he was as devout in his Catholicism as in his nationalism. Before his daily training sessions, he spent fifteen minutes in prayer. His militancy was the product of his experiences. Like most of his countrymen, he had been traumatised by the return of the communists and the mass deportations. With thousands of other young men, he had fled to the forests and joined the Forest Brotherhood to fight dictatorship. But having left his homeland to seek help, he was tortured by his absence from the fight. His letters from his training camp in 1948 to his Lithuanian fiancée, sick in a French sanatorium, were melodramatic but nevertheless sincere: 'I can't understand why I am here. I left the bloodstained fields of Lithuania. Our beloved Lithuania which is so crucified, screaming with pain, and I am not suffering the same death as thousands of others. I feel the cries of hell and try to see the faces of the horrible nightmare and with my tears I try to lighten my feelings. But I constantly see long corridors filled with friends who are marked by death. I yearn to live, yet I also long to have my bones laid alongside those of my friends who are the real freedom fighters.' Inevitably, Luksha's anguish intensified when through his open bedroom windows he listened to the sounds of a Parisian summer: 'laughter, plenty of happiness, no worries and screams of coquetting women. Things become so precious when they are so difficult to obtain.' The pressure of inactivity was excessive, especially 'the deafness to our cause. I hate the people whose silence helps to crucify our nation.'

On the eve of his move to Munich, he was married by Krupavicius. The groom called Nijole, his bride, his 'second wife'. Lithuania was the first. After a six-day honeymoon, they separated and barely met again. He made little attempt to disguise his expectation and even hope that he would die for his cause.

Luksha had no doubts that the CIA was his salvation: 'Finally I'm with people who think that we are worth our freedom.' This was exactly what Belic needed: intelligent, dedicated idealists. Yet in their conversations, Luksha had disturbed Belic by his conviction that SIS's network in Lithuania was already penetrated by the KGB. 'Our man,' Belic told McKibbin in London in June 1950, 'believes that Deksnys has been turned. What have you heard from him since his return?'

McKibbin had anticipated the question. The hostility between the British-sponsored VLAK group, which was led by Deksnys and Zymantas, and VLIK led by Krupavicius had worsened since Deksnys' return. Three radio messages had been received in June from Bredis, Deksnys' operator, since their arrival on 1 May. All had been judged reliable but a fourth was suspect. The message was eerily propagandistic and it arrived simultaneously with a message from Piplys, the third agent on that mission, asking if SIS knew about the circumstances of Deksnys' disappearance.

Deksnys and Bredis had in fact been arrested. Nothing more was heard of Bredis; he was presumably executed. Deksnys, however, had agreed to collaborate with the KGB. Four months later, Piplys would be killed in a forest battle with the KGB.

In London, McKibbin knew that the CIA had good grounds for suspicion but he had no intention of encouraging that uncertainty by revealing to the American that Deksnys, in reply to a trick question contained in a recent letter, had failed the test. Nor did he pass on Zymantas' claim to have been the unsuccessful target of a KGB assassin in Sweden. McKibbin took his lead from Zymantas who, in the final resort, could never doubt anyone's loyalty.

'We're in contact with Deksnys,' McKibbin reassuringly told Belic, 'and while there must always be doubts, we believe that he's perfectly reliable.' Belic returned to Munich reassured and committed to the Luksha mission.

The Western intelligence services and the émigrés all believed that partisans with machine-guns and radios were on the way to the overthrow of Stalin. Since 1945, the émigré leaders had urged that their people were just waiting for the sign to revolt against the communists. Hundreds of petitions from lobby groups representing millions of East European migrants had arrived at the White House and State Department, stridently urging

American politicians to believe that there were movements behind the Iron Curtain fighting Soviet oppression which needed support. That pressure had persuaded Congress in 1950 to hold well-publicised hearings on 'Communist Aggression', and the politicians joined the vanguard in urging the Pentagon and the CIA to support the partisans. When Belic returned to Munich from London, the moment could not have been more propitious for the émigrés to prove that their words were not the product of a dream factory.

No one paused to reflect that the inhabitants of the Baltic States, like the Ukrainians and other Soviet nationalities, had suffered unceasing deprivation, occupation and war for ten long years and were exhausted. Moreover, Belic and others in the CIA had received neither reliable eye-witness reports nor intelligence summaries about the KGB's latest strategies to crush the partisans: the forced collectivisation of farms, the deportation of 350,000 Lithuanians to Siberia, and the slaughter of thousands of partisans in pitched battles. Belic preferred to accept Krupavicius' and Colonel Sova's assertion that 'They've got the stomach to fight.' No one in Munich doubted their wisdom. And no one paused to contemplate how long it would take to build a reliable resistance and spy network behind the Iron Curtain because everyone assumed that a framework existed. When occasionally, at the end of a day, as they sat in the requisitioned villas around Munich, the odds seemed so daunting that the spirits of even the most dedicated and brave agent floundered, Belic would step in to deliver a pep talk: 'We're fighting for freedom.' He was sincere and his agents' spirits revived, but only temporarily. Belic then turned to Sova or Krupavicius to supply the inspiration that their cause was worth their sacrifice. What remained unspoken was that the offering was also important for the émigré leaders personally, since the missions demonstrated their political influence and bolstered their reputations.

A letter from Luksha at the end of September 1950 caused Nijole to sense that her husband was on the eve of departure: 'If my destiny is that I'll be killed, then dream that I am happy somewhere and make your own happy life. I'll become just a bit of our country's dust which is already soaked with blood.'

On 1 October Luksha and two others, Benedictus Trumpys and Paulus Sirvys, the radio operator, bade Belic farewell. Luksha, who had adopted the codename 'Skrajunas', handed the branch chief his silver cigarette case, smiled, and strode confidently to a waiting truck. All three, dressed in combat fatigues and without even forged identification cards, accepted that they would never return to the West. Six hours later they were at the US Air Force base in Wiesbaden. Two Czechs, wartime RAF pilots, were already plotting the north-easterly course which the unmarked C47 would follow to the dropping zone. Since their first drop of two Ukrainians one year earlier, they had perfected a fail-safe routine, flying at 200 feet across the Russian border and climbing at the last moment to 500 feet, the minimum height for a safe parachute drop. They prided themselves that the enemy's radar had so far failed to alert interceptors.

Two days later, on 3 October, in perfect weather, the C47 took off. Besides their equipment, each agent had been given ten watches, 3,000 roubles and $2,000. Julijonas Butenas, a successful Lithuanian journalist who watched them jump, wrote six days later to Nijole that each man looked calm and resolute as he stepped into the darkness 'and left me with a feeling of emptiness. I send you Juozas' last kiss'.

The three agents landed in the Taurages area after a thirty-second fall. In the pitch darkness, Sirvys heard Luksha swear that his shoulder was badly injured while Trumpys cursed that one parachute carrying half of their equipment and food had disappeared. 'It's too dark for us to search and we must clear out,' decided Luksha in evident pain. With the remainder of their equipment buried, and gripping their Schmeisser sub-machine-guns, they began walking through the night in search of a barn and cover. Daybreak revealed that they were one hundred miles from the intended landing zone. One week later they were finally reunited with old comrades of the Forest Brotherhood.

The news was not encouraging. A Red Army division had just completed another sweep through the forest, the latest of a long series of bitter battles, killing about one hundred partisans. The reality was harsh: the war which had been waged for five years was nearly over although the forests were still relatively safe.

In the first coded message for Munich that Luksha handed to Sirvys for dispatch, there was no mention that the war was lost, only a report of their safe arrival. Sirvys' first attempt to transmit the message on 21 October failed. The batteries which had been recovered from near the landing zone were damp. Using an improvised generator, Sirvys was sure that the transmission the following day was successful, especially as he received an acknowledgement from Munich. The session completed, the radio was packed up and hidden in a bunker. Luksha set off to discover the state of the partisans and Sirvys settled down in a forest hide-out to an inactive life, listening for signals and ready to dispatch Luksha's messages if required.

'Their message is garbled,' Gordon Stewart told Vaivada on 22 October. The Lithuanian expert from Washington had taken leave to be in Germany when Luksha's mission set off. Anxiously, he had waited with the CIA chief in his Karlsruhe headquarters to discover the outcome. Stewart's news frayed his emotions: 'We should never have sent them. The whole organisation is penetrated. Deksnys betrayed them.'

In Munich, Belic accepted Vaivada's doubts as reliable. 'They've possibly been captured and turned,' he told Colonel Sova. The VLIK military chief was shocked. The risks being taken by the intelligence service were far greater than he had imagined. 'It's madness to think that you can build a resistance network this way,' he shouted at Belic. 'It takes years. I know the Russians.' Two weeks later, another message was received from Sirvys. The radio operator had been given Luksha's encoded signal by a messenger and although he did not know its precise contents, Sirvys believed it confirmed that the partisans' plight was worse than had been expected and added that there was no evidence of Russian mobilisation. This further convinced Belic and Vaivada of treachery: if the Pentagon and the politicians believed that Russia was preparing for war and Luksha was reporting the contrary, there were good grounds to suspect that he had been arrested and turned. The intelligence famine fed its own distortions. Belic was given clearance to return to London.

There was no hint of antagonism or recrimination when Belic outlined his suspicions to McKibbin in a bare interview room at Broadway. Once again he voiced his fear that Deksnys was the traitor, and once again McKibbin told him that while there must always be suspicions, SIS trusted Deksnys.

Belic flew back to Munich and filed a report to Washington explaining his suspicions but offering no solution. Coincidentally, Carr was due to arrive in Washington for further consultations with Rositzke. The American had been persuaded that the Lithuanian operation had been betrayed by a British-sponsored agent and wanted a face-to-face meeting, although operations into the Ukraine were the most important subject on the agenda. According to Vaivada, Deksnys' credibility was uncertain. 'How can any man,' he asked Rositzke, 'get out of Russia twice and so easily?' For Carr, this was just another route to rehashing tiresome émigré politics. It was VLIK versus VLAK and not the business of espionage. Philby was present at the meeting, once again the recording secretary, as the two Harrys gradually raised their voices at each other.

'Do we know which of these operations is already under Russian control?' asked Rositzke.

'Ours isn't,' replied Carr.

'How can you be sure that your agent isn't under control?' snapped Rositzke.

'We're sure.'

'But how can you be?' persisted Rositzke.

'Because we've made our checks. Our group is water-tight.'

'So's ours,' expostulated Rositzke, 'but one group is penetrated.'

'Harry, I think we know our business on this one,' insisted Carr.

Throughout, Philby silently scribbled down the exchange verbatim. As he later recalled, 'Both SIS and CIA had their Baltic puppets, whose rival ambitions were usually quite irreconcilable. It was with some relish that I watched the struggling factions repeatedly fight themselves to a standstill. On one occasion, the position got so dangerous that Harry Carr, the North European expert in Broadway, was sent to Washington in a desperate bid to stop the rot. His visit ended disastrously, with both Carr and his opposite numbers in the CIA accusing each other, quite justifiably, of wholesale lying at the conference table.'

Even Philby was not fully aware of the ironies. Although he knew about Deksnys, the SIS agent, from his period as head of Section IX, he did not know in 1950 that the Lithuanian was under KGB control. Philby's message to Moscow Centre reported the argument and Carr's concluding sentiment: 'The proof of our certainty is that we are stepping up our activities.' In December, two Lithuanian agents were due to be landed on Palanga beach in Lithuania by Klose. Algis Lechmanas and Paul Janitzkas, both trained radio officers, were due to meet Deksnys. Thirty years later, Carr bitterly regretted that uncharacteristic indiscretion.

As Carr boarded an Atlantic liner for his return to England, the headlines in the New York newspapers justified the wisdom of dispatching more agents. At the end of November, the communist Chinese had launched a counter-offensive in Korea. By the second week of December, as Carr set sail, the newspapers reported that the American army was retreating in disarray. Some experts were already speculating about the magnitude of

164

the inevitable disaster. What had been a local war on the other side of the globe was now verging on a major American defeat, which could have dire consequences in Europe. The enemy victories seemed overwhelming: Eastern Europe and China had gone communist; there was a Russian atomic bomb; even France seemed to be on the brink of falling victim to communist subversion. On top of it all, Klaus Fuchs, an atomic scientist sent by Britain to Los Alamos during the war, had been charged with being a Soviet spy. For Carr, it was just the latest evidence that the Communist International was a perfect spy network. More than ever, he reasoned, SIS needed agents inside the Soviet Union to warn of a pre-emptive attack.

In London, McKibbin's three Baltic lieutenants had been energetically recruiting their countrymen for training. Lithuania House in Holland Park, west London, was occupied by young men who had come to Britain under the Westwood Ho scheme as farm labourers and had subsequently been employed by London Transport. As they relaxed in the evenings over a drink with their countrymen, the dominant topic of conversation was the possibility of a new world war to defeat communism. Circulating among the workers were older Lithuanians who had been soldiers, civil servants and politicians in the pre-war free state. Methodically but unobtrusively they pinpointed those who would suit SIS purposes.

Zigmas Kudirka, a 24-year-old, had been kidnapped from school by the Germans in 1944. His whole class had been forced to march westwards, digging trenches for the retreating army. Christmas 1950 was the first occasion since his abduction when he could seriously contemplate his ideal future: to emigrate to Canada where he would eventually graduate from university. Just after the holidays, as the Allied army evacuated Seoul and defeat in the Far East seemed inevitable, Kudirka and two friends were invited to visit the office of Colonel Sutkos, a veteran Lithuanian officer. The colonel's introductory comments were by then well-rehearsed: 'War is certain to break out

165

soon in Europe. Our country will be liberated. We need volunteers to join the huge partisan army in Lithuania and help the British to fight for our freedom.'

'How can we do that?' asked Kudirka.

'By joining the British secret service.'

Kudirka, an intelligent but uneducated London Transport worker, was stunned: 'A Lithuanian become a member of the British secret service?'

'It's for your country and there are rewards. You'll be paid five pounds per week for all the period you are in service and they promise you British or any other nationality when you return.'

Kudirka, who desperately wanted both the money and the possibility of an adopted nationality to enable him to study at university, accepted the offer instantly. His two companions, moved by the patriotic appeal from their elder, also agreed. Two weeks later, they arrived at the 'School' at 111 Old Church Street.

Colonel Alphons Rebane, the former Estonian SS officer, had been similarly active and successful. Väino Pärtel, his adjutant, had worked through the roster of Rebane's wartime SS division and selected about fifty former SS officers working in British mines, textile factories and on farms, who were invited to the Embassy in London to meet their old commander. Rebane, whose SIS codename was 'Robert', positively relished his reincarnation after the degradation of employment in a textile mill. The self-styled courageous war hero could, courtesy of SIS, now afford to drink at least one bottle of Scotch every day and play high stakes poker throughout the night. In the weeks before Christmas, he gave his troops a pep talk, stressing the imminence of the Third World War and the urgent need for radio links with the underground in their homeland to liaise with the Allied armies when they launched the invasion. To his audience, Rebane was a demi-god and his patriotic appeal was irresistible. By late 1950, he had found forty volunteers and, to his satisfaction, the first six were already under training in Old Church Street. On 24 February, the six were invited by Ambassador August Torma to Estonia House to celebrate their country's Independence Day. Torma, with Rebane wobbling slightly at his side, spoke excitedly of the coming conflict: 'War is about to break out, mark my words.'

In the forests of Latvia, the winter of 1950/51 had meanwhile taken its toll of SIS's two agents, Berkis and Galdins. The mosquitoes of the early summer had been followed by blood-sucking fleas. In November, the irritant of insects had been replaced by humid, sub-zero temperatures which rarely rose above minus fifteen degrees. Life in the bunkers had become harsh for both the 'partisans' and the SIS officers. Berkis' messages to McKibbin were punctuated by regular complaints about the physical discomfort in which they lived. There had been some lighter moments when the partisans had obtained special supplies of food from local peasants, although neither Berkis nor Galdins ever witnessed the method of extracting supplies. Had both dared to venture from the safety of the camp, they would have been somewhat surprised to discover that Gailitis picked up the food from a hiding place in the undergrowth, where it had been delivered earlier by an unmarked car driven from Riga. There was excitement too when they met another band of partisans. But an agreement to meet again four days later had been abandoned on Gailitis' recommendation that 'it was too dangerous'. Unknown to the two SIS agents, others did meet the partisan band and dispatched them, after interrogation, to Siberia.

Berkis had begun regularly complaining to London that he was short of money. The partisan group, he fretted, depended upon him. London, still suspicious, never replied to his plea. In the forest, Gailitis offered a solution. A bank courier was known to ride regularly on horseback along a desolate road near the coast. Perhaps they could steal the money?

Berkis agreed, and four partisans waited with the two

SIS agents throughout one day for the armed courier to appear. Eventually, he did, and was successfully robbed. 'I had to take part in a hold-up,' Berkis wrote in a letter to London, 'which has endangered the whole operation. We could have been traced by the Soviet security forces.' The fear that the KGB's tracker dogs might trace their scent persuaded Galdins never again to venture more than a few yards from his bunker. In Riga, Lukasevics inserted in his operational records that 12,883 roubles had been 'stolen' in his carefully arranged 'crime' and noted that the ruse might prompt London to send more agents.

While they waited, anxious about Broadway's silence, Berkis drank increasing amounts of vodka to stave off the effects of the bitter climate. Whenever supplies ran low, he would sip and gargle the alcohol to prolong its effects. But even drunk, Berkis remained an excellent shot. With his pistol pointed over his shoulder, aiming at his target from its reflection in a mirror, the gently reeling agent could score an impressive hit. It was just before Christmas, in the midst of a regular bout of drunkenness, that he fell into a freezing marsh. Extracting himself, he fell asleep inside his bunker, still wet. On awakening, he was practically paralysed. Anxious that the operation should continue, Gailitis tried to improve conditions in the bunker and said that he would seek out a sympathiser near the forest who would be prepared to hide the ill man.

While Berkis lay in pain but uncomplaining, the partisan radio operator he had trained, Kipurs, continued to transmit messages to Broadway. In March 1951, their patience was rewarded. 'Gabriel' (Silarajs) signalled that a new team of agents would arrive shortly. Berkis and Galdins were delighted. London, they both told Gailitis and the other partisans, clearly had confidence in their work. Quietly they celebrated and agreed that Gailitis should search for more food.

When the news reached Lukasevics, he was pleased but not surprised since he had already heard the news from London. One of SIS's newly trained radio officers bound for Latvia was a member of the KGB. He had been recruited in a German DP camp by John Ransome, a British intelligence officer attached to the 'Technical Section' of the British Control Commission.

SIS's final preparations in April 1951 for sending four agents to Latvia coincided with the arrival in London of six CIA officers for a three-day conference with Carr and other SIS officials. The agenda was to survey all Anglo-American operations in Russia and some satellite countries. Leading the Americans was Rositzke who, as the Korean debacle continued, had arranged to be posted to Munich for a tour of duty as chief of base in place of Charlie Katek. He had left behind in Washington 'a city gripped by paranoia'. The trial had just started of Julius and Ethel Rosenberg, charged with passing atomic secrets to the Russians. On Capitol Hill, Senator McCarthy was launching his investigations to expose the communist bacillus which he claimed was rife in American society. In contrast, the US administration was receiving no reliable information from inside Russia. The existence of an invisible but omnipotent communist onslaught had been instilled into each of the CIA officers who arrived at Broadway in April.

Rositzke was accompanied by Vaivada who was convinced that, betrayed by Deksnys, Luksha was under Soviet control. However anxious to continue operations, he wanted to re-examine the facts. A fifth message had been received recently from Luksha requesting the urgent dispatch of a new team which would include a 'political indoctrination officer' to encourage the partisans. Although passionately committed to their cause, Vaivada had opposed further missions until he was convinced that there was no Soviet penetration. 'They're just sending us cold turkey instead of hard facts,' he insisted. Washington wanted the evidence which everyone knew existed that the Russians had mobilised. The Pentagon wanted to know troop displacements, the movements of railcars, industrial output and airfield activity. Only the Russian Intelligence Service would send this 'patriotic nonsense about the problems of the partisan war', Vaivada concluded. He did not realise that Luksha was no longer fighting for his nation's liberation but for his personal survival and that the single battery powering the radio was running low.

'Let's hope to God,' Vaivada said to Rositzke as they approached Broadway, 'that this will be useful.' Privately he thought the British had muddled through but had succeeded, so something could be learnt from them.

Dressed in a dark pin-striped suit, which to the Americans epitomised 'experience and discretion', Carr looked and sounded the proverbial English gentleman as he welcomed the visitors to his office. Vaivada in particular interpreted the warm greetings between the two Harrys as testimony to the special relationship. Their recent differences in Washington were 'a family row' and easily forgotten. But there were no jokes as they sat down.

'To business,' said Carr.

'Harry,' began Rositzke, emphasising the seriousness of their purpose, 'we're looking for an open and frank exchange. Let's compare notes and see if we have any problems in common.'

Carr outlined SIS operations, disclosing nothing that was not already known, with one exception. More agents, he revealed, were about to be landed. 'As a precaution, however, we are not alerting our people over there about the specific landing zone or time of arrival. We are as concerned as you and are being cautious.' He was not specific, and the Americans realised that he was giving them a palliative rather than sharing a secret. Yet, by the end of the morning, Carr had agreed that Vaivada should have 'a full brief from McKibbin about our Lithuanian activities'. The conference adjourned for lunch, hosted by Carr, which ended in the late afternoon. There was no more work that day.

The following morning, Vaivada met McKibbin and was instantly attracted to the man who was more Baltic than English. 'I was on the same wavelength,' he told a colleague after a session working through McKibbin's files. Struck by McKibbin's seriousness and sense of responsibility, Vaivada felt reassured, especially when the SIS officer promised to forward at a later date an assessment of the Latvian partisan movement for CIA use. They adjourned for lunch and agreed to meet for dinner that evening.

In Broadway, Rositzke and Carr had not enjoyed such an amicable meeting that day. OSO officials in both Munich and Washington were convinced that SIS's close relationship with Stefan Bandera, the Ukrainian nationalist, was damaging their own effort to recruit and dispatch agents to support the partisan war in the Carpathian mountains and elsewhere. The Americans claimed that while they were not averse to using Nazis and even war criminals as agents against the communists, Bandera's appalling record of collaboration with the Nazis during the war was positively counter-productive and there was insufficient evidence that he commanded any support in the Ukraine. Their argument was supported by Reinhard Gehlen, the former German intelligence chief who had become a permanent adviser to the Americans. Gehlen warned the Americans that not only was Bandera's past a millstone but his organisation inside Russia was in all probability penetrated. 'We're hitting real obstacles in our relationship with the Ukrainians,' said one OSO officer at the Broadway meeting, 'because of your support for Bandera.' Carr's trust in Bandera, however, whom he had known for nearly fifteen years, and his disdain for the nouveaus from Washington led him to reject every attempt by the Americans at the conference that day to break the relationship.

The pattern of convivial socialising, smothering every suggestion of acrimony, was repeated on the third day of the round-table conference, and then, after warm farewells from their generous hosts, the American team set off for Munich. Vaivada felt uneasy. 'We accomplished nothing,' he confessed to Gerhardt Meyer, the Washington head of

171

the Baltic Branch. 'The Brits just humoured us. We went round in circles, rehashing the past. I feel I've just spent three days chewing cotton.'

'*C'est la vie*,' replied Meyer. 'We gotta push on. We need some success.'

Among those stepping off the plane in Munich was David Murphy, a gung-ho military intelligence officer with war-time service in the Far East and subsequently in Berlin. Murphy, who was once described as 'always handsome, always articulate and always wrong', was to organise the 'Russian training centre' for the Ukrainians and replace Belic as head of Soviet Operations. During the three-week transition, Belic watched in amazement as his shoe-string enterprise ballooned six-fold into a huge operation. The inspiration for the expansion had been the newly appointed Director of Operations in Washington, Allen Dulles, whose love for and trust in the efficacy of cloak and dagger intrigues found no equal. Dulles passed on to his subordinates his credo that clandestine operations were the real stuff of successful espionage. He shared SIS's conviction that communist subversion could be defeated by stimulating and supporting the nationalist revolts inside the Soviet Union.

The bible for that belief was the National Security Council Directive NSC 68, whose evocative terms provided believers with a sermon to fight the Cold War. 'The Soviet Union, unlike previous aspirants to hegemony, is animated by a new fanatic faith, antithetical to our own, and seeks to impose its absolute authority over the rest of the world . . . The design, therefore, calls for the complete subversion or forcible destruction of the machinery of government and structure of society in the countries of the non-Soviet world and their replacement by an apparatus and structure subservient to and controlled from the Kremlin. To that end Soviet efforts are now directed towards the domination of the European land mass. The United States, as the principal centre of power in the non-Soviet world and the bulwark of opposition to Soviet expansion, is the principal enemy whose integrity and vitality must be subverted or destroyed by one means or another if the Kremlin is to achieve its fundamental design.'

To defeat the 'world-wide revolutionary movement . . . the inheritor of Russian imperialism', the OSO and Office of Policy Co-ordination (OPC) staff was increased to 1,400 officers. In the storm of hyper-activity, it was hard for insiders in Munich to judge whether it was Murphy or Rositzke, newly named 'Harry the Rose', who was the more impassioned, the more hard-working, and the more fanatical, but the balance usually tipped towards Murphy. His will to succeed inspired and intoxicated those who joined the excitement of the chase. Murphy placed himself in competition with Michael Burke, the danger-loving OPC chief in Germany who was enmeshed in the Albanian operation. Burke had served with the OSS behind the lines during the Second World War; Murphy was not an OSS veteran, but sought to emulate the legend. For Murphy, there was no distinction between the Russians and Germans – both were enemies to be defeated. The cynic had not yet arrived who would quip, 'Murphy thinks that if he puffs out a lot of hot air, he'll blow the Russians away.' In April 1951, when General Douglas MacArthur had just been dismissed as commander of the Allied forces in Korea and the fighting in Asia had reached a bitter nadir, no one questioned Murphy's judgment in sending out many more agents.

A second CIA team was to be sent immediately into Lithuania. A Latvian section, established by Belic under a Latvian-born American, Paul Hartman, was to bring a trained team of recruits from Sweden under Fred Launags and make them 'mission-ready'. There were to be extra missions into every area of the Soviet Union. Murphy was particularly keen to use White Russian agents regardless of their Nazi connections. His rationale silenced the doubters: 'Even if they die, it's causing the Soviets problems. We're tying them down, tiring them out, frightening

173

them, setting them off on a wild-goose chase.' This was the beginning of a new world conflagration and winning wars required taking risks. Just five years after the last world war, it was not unusual to expect men to die for a cause. The new breed of intelligence officers would emulate and even outclass the bravery and derring-do of the OSS.

Day and night, at a pace which, in retrospect, Belic, Vaivada and Rositzke uniformly considered 'madness', the young intelligence officers conspired, schemed and gave orders which they hoped would establish a network of agents inside Stalin's empire. Twenty-four hours every day of the week, forsaking holidays and sleep, driven by Murphy and encouraged by Rositzke, the Russian Operations Group sought the means to obtain information about their foe. Emotions were so raw, so intense, that many would soon suffer serious mental problems. Only one thing mattered: the CIA must be able to reassure the Pentagon that they had assets behind the Iron Curtain. No one doubted that the demands could be fulfilled. The equation was simple: Resources + Manpower = Success.

'It's a peasant society,' Murphy quipped to Rositzke who nodded in agreement. 'Just peasants and women in horse-drawn carts. No problem for us.' No one pushed the argument the other way to ask: 'Then what are we afraid of?'

Murphy was emulating a mentor, Frank Lindsay, OPC's deputy chief who by then was immersed in a myriad of operations throughout Eastern Europe, including Albania. For professional and personally ambitious men of the Murphy/Lindsay mould, success depended upon dispaching agents into Russia. Their motive was patriotism and their motor was gamesmanship. No one could imagine that the security services of a backward society might be more effective than the German secret services, whose offer of help in the person of Reinhard Gehlen had been gratefully accepted.

The drop into Lithuania was brought forward to 19 April, in the midst of the transition period. Secrecy

174

disappeared in the celebrations to wish the second team luck, although its leader, Julijonas Butenas, fearing the outcome, had broken down in tears on several occasions before the departure. Dropping with him was Jonas Kukauskus, a radio operator.

The two landed on target in a forested area, buried their equipment and contacted a local partisan group. Butenas set off to find Luksha while Kukauskus, accompanied by a partisan, was taken to Sirvys, the radio operator, in his forest hide-out. When the emotional greetings were over, Sirvys detailed the harsh conditions of his survival over the past year: 'Everyone's petrified of the Russians. They have informers everywhere. Life is constant tension.' Luksha, whom he had not seen since their arrival, was 'safe and working in another area'. Kukauskus and his guide were taken to a bunker while Sirvys and three friends set off to recover the newcomer's buried equipment. On their return the following day, a farmer warned that there had been heavy shooting and explosions in the forest. The four fled and returned two weeks later to discover that their bunker had been destroyed, the guide was dead and Kukauskus had been arrested. Sirvys was certain that they had been betrayed by a farmer's wife.

A chain of disastrous consequences rapidly unfolded. Soon after his capture, Kukauskas, threatened with torture, agreed to collaborate. In the forest, Butenas, unaware of his colleague's arrest and attempting to contact Luksha, was relying upon partisans who also were betrayed. Two weeks after arriving, Butenas' hide-out in the forest was surrounded by a KGB detachment. To escape capture, he swallowed cyanide. Meanwhile the KGB, using Kukauskas as a stooge, had arranged a meeting with Luksha. The partisan leader was suspicious but ignorant of the fate of Butenas and his colleague. He approached the rendezvous having ordered his bodyguards to shoot him if the meeting was a trap. His unmarked grave has never been discovered and his sacrifice never properly acknowledged.

At the end of April, Sirvys was alone and on the run. His radio had been hidden in the bunker destroyed by the KGB's explosions but he had retained Butenas' set after its recovery from the landing zone. To his frustration, on the first attempt to transmit a message to Munich he realised that the set had been damaged and was beyond repair. 'We're cut off,' he told the group of partisans watching. 'I'll write a coded letter to a cover address, warning them of our problems.'

In Munich, in early May, Murphy and Vaivada already knew that the mission had failed. A series of correctly coded messages had been received from Lithuania but their contents – 'more patriotic nonsense,' cursed Vaivada – proved to their satisfaction that the sender was under control. Unknown to Sirvys, the KGB had extracted the radio set from the bunker and caused the forest explosion to disguise their deeds. Using Kukauskas to send messages to Munich, their intention was to encourage the dispatch of more agents.

Vaivada's suspicions burst in a tirade directed personally at Murphy. 'It's too dangerous. We need to rethink this whole operation.'

'You're too emotional,' retorted Murphy. 'You're going back to the States.'

That same week, as the Baltic Branch in Munich reeled amid retribution and accusation, the news arrived from London that two senior Foreign Office officials, Donald Maclean and Guy Burgess, had disappeared. After years of patient investigation, the FBI had proved to the Foreign Office that Maclean was a Soviet spy. At the end of the month, the CIA demanded that Philby, SIS's liaison officer in Washington, be recalled. The spy, who was privy to the mounting evidence against Maclean, was suspected of having tipped off his colleague and provoking the escape. To Rositzke and Murphy, the cause of their Soviet disasters was now self-evident. Vaivada added an epitaph: 'There's a Lithuanian proverb which applies: "I feel like I've bitten on a fly." We were betrayed by the Brits.'

Few in Broadway shared the American suspicions about Philby. Menzies and most of his staff rejected the allegation that their respected colleague was a traitor. Among the small minority who in 1951 accepted the American evidence was Menzies' deputy, Air Commodore James Easton, who had sent Philby a hand-delivered letter warning of his impending recall. Already treated as an outsider, Easton became an outcast for daring to believe the worst about a trusted member of the Firm and he was cut out of the loop in the discussions about Philby's treatment.

Carr and McKibbin belonged to the overwhelming majority who initially believed in Philby's innocence. As liaison officer in Washington, Philby had known details about the Ukrainian drops, but the CIA had been kept deliberately uninformed about SIS's Baltic operations, so little of relevance passed through Philby's office. Carr and McKibbin could congratulate themselves that the tight security surrounding a group of agents who had just landed in Latvia had not been compromised by the new spy scare. The four men had arrived unannounced with a warning to be ultra-cautious before and after contacting the 'Maxis' group.

Six

TOTAL DECEPTION

Harry Carr was aware that his obsession with security irritated McKibbin but ruffled emotions were peripheral where the nation's security was concerned. 'Biffy' Dunderdale's recent retirement had been accompanied by whispered suggestions that the White Russians he had employed were totally penetrated by the Soviets. Carr, proud of his senior status in the service, was satisfied that the same would never be said of him. Fortunately, security in the Baltic operations did not depend entirely upon McKibbin who, Carr felt, was too close to the émigrés. There was John Liudzius ('Big John') and John Crofton ('Little John') at the School in Old Church Street who would pick up anything suspicious about the recruits. Failing their scrutiny, there were the specialist trainers who would be alert to any hints. At the final hurdle, the three émigré Ambassadors would be able to see through their own countrymen, although the Burgess/Maclean business was a nasty reminder that even the best could be treacherous. Unspoken by Carr was the bottom line: that it was foreigners whose lives were in danger; they were all volunteers and knew the risks. After all, both Brits and Balts shared the common aim to destroy communism and SIS was giving the agents a privileged opportunity to help their countries recover their independence – in the long run. If this latest mission proved satisfactory, SIS could slightly increase its support.

These were the practical and honest thoughts of a

178

dedicated officer but not of an intellectual. Indeed, had anyone proffered the opinion to Carr that SIS's weakness was the lack of eggheads among its staff, he would have abruptly replied that the Firm was the better for their absence. For as Carr set in motion SIS's first major penetration of the Soviet Union for nearly thirty years, he was convinced that his short childhood in Russia and long experience in Scandinavia eclipsed any insight which a newcomer might contribute to the art of espionage. In common with so many of SIS's original intake, Carr disdained those who sought a deeper analysis of what in later years would be called 'a wilderness of mirrors'. Yet the web of deception as perfected by the KGB certainly required that critical perception.

In 1921, as the Trust was being established, Lenin had instructed Feliks Dzerzhinsky: 'Tell them what they want to hear.' In common with other Western intelligence agencies, SIS had been deceived because Yakushev delivered information which confirmed SIS's preconceptions and desires. London needed little convincing that an anti-Bolshevik movement existed and that it would naturally seek links with the West. Twenty-five years later, Carr was equally certain that an anti-Russian underground existed in the Baltic States. Paradoxically for an officer who had deliberately allowed the Trust markedly to influence his professional life, Carr's qualities were too limited to enable him to detect an identical deception. Whenever any hints of doubts surfaced, they were partially smothered by the self-interest of McKibbin and the émigré agents in London and Russia, and totally extinguished by his own obsessive belief in secrecy. Denying others insight into his operations precluded any objective appraisal. Lukasevics' deception could only flourish because it developed best in the very conditions which Carr believed prevented the danger.

Lukasevics' agent among the four men who had just landed in Latvia was Janis Erglis, whose SIS codename was 'August'. He had spent four years fighting the partisans in the forests when it was agreed in 1949 that he had sufficient experience to pose as a partisan himself. Following the established pattern, Lukasevics sought the sponsorship of an anti-communist whose judgment would be trusted by the émigrés. The candidate was a Catholic priest, Antonys Springovitch, a partisan sympathiser whom Lukasevics knew was seeking ways to establish contact with the Vatican. Posing as an ardent Catholic, Erglis was surreptitiously introduced to the clergyman and offered to serve the Church's cause. Convinced of his honesty, Springovitch entrusted the KGB agent with a fulsome letter of introduction to a Latvian bishop who had fled to West Germany.

In 1950, Erglis was dropped on the Gotland coast and, after successfully convincing Bertil Bonde of Swedish intelligence that he should be granted political asylum, was allowed to travel to Germany. Soon after his transfer to a German DP camp, Erglis was spotted by a British 'Technical Section' officer as a potential recruit, prepared to fight for Latvia's freedom. As instructed, Erglis was initially reluctant to become involved but was finally persuaded and was brought to Old Church Street.

Lukasevics' skill and patience had at last, after two years, paid off. With an experienced KGB officer placed at the heart of SIS's operation in London, he received the feedback which is the essential nutrient of a successful deception operation. Accordingly, his ambitions grew and he decided to spread his net wider. Through Berkis, McKibbin was told that another partisan group codenamed 'Roberts' was known to exist. Although it had links with other partisans who hid in the Vidzeme forests in Courland, 'Roberts' leaders were Latvian professionals who lived quite legitimately in Riga. Once the news was planted, it was not long before McKibbin's own ambitions grew. SIS, he calculated, would utilise 'Roberts' for a new operation, to be organised by Erglis whose three months of training had proved his natural talent as an intelligence officer. Silarajs, SIS's Latvian recruitment and training officer, explained to Erglis that his mission would be to build an intelligence network of 'legal' agents, that is legitimate Soviet residents, from Leningrad to Siberia. Erglis was to find informants in every major Soviet city, pinpoint fields suitable for parachute drops, and hire fishermen who were prepared to meet British ships offshore. The only caveat was that he was to pose strictly as a nationalist. None of his contacts was to realise that he was acting on SIS's behalf. Since they would be Soviet citizens who had perfect cover as legal citizens, Erglis could mobilise them to serve their own ambitions.

Lukasevics' web had another strand firmly in place.

One year after Erglis arrived in London, Lukasevics received a message via the Resident at the Soviet Trade Mission in London that Erglis would shortly be departing. It arrived just weeks before the team flew to Hamburg.

Klose landed the four agents at the mouth of the River Venta near Ventspils. Before the rubber dinghy had been hauled back on board, the four had split up into pairs and gone their separate ways. Although ensnaring three more British agents was a coup for Lukasevics, it also increased the difficulties of maintaining the deception. The intent of 'Operation Lursen-S' was to keep SIS's activities within a tightly controlled web. Clearly, three genuine agents could not be allowed to roam unsupervised inside Russia or to have more than the barest contact with each other.

Erglis, accompanied by Janis Berzins, a radio operator codenamed 'Toms', set off for Riga, one hundred miles distant, as instructed by Silarajs. Even for those with valid passes, travelling across the flat farmland interspersed by forests was fraught with difficulties. The combination of international tension and Stalin's draconian presence intimidated all but the bravest of citizens who were regularly stopped at frequent and unexpected checkpoints. The SIS instructors had never hidden from their recruits the efficiency and brutality of their Soviet adversaries. 'They pull out your fingernails, burn cigarettes on your body, poke out eyes,' Silarajs recounted to those who had

181

pledged their lives to the fight for freedom. The cyanide tablets issued on the eve of departure in Hamburg were their only salvation.

As Erglis and Berzins emerged from a forest, making their way towards a railway station, they were stopped by two armed militia men. Berzins paled as their papers were inspected and deemed to be unsatisfactory. As they were marched towards the local village, Erglis engaged one of the militiamen in conversation. Suddenly the four stopped. Erglis handed over 1,000 roubles and whispered to Berzins, 'Run!' Thirty seconds later there was a crack of rifle fire but the bullets went wide. One hour later the two fugitives collapsed exhausted in the forest. When they eventually arrived in Riga, Berzins, his body still shaking with fear, vowed he would never leave the apartment, which Erglis had guaranteed was safe. He would rely upon Erglis to gather the intelligence for transmission to London, for which they were well-equipped. Besides radio sets, maps and weapons, they had 190,000 roubles.

The two other agents had been briefed for different tasks. Lodis Upans, a Latvian codenamed 'Peter', was to contact the Maxis group and report to London whether Berkis and Galdins were free or under control. 'Gustav', an Estonian, was to cross the border and establish contact with the underground in Tallinn. To protect the operation's security, McKibbin had insisted that Maxis should not know the location or time of the agents' landing. Yet Berkis, on the advice of Gailitis, the 'partisan' leader, had warned London that 'the new agents should not wander freely for long in case they are suspected of being KGB agents by the partisan groups roaming the area'. Silarajs, having judged the advice reasonable, had asked Berkis in reply for the address of a safe house where the two agents could take temporary shelter. Gailitis had willingly found a suitable location, a house not far from the coast. Accordingly, SIS's wise precautions were short-lived. Upans walked straight into the web and asked his host to inform the Maxis group of his safe arrival. 'Gustav'

Top: Harry Rositzke established the CIA's first Soviet Division to infiltrate agents into Russia.

Bottom left: George Belic was the CIA's Soviet branch chief in Munich between 1948 and 1951.

Bottom right: Paul Hartman was responsible for the CIA's disastrous operations in Latvia.

Top left: Edvins Osolins was in the first team parachuted by the CIA into Latvia. On arrival he worked for the KGB and enticed subsequent CIA agents Leonids Zarins (*top right*) and Leonids Bromberg (*left*) into the KGB's web.

Opposite page, top: Juozas Luksha was married shortly before his drop by Monsignor Krupavicius, sitting on his bride's right. (*Bottom*): Luksha (crouched left) with members of the Forest Brotherhood partisans in 1947.

Top left: Zigmas Kudirka (right) was trained by SIS in 1950 to become a radio operator in Lithuania for the partisan leader 'Edmundes' (left).

Top right: Margers Vitolins, posing as a partisan, was sent to London by the KGB to reassure SIS that their networks were secure. Today he is an artist.

Bottom right: When SIS uncovered the KGB's deception, Janis Klimkans was sent to Britain by the KGB and was interrogated by 'Scott' (*bottom left*).

Top: The KGB headquarters in Lenin Street, Riga, from where the deception operation was controlled.

Bottom: The former British Embassy in Riga which became an important base for SIS's operations in Soviet Russia after Latvia's independence in 1920.

In 1949 Bolislav Pitar
was a pastry cook in
Peterborough. After
training by SIS he wa
dropped on the Latvi
coast to establish a
radio link with Lond
He was arrested in 19
and now lives in Latv

Elmar Remess was
released from Siberia
imprisonment to wor
for the KGB. He was
'host' for two SIS
agents in Riga.

Nora Dashwood, McKibbin's secretary, as drawn by the KGB's infiltrator Margers Vitolins when he lived as an 'SIS agent' in London.

John Liudzius, the British-born SIS officer who supervised the training of agents in Chelsea.

Top: In November 1955 Kim Philby denied that he was the 'third man' in the Burgess-Maclean affair.

Bottom: In November 1987 General Janis Lukasevics and Philby met in Riga. Philby told Lukasevics he knew nothing about the SIS or KGB operations.

was also compromised since he had not yet left Upans to travel into Estonia.

Security completely disappeared when, four days later, the two agents met the Maxis group. 'Vitolds!' shouted Upans with pleasure when he saw Berkis, who was still known to the partisans by his partisan codename 'Urbis'. The two had been friends in the Latvian air force and later as officers in the German security service.

'My instructions,' Upans told Berkis, 'are to check on all the partisan groups in the forests and in Riga.' Lukasevics had already anticipated that London would want to recheck the partisans' activities and, in the previous weeks, sent KGB officers into the Vidzeme forests to act as if they were members of the 'Roberts' partisan group. Upans was to be introduced to that group. Smiling, the major had joked with his chief, General Vevers, 'It's all becoming a gigantic game.' But Lukasevics had not anticipated other instructions brought by Upans. On Klose's next foray, explained the new arrival, he was to return to Hamburg with either Berkis or Galdins and the Maxis leader, Gailitis.

The opportunity of returning to Britain after nearly two years in the forest appealed to both agents – Berkis because he was ill and Galdins because, as he repeatedly argued, he felt that the operation was failing. 'We should have travelled more,' shouted Galdins in one dispute with Berkis, 'and killed a few Russians as well.'

The outbursts convinced Lukasevics that under no circumstances could Galdins be allowed personally to voice his dissatisfaction in London. 'Tell him that he's too important to go,' the KGB major instructed Gailitis and added that it was about time that a man who had boasted about his wartime activities in an execution squad was brought to justice. Berkis, on the other hand, of whom everyone had grown fond, could be relied upon to deliver a favourable report when he had recovered from his sickness. In his frequent conversations with Gailitis, Berkis had promised that he would urge Silarajs to increase SIS's assistance. Kipurs transmitted Lukasevics' proposals that only Berkis should return to Broadway. In the meantime, the new arrivals, 'Peter' and 'Gustav', needed to be processed and contained.

'I'll live in turn with Maxis, then the Roberts group and finally travel to Riga before submitting a report to London,' Upans told Gailitis. Satisfied after just a few days that Berkis was a free agent, Upans set off to meet the Roberts group in Stende. 'Gustav' left the camp with him. Upans insisted on travelling unaccompanied by any of the Maxis partisans. He wanted to establish his independence and give 'Gustav' a chance to travel unseen into Estonia. Lukasevics had no objection; it served his purposes for Upans to gain the impression that the partisan groups were not connected. Upans arrived at his destination without difficulty having, as arranged, separated from the Estonian en route.

The exact circumstances of 'Gustav's' fate remain unclear, since in the KGB's files they would be deliberately obfuscated. However, it was commonly agreed that on 24 April 1951 the Estonian headed north towards the border. Some hours later, his body was recovered from the fast-flowing River Ujava.

It would appear that in the few days since Upans and 'Gustav' had arrived, Lukasevics had been unable to ascertain whether the Estonian KGB would be able to control the British agent, which was indicative of the temporary lack of co-operation between the two neighbouring states and Moscow Centre's failure to co-ordinate the deception operation. Lukasevics therefore ordered that the Estonian be arrested soon after he separated from Upans. This simple task had been botched and 'Gustav' managed to swallow his cyanide tablet. For Lukasevics, even the suggestion that 'Gustav' had been stopped by border guards was dangerous. Berkis would pass the message on to Broadway who would assume that the KGB had initiated an inquiry and sit tight to await the consequences. The KGB's operation, so painfully constructed, would grind to a halt. Accordingly, the corpse was left in the river to form part of a cover story which it was hoped would arouse minimum alarm when it was transmitted to London.

Berkis heard the news of 'Gustav's' death from a courier sent by the Roberts group. He and Gailitis left for the spot immediately and found a 'peasant', an eye-witness to the tragedy, who described to Berkis how 'Gustav' had been stopped by a herdsman who was suspicious of any stranger travelling in the border area. The 'peasant' explained that 'Gustav' had not replied when the herdsman hailed him – the Estonian spoke no Latvian – and border guards were summoned. While they were trying to arrest 'Gustav', he bit a pill and fell head first into the river, drowning as the cyanide took effect. Another 'eye-witness' embellished that version with a description of how the fleeing man had been shot. When Berkis eventually saw the body, there was indeed a wound. Kipurs transmitted Berkis' encoded message to that effect. Broadway's silence was interpreted positively.

Upans showed no emotion when told of 'Gustav's' death although his fellow partisans noticed that he became distinctly nervous. Lukasevics had by then understood that SIS had selected Upans to investigate the network. He was naturally suspicious and clearly harboured a deep loathing for communism. One member of the Roberts group, Alberts Dabols ('Furst'), passed on his alarm about the new arrival's sentiments to KGB headquarters. 'When we finish with the Russians,' Upans would snarl, 'I'll shoot every communist I can find in the morning, then have lunch with a lot of vodka, and carry on shooting in the afternoon. It'll give me a good appetite for dinner.' To emphasise his commitment, Upans was always playing with his revolver, occasionally standing up and drawing it from his pocket cowboy-fashion: 'Pow, pow. There goes another commie.' Dabols' report to headquarters warned that the slightest slip by any operative in Upans' presence – 'a very self-confident man who insists on being on top' – would cost that KGB agent his life. The instability was compensated for by Upans' indiscretions. During his first days with the Roberts group, the SIS agent revealed how many more Balts were undergoing training in Old Church Street, their identities and even their codenames. His boasts suggested that SIS was planning a major operation. Lukasevics was puzzled about the absence of security. Surely the British could not be so amateur? Keeping Upans alive and content was vital in order to discover the answer and guarantee the success of the KGB's response. In early May, Upans sent a coded message to London: 'All's ok.'

In the Maxis camp they now awaited Klose's arrival at the end of the month. Berkis was to return to Britain with Gailitis, as requested by Broadway. A boat was obtained from a fisherman and, on the date signalled from London, they rowed quietly out to their first rendezvous with S208. The patrol boat failed to arrive. To Berkis, the delay was inexplicable and nerve-wracking. One hour before daybreak, on Gailitis' suggestion, they returned to the shore.

Klose had in fact sailed to within five miles of the two men with three more agents on board but had been taken by surprise. A Soviet naval patrol had noticed S208 on previous forays and had lain in wait to intercept the intruder on its next visit, unaware that another department of the Soviet security service was anxious that the craft should arrive safely. Standing in S208's wheelhouse, Klose caught sight of the Soviet ship as his boat began to inch through territorial waters towards the shore. With a sharp command, S208's powerful engines had effortlessly revved to produce 50 knots, outclassing the pursuers but not before a Russian cameraman had filmed the fleeing craft. In the wake of Klose's return to Hamburg were the makings of a major international incident.

Vyacheslav Molotov, on instructions from the Ministry of Defence in Moscow, personally complained to Bevin about 'an unacceptable incursion' into Soviet territorial waters by a 'spy ship'. Bevin feigned puzzlement and scoffed. Uninitiated Foreign Office officials in the Northern Department commented on Royal Navy reports of a huge and inexplicable concentration of Soviet warships in the

Baltic near Ventspils and later of their equally inexplicable dispersion. Molotov's protest was not followed up; General Kruglov had discreetly informed the Ministry of Defence that their diligent protection of the motherland had interfered with a top-secret operation. In Hamburg, with the prospect of the longer autumn nights just weeks away, Klose began preparing to return to the Baltic.

Towards the end of September, the same three agents were flown from Britain to Germany. Bolislav Pitans, a radio operator, had been recruited in 1950 while employed in a London bakery. A former member of the Latvian SS Legion, he had arrived in Britain under the Westwood Ho scheme. 'I was a foreigner in Britain,' he later explained to the partisans, 'and I wanted to return to my homeland.' His contract with SIS stipulated that his £5 weekly wage would be paid into a Swiss bank account. His companions, Leo Audova ('Ants') and Mark Pedak ('Otto'), were both Estonians who, according to Broadway's plans, were to be helped into Estonia by the Maxis group. Both were former members of the Estonian SS, although since the war Audova had become intensely religious and always carried a copy of the New Testament. Their task was to undertake 'Gustav's' original mission and establish contact with the Estonian underground.

Anticipating possible landing problems, Broadway had transmitted a stream of messages to Maxis advising on the procedure for S208's arrival, including the use of battery-powered radio beacons, Morse messages and flashes of the letter 'K' using a red torch. The location chosen for the landing on 28/29 September 1951 was a bay six kilometres from the Ujava lighthouse which was a blind spot for the Soviet radar network.

After the three agents had been entertained for the last time in the clubs and brothels along the Reeperbahn, they embarked on Klose's flagship and settled down for the 600-mile journey. In the hold were nine huge bags containing four radios, code books, forged Soviet passports and duplicate rubber stamps, invisible inks, three sub-machine-guns, six pistols, 2,000 rounds of ammunition and 150,000 roubles in small denominations. The horde testified to Broadway's conviction that their Baltic networks were loyally serving their cause.

On this occasion, as he edged towards the moonlit shore, Klose felt confident he had outwitted the Soviet patrols. From land, half a mile away, a red light flashed 'K' towards S208's muffled sound and a rubber dinghy called *Lady Jane Russell* was lowered into the water. On the beach, Berkis bade farewell to Kipurs: 'I'll do the best I can for your group when I get back. What can I send you from London?'

'A good watch,' replied Kipurs, 'more money and more guns.'

Berkis noded and pressed a package into Kipurs' hands – blank Soviet documents. 'You'll be able to legitimise yourself,' whispered Berkis and waded through the dark water towards the dinghy. Gailitis meanwhile was seen to stoop down and take a handful of sand which he poured into his pocket. 'Bit odd,' thought Kipurs. KGB officers were not renowned for sentiment or emotion.

As Berkis and Gailitis were pulled on board, Klose presented each with a bottle of brandy and a large cigar: 'A present from Uncle Sandy,' he laughed.

The three new agents, helped by an eager team carrying the baggage, had by then disappeared into the undergrowth. At daybreak in the Maxis group camp, Pitans extracted a large envelope from his pocket. It contained a thick letter from Silarajs, which Pitans read out aloud to the assembled partisans. It was rich with nationalistic and patriotic appeal and ended: 'You are the fighters and you will never be forgotten.' Kipurs, who had become Upans' radio operator, led the applause. The future success of Lukasevics' operation now depended upon how Gailitis fared in London.

The arrival of the leader of Maxis and the safe return of Berkis were considered so important that both Silarajs and Rebane were awaiting S208 when it docked in Kiel. Theirs was a warm, unreserved welcome. Both were to be flown directly from Gütersloh to Fairford but first, as a precaution, they would change all their clothes, leaving their forest garments in Hamburg: 'To protect you if the Chekists arrest you on your return,' Silarajs explained to Gailitis. En route to Britain, Gailitis began telling Silarajs of the partisans' successes and problems: 'There are many bands throughout the region,' he reassured his eager audience, 'never more than seven strong, but they need more weapons, money and documents.' Silarajs nodded his agreement: 'Don't worry, we'll help you. You'll be sent to a special school where you can be trained as a cadre to expand our intelligence networks.' The Latvians had established an easy rapport by the time the plane landed. The KGB officer believed that his task would be less difficult than Lukasevics had imagined.

In London, the group separated. Berkis needed immediate hospital treatment while Gailitis was taken to an office in Victoria for intensive debriefing by Silarajs. The atmosphere was studiously relaxed. The Korean war had lapsed into an unpredictable and bloody stalemate and although the imminent threat in Europe had receded, the tension remained. Yet, over the following days, Gailitis gradually realised that Silarajs, who admitted that he was 'Gabriel', was a hawk compared to 'Uncle' McKibbin. His fellow Latvian seemed puzzled that the partisans had not used the weapons supplied from London to engage the Russians not just in skirmishes but in a general war which he imagined was Latvia's only hope for independence. McKibbin, in contrast, whom Gailitis met in separate sessions, seemed repelled by the idea of bloodshed and wanted the partisans to deliver more intelligence which could be used by the West to undermine Soviet control. The undisguised split within the department was significant but faded in the KGB agent's mind as the pressure of his deceit intensified during the daily debriefings. Approximately four weeks after his arrival, his nerves broke. Silarajs signalled the Maxis group that their leader had suffered a breakdown and was being treated in hospital; his return was delayed. Lukasevics suspected that Gailitis and the operation had been exposed, but it was imperative to continue as normal.

Pedak and Audova had, in the meantime, made their way safely into Estonia. Pedak's orders were to contact Rebane's old friend Sirel who was a partisan leader. 'First ask him for his watch,' Rebane had instructed. 'On the back should be an engraving, "To Sirel. With memories of the eastern front. Rebane." That should prove you have met the right man. But to make sure, here is a list of personal questions, and here are the answers which only he would know.'

Pedak obeyed. In a house outside Tallinn, the Estonian capital, he met Sirel who, after a slight delay, found the watch which he handed over for inspection without demur. In response to Pedak's questions, he gave the correct answers, occasionally seeming slightly unsure, although he was more certain the following day. Throughout, Pedak remained unsuspicious and after a few days signalled London, 'All's well.' Since the coded message did not contain the letters which would have indicated that Pedak was under Soviet control, Rebane told McKibbin that more agents could safely be sent. Unknown to Pedak, the real Sirel was under KGB arrest and, threatened with torture, had previously briefed his substitute, 'Känt', about every aspect of his life with Rebane. Since McKibbin had decided that temporarily the Latvian route was the safest for infiltrating agents (others would later be delivered by speedboat from Finland), the growth of the Estonian KGB's web would be dictated by events across the border.

Throughout the summer, Upans, Kipurs and four others had functioned as the Roberts group but the 'partisans' found the strain considerable. Kipurs explained to Lukasevics that living in close proximity with the SIS agent, amid the mosquitoes and the damp, imposed a constant fear of self-betrayal, especially when they slept. 'Upans is now demanding that the partisans launch attacks on KGB officers,' reported Kipurs. 'This could become very dangerous.' Lukasevics' solution was a KGB attack on the partisan camp. The surprise raid forced the Roberts group to scuttle for cover; it also aggravated Upans' fears of his precarious existence and he would cock his revolver at the slightest sound. Lukasevics' ruse was soon judged to have been counter-productive.

As snow began to fall, the KGB major agreed that the strain of survival in the forest for a second winter was excessive. The network of anti-Soviet sympathisers which had been contrived in Riga was activated. Doctors, engineers, writers and teachers were recruited who could house the SIS agents while their regular handlers enjoyed some leave with their families. Upans was assigned to live with Elmar Remess, a 30-year-old journalist who had been specially recruited by Lukasevics to 'nurse' the British agent.

Remess' recruitment was unspectacular but noteworthy. During the German occupation, the journalist had shared his middle-class family's toleration of the Nazis and their antagonism towards the communists. He had willingly joined the German army and was posted as a quartermaster to Poland. In 1944, as the Red Army advanced, he evacuated with the retreating Germans but later returned to Riga to resume his studies. Instead he was arrested by the KGB and sent to Siberia. Two years later, he was inexplicably released and allowed to return home. Only subsequently did he understand the background to his unexpected rehabilitation. In 1947 Lukasevics was searching for citizens who would not provoke SIS's suspicions, and Remess was of particular interest. Before the war Remess had been, at the insistence of his parents, particularly close to the resident British community. As a young man his politics had remained innocuous and any SIS investigation would unearth neither left- nor right-wing activities but would reveal a pro-Western bias. All that made him an ideal candidate for the KGB's deception operations.

When Remess received at the end of 1947 a standard letter to report to the military office in Riga to check on his continuing suitability for the draft, he assumed that it was merely routine. At the informal interview, he barely noticed the taciturn officer seated beside the questioner. The meeting was brief and he was asked to wait outside. Fifteen minutes later the silent officer approached and began a conversation about events in their country since the war. They parted amicably and several more meetings followed, the conversation surreptitiously eliciting Remess' attitudes in a friendly and amusing manner. When the unknown questioner's identity was finally revealed as Major Lukasevics of the KGB, Remess realised how adroitly the officer had prepared the ground, psychologically, before making his offer. 'We want you to give a few years of your life in service to the nation. Thereafter, you'll have no problems; only our gratitude.' It was an offer which could not be refused. For two years Remess was posted to Moscow with the task of posing to Western diplomats as a disgruntled anti-communist, in the hope that they might be lured into a trap. In 1950, when Lukasevics was searching for safe houses for the partisans, Remess was summoned from Moscow to pose as a member of the Maxis group and provide Lodis Upans with a safe house in Zala Street, Riga. 'You need do nothing other than keep him content and as sterile as possible.' Dampening Upans' ardour seemed to Remess an uncomplicated task until their first meal when he realised that his guest was both actor and author of his own wholly unpredictable and impromptu script.

Upans was both restless to build a network and nervous about the dangers of encountering the KGB. The agent's solution was permanently to carry in his pocket a loaded Walther pistol which he automatically cocked whenever entering or leaving the fourth-floor apartment. Beside his bedroom window he laid a coiled rope for a fast escape. Whenever he and Remess travelled by car, Upans would place a loaded Schmeisser sub-machine-gun across his lap. Eating meals in the apartment became particularly dangerous. Upans frequently waved his loaded pistol at Remess while repeating with frightening vehemence: 'We won't use bullets against the communists, we're going to hang them individually.' The returned émigré's delight at the prospect of a bloodbath chilled Remess; he was aware that he would be among the early victims.

'Surely the British are more civilised than to go around killing people?' asked Remess.

'It's nothing to do with them,' replied Upans, 'We'll be in control.'

Remess nodded.

'When we take over,' continued Upans over one memorably raucous and drunken dinner, 'I'll get lots of money and be given a position in the government.'

Upans could be quite amusing when drunk but Remess broke out in a cold sweat when his guest began reminiscing about the war and boasted about his part in the Arjais execution squads: 'We killed them all. Communists, Jews, men, women and children.'

Lukasevics later checked the archives to see whether Upans had indeed been a professional murderer but found no evidence. It was possibly an empty boast but revealed an unexpected and unsavoury alliance between the Latvian nationalists and the British government which, in Remess' view, more than justified the KGB's concern.

While Upans was in the care of Remess, financed by SIS money, he regularly went out into the town to collect information and search aggressively for recruits. He would give Kipurs, via Remess, voluminous messages to transmit to London. The KGB radio operator was not in the forest, however, as Upans imagined, but had returned to his family in Riga and commuted daily to work in Lenin Street. His chauffeur-driven limousine was equipped with black windows in case Upans should spot him as he walked the streets of the small town.

By early March 1952, Lukasevics had received sufficient information from other sources in London to believe that Gailitis' illness was genuine. The passing months, however, were uneventful. No new agents arrived and he was stretched to keep the radio operators of both the Roberts and Maxis groups supplied with proper intelligence. His predicament was compounded when Broadway asked Upans for a list of all the naval ships in Ventspils harbour.

Remess carried the coded message from Kipurs to Upans. After decoding, the SIS agent asked Remess to obtain the information. Lukasevics notified Moscow Centre of London's request and required clearance to send the information. To his surprise, his liaison in Moscow replied that the Ministry of Defence opposed giving the British the truth and insisted that London should be told of a reduced number of ships in the port. Lukasevics' arguments that Swedish and French cargo ships visited Ventspils port and their reports on their return home would refute the partisans' information were curtly dismissed. The KGB, Lukasevics was compelled to acknowledge, clearly did not reign supreme in the bureaucracy. Accordingly, Remess brought Upans the false information which Upans coded and handed to Remess to be passed to Kipurs for transmission to London. Some weeks later, London signalled that it had noticed a discrepancy in the information and urged greater attention to detail. The message included another request: an agent was to travel to Gorky and report on a new submarine which other sources had revealed was about to sail from Baku along the Volga and the canal network to the White Sea. Since the Ministry of Defence in Moscow was most unlikely to permit the release of the intelligence, Lukasevics decided that drastic measures were necessary.

Gailitis must return. Without him, the momentum of the deception operation was slackening and the dangers of exposure increasing. The stakes, Lukasevics judged, should be raised. Broadway must be persuaded that the partisans were in danger and more agents were needed. Two messages were transmitted in early April 1952 to cause alarm in London.

'"Meonis" has died of illness,' was the first message. 'Meonis', or Galdins, had asked Berkis to send drugs for his appendix which was painful. Silarajs interpreted the death notice to mean that the drugs had been needed more urgently than realised. The death was unfortunate, but the truth was worse.

Galdins, whose behaviour and reminiscences about his wartime career had swelled his unpopularity, had spent the winter in the house of a sympathetic 'forester' and his wife. A row erupted between the two men when Galdins made an apparent advance towards the woman. Galdins was therefore 'forced' to seek another hide-out and it was agreed that he should travel first to Riga. The identical fish transporter which had brought him to the forest three years earlier was used for the drive to the city. En route, it stopped for petrol, a militia patrol appeared and the group was asked for identification documents. The driver obliged and, pointing at Galdins, said, 'He's a hitch-hiker. Never seen him before.' Galdins confessed that his papers were missing. While one militia man covered him with a rifle, the other searched his clothes and produced a pistol and maps. 'We've caught a spy,' said one with apparent surprise. Galdins was interrogated, tried and sentenced to death. He was deliberately denied any knowledge about Lukasevics' web in case he should ever escape. Shortly after his execution, the brief message was transmitted to London reporting his unfortunate death. A few weeks later, a letter written in secret ink arrived at a cover address in Western Europe. It gave details of his 'burial with honours' and the co-ordinates of the site of his grave 'near three oaks'.

Janis Berzins ('Toms') was also sacrificed in Lukasevics' plan to alarm London. To settle his fate, Lukasevics set about constructing two stories. The KGB record would state that 'Toms', constantly fearing surveillance and capture, finally lost his nerve and threw himself out of the window of the fifth-floor apartment in Riga.

The second account, which was transmitted to London, stated that Berzins and an assistant had been caught in Riga by the KGB en route to send a radio message. Both had drawn guns. The assistant was immediately killed while Berzins was wounded. Rather than be captured alive, he had heroically shot himself in the head. Regrettably, ended the message, the radio set and schedule had been found by the KGB but the codes were safe. The bad news provoked the desired result. Maxis was alerted that Gailitis and three more agents were to arrive in April.

The days before Gailitis' transfer to Germany were hectic, but among them there was one moment of farcical solemnity. Silarajs had spent many hours conferring with the partisan leader about the chance of a general armed uprising to liberate Latvia. The conversations had been hampered by the partisan's illness but nevertheless Silarajs believed that they had agreed upon an aggressive strategy which blithely ignored McKibbin's instructions. The climax of these discussions occurred just before Gailitis' departure.

An unusual frown crossed Silarajs' face as he rose and addressed Gailitis. Extracting a sheet of paper from a folder, the SIS officer explained: 'There is an important formality which we must conclude. I would like you to sign this document.' Gailitis took the proffered sheet: 'I, Arvits Gailitis,' he read in Latvian, 'know that I bear responsibility before Latvia, the Latvian people and God and I swear that I will never say anything about my work or these objectives. I understand that were I to reveal anything, I am liable to be sentenced to death. I agree that I can only be released from my oath of silence if the Latvian government grants permission.' When Gailitis had finished reading, Silarajs spoke in a grave tone: 'You are to swear to God and the government to fight for a free Latvia.' The KGB agent was sufficiently sane to appreciate the piquancy of the circumstances. He was required to swear an oath equivalent to the Official Secrets Act. Silarajs was rewarded with a firm signature and a smile.

It was a brief interlude in what were otherwise fraught days. Gailitis' nerves were again fraying. 'I don't need all this luggage,' he shouted pointing at the bags of equipment being prepared. 'The forests are full of Chekists.' Silarajs took no notice. They travelled together to Hamburg. On the eve of embarking on S208, Colonel Rebane offered Gailitis his encouragement for the future struggle against the cursed Stalin. Screaming that no one should take the great Stalin's name in vain, the Latvian lunged at Rebane and had to be forcibly restrained from throwing the terrified colonel through a window. Silarajs still failed to draw the correct conclusion.

On the night of 20 April 1952, Klose once more manoeuvred his boat towards the flashing red light on the landing spot close to the Ujava lighthouse near Ventspils. On board were Gailitis and three new agents: Ancietas Pershlotas ('Mike'), a Lithuanian; Albert Kusk ('George'), an Estonian; and a Latvian, Janis Pilsetnieks ('Hugo'), who was trained as a forger and radio operator. As the dinghy neared the shore, the oarsman, Zigmas Kudirka, the Lithuanian who had been recruited one year earlier in London, called to the group on the beach, 'We come from Gabriel.' Pitans, who was in charge of the reception, replied precisely as Silarajs had advised: 'Lucifer is waiting for you.'

As the four men clambered out of the dinghy, one man was helped on board. Lodis Upans was returning to Britain, a nervous wreck. Lukasevics had decided to recommend his return not as a humanitarian gesture but because after Gailitis' nervous breakdown, Silarajs and Broadway needed to be reassured that the network was still operational. Upans would perform that role admirably since in his last months he had eagerly set up a network of contacts throughout Riga, many of whom were innocent and genuine sympathisers. Following instructions from Silarajs, during the month before his departure Upans had passed on everything he had been taught in Old Church Street to Kipurs, including all his codes. After Upans was hauled onto the dinghy, a 50-year-old Lithuanian was also helped on board. His codename was 'Edmundes'. Lukasevics knew nothing about 'Edmundes' other than Moscow Centre's warning of his arrival from Vilnius: 'He is to be treated as a member of the Lithuanian partisans and put on the boat to London.'

The exchange of nervous wrecks completed, Gailitis

was 'retired' from the partisans. His debriefing was judged 'a disaster'. In Stalin's era, his colleagues had little sympathy for their own casualties. Upans was debriefed in London and remained on SIS's payroll until 1955. He never recovered his mental stamina and now lives in a bare council flat in north London.

Silarajs, McKibbin and Carr still believed that the Baltic operations were in comparatively good shape. The messages from Roberts convinced Broadway that SIS was building a spy network across the Soviet Union. Maxis continued satisfactorily. The Lithuanian network had been problematic after it was decided that Deksnys had been turned, but new contacts had been established and 'Edmundes', the partisans' senior representative, was coming to London to discuss a new strategy. Finally, contacts had been firmly established with the Estonian underground networks.

The Estonian agent Albert Kusk confirmed his safe arrival in Tallinn to Rebane in a short signal transmitted by his contacts, whom he believed were members of the imprisoned partisan leader Sirel's network. The Estonian KGB were surprised by his sudden arrival since Moscow Centre had agreed that Kusk should remain for some time with the Maxis group in Latvia. But that arrangement had changed abruptly when the 'partisans' noticed that the Estonian was sweating profusely and disappeared regularly into the forest. After one week, Kusk confessed that he had caught venereal disease, probably during SIS's big night on the Reeperbahn. Self-interest superseded professional duty and Lukasevics bowed to his officers' demands that the agent be sent immediately to Estonia before the disease spread.

Kusk's misfortune was signalled to London. Rebane's response was explicit: 'Don't contact doctors, use penicillin tablets.' Suffering considerably, he was hidden in the countryside while a safe house was found in the city. The irritant of an incapacitated agent was outweighed by the evidence he brought of the growing sophistication of the Allied intelligence services.

Among the thirty-five kilos of baggage, the SIS agent had brought a stack of blank Soviet 'passports', identification cards, work permits and an array of rubber stamps which could produce 'legitimate' documents. SIS obtained some of the documents from the CIA's 'Technical Services' which had established a specialist factory in the basement of the Agency's E Street headquarters in Washington. The KGB's experts were impressed with the progress towards good-quality forgeries made by their adversaries.

When the news first arrived in the West in 1949 that the Soviets had begun to introduce new passports, both the CIA and SIS regretfully acknowledged that the relatively easy adaptation of the documents which had been surrendered by refugees was curtailed. Their agents could also no longer resort to the excuse that their papers had been lost or confiscated by the Germans during the war. Instead, both agencies needed to produce forgeries. The major proviso was to avoid the pitfall committed by the wartime German intelligence service who, in their quest for perfection, had produced forgeries which were of better quality than the originals. What betrayed the forgeries were the staples. The Soviet metal used for staples was of inferior quality and rusted easily, staining the passport paper. German staples were pure steel and never rusted. This was one tiny but damning clue which the CIA's new specialist factory sought to avoid.

In Washington, Technical Services recruited one hundred specialists to analyse the new Soviet passport and produce a replica. The problems were enormous. Experts were required who could unlearn the developments and improvements of the past century and master the technology of producing shoddy paper. The next step was to find old machinery. When that search was unsuccessful, the CIA built its own paper mill to reproduce the Soviet's olive-green paper which suffered a waffle effect. The forged paper was shaded pink to blue in one operation from top to bottom and a distinctive watermark added. The same mill also produced and wove the poor-quality cotton reddish-brown covers. The next stage was to unearth a century-old printing press.

An exhaustive search eventually located a suitable machine in the basement of a Vienna bank. Chemists were recruited to produce the distinctive and various Soviet inks used in the fifteen different Soviet republics where the agents were to be sent. Émigrés educated in those regions were hired with similar handwriting styles to those of their former countrymen, now employed in the Soviet ministries. Finally, 'to duplicate three years' sweat' and give the forgeries the authenticity of daily use in the pockets of the bearer, the CIA forgers pushed the completed passports into their hip pockets and allowed Washington's humid atmosphere to complete the job. The result was impressive for amateurs although the case officers warned their agents that the Soviets' rigorous security apparatus severely limited the use of the papers. Similar warnings were not given to SIS agents destined for the Baltic, who were issued with the Agency's reproductions.

Among those agents was Zigmas Kudirka, the Lithuanian who had rowed the dinghy during Klose's last trip. Kudirka had been selected to travel on Klose's journey in autumn 1952. He would serve as the radio officer for 'Edmundes', the Lithuanian who had been collected with Upans and was being briefed to return and re-establish SIS's network.

'Edmundes' had remained an enigma throughout his stay in London. Adamantly, he refused to reveal to Zymantas his real identity. Quoting security and his fear of the KGB in London, he insisted that he had been sent by the Lithuanian partisans. Zymantas, trusting as ever, accepted the explanation although he had been told by one émigré that 'Edmundes' looked very similar to a prison governor in Kaunas. No one even commented upon the peculiarity of a partisan leader visiting London buying a wig to conceal his baldness. It suited Zymantas to ignore the warnings; equally, McKibbin preferred not to be alarmed.

During those months while 'Edmundes' was in London, Kudirka, whose SIS codename was 'Conrad' and whose name on the forged passport was Zigmas Durba, was assured by Zymantas and more importantly by John Liudzius and John Crofton in Old Church Street that SIS's operations were still totally secure. 'Look at the uninterrupted traffic of agents through Latvia,' he was told on several occasions by 'Big John' Liudzius. Although the two SIS liaison officers knew nothing about other SIS operations into Russia, they sensed that the Baltic infiltrations were Northern Area's 'jewel in the crown'.

Unknown to both men, there was already a hint of alarm inside Broadway, aroused by the growing evidence of failed operations in Albania, Czechoslovakia, Poland and the Ukraine. In addition, there was a gradual accumulation of evidence against Philby. Not surprisingly, however, since the pace of the mole-hunt was languid, there was no consideration whatsoever of launching a search for weasels. The aroma of perdition in Special Operations was imperceptible to all but the most sensitive, and those were rare creatures in that monolith building. The majority, like Carr, resembled those covert specialists about whom William Colby, a future Director of the CIA, later wrote: 'Socially as well as professionally, they cliqued together, forming a sealed fraternity. They ate together at their own special favorite restaurants; they partied almost only among themselves; their families drifted to each other, so their defenses did not always have to be up. In this way they increasingly separated themselves from the ordinary world and developed a rather skewed view of that world. Their own dedicated double life became the proper norm, and they looked down on the life of the rest of the citizenry. And out of this grew what was later named – and condemned – as the "cult" of intelligence, an inbred, distorted, elitist view of intelligence that held it to be above the normal processes of society.'

Dedicated to serving his country and cocooned from objective appraisal of his operations by either the retiring

201

Menzies or his successor, John Sinclair, Carr remained oblivious of the signs of misadventure. In 1952, SIS still lacked a director of operations who would initiate any self-investigation. SIS fed its own deception by its willingness to believe in its own success.

In Washington, the CIA was suffering similar problems, but the new Director of the Agency, General Walter Bedell Smith, had launched a thorough review which he hoped would unearth the very cancer which infected SIS.

Seven

MOSCOW'S BLUNDER

Looking down at the Agency's car park in early 1951, 'Beetle' Smith saw that his inheritance as the new Director of the CIA had already become a casualty of its own short history. Those like Rositzke at the Office of Special Operations (OSO) were government careerists who drove conventional Plymouths and Dodges. In contrast, the Ivy League types in the Office of Policy Co-ordination (OPC) were recruited on temporary assignment from banks, law firms and big business by Frank Wisner and they boasted flashy sports models. No one sought to disguise the fact that the unpleasant social divisions within the organisation were reflected in bitter professional rivalries. During the past year, both groups had multiplied and re-multiplied their personnel, resources and ambitions but their mutual distaste was undermining their common zeal to destroy communism. To some degree the operations were undertaken to enhance the Agency's policital reputation rather than to satisfy an intelligence strategy. In 1951, Smith had appointed Allen Dulles to manipulate a merger by consent which would eradicate duplication and effect control, but the new man's bureaucratic efforts were not immediately successful. Dulles' appointment had encouraged both OPC and OSO to increase their serious espionage missions but also to indulge in fanciful pranks.

The brilliant Wisner, whom Philby would unkindly describe as 'running self-importantly to fat', had recruited anyone and everyone who had been recommended by 'someone' on the network. The same organisation which was spending huge sums in support of Ukrainians, Byelorussians, Georgians, Albanians, Balts and Poles was also launching hot-air balloons carrying baskets of propaganda news sheets across the Iron Curtain, sending glossy printed invitations to non-existent receptions at Soviet Embassies in West European capitals, and dropping stink bombs into youth rallies in East Berlin. Between the extremes, the US government was committed to 'Psychological Warfare', to winning the hearts and minds of important personalities by financing radio stations, publishers, newspapers and corporations. In the early fifties, when the battle between the ideologies was as much intellectual as military, the Psychological Warfare Board headed by General Robert McClure was deemed to be a vital adjunct in the conflict. Yet to Smith, both the black propaganda and the black bag missions seemed to have run out of control.

Smith summoned his friend General Lucian Truscott from retirement to reassess his Agency's covert operations into Russia and the satellite countries. Truscott, an astute, no-nonsense combat soldier who had commanded the Fifth Army until 1945, was quite certain about his new task: 'I'm going over to Germany to see what those weirdos are up to and put the lid down.' He arrived in April 1951 accompanied by two young aides, Peter Jessup and Tom Polgar, who were both prejudiced against the OSO and OPC types who 'could so easily have wool pulled over their eyes'. Among their early targets were Michael Burke, who was continuing the Albanian venture after the British withdrawal despite evidence that it was compromised; and Walpole Davis, whose multi-million dollar support of a Polish underground group called WIN was, he told Truscott, 'too secret to be committed to paper'. Truscott's earthy scepticism irritated those such as Burke who was co-incidentally enjoying a comfortable life with his wife at OPC's expense, and the feeling was mutual. Truscott's confrontation with the 'snobbish complacency' reached a climax when he lobbed a glass of wine at Burke's face. The incident hardly recommended the general to Harry Rositzke and David Murphy.

Truscott and Polgar inspected the OSO training camps, still being expanded, in Kaufbeuren in early 1952. They were shown the numerous requisitioned houses in the woods and alongside the lakes of southern Bavaria where dozens of agents were undergoing training for clandestine missions. Rositzke's and Murphy's enthusiasm as they extolled the unit's ambitions and chances of success evoked a cool response.

'These agents won't survive,' declared Truscott. 'They're known among the émigrés and the émigré groups are certain to be penetrated.'

'And what are they meant to do when they get there?' asked Polgar who had been dubbed 'Rasputin' by his detractors. If 270 German divisions had failed to topple Stalin, he could not understand what these émigré agents hoped to achieve.

Convinced that resistance movements existed across the border, Murphy dismissed their doubts. 'Even if they don't send back good intelligence, we're causing the Russians a lot of headaches.'

'Those in the Kremlin must be scared shitless,' added Rositzke who would write in his memoirs how he spent long hours 'in an atmosphere of impatient tension [while] our agents' lives were at stake [fighting] the Bogey with a Blueprint for World Conquest.'

'The only thing you're proving,' scoffed Polgar, 'is the laws of gravity.'

'Lives are being risked just to see what happens when men put their feet in the water,' concluded Truscott, 'but they're finding nothing. We're not getting any intelligence.'

Among the ventures which Truscott would subsequently query as reckless was OSO's dispatch of two groups of Lithuanians who were landed on the Polish coast. In preparing both operations, the CIA case officer Mike Aniki-eff had liaised in detail with the Reinhard Gehlen group which would become West Germany's foreign intelligence service and was sure that security was perfect. Yet the landings had ended in swift disaster. Guards had surprised the agents on the beach and everyone had been killed. In Truscott's view, these events should have alerted OSO at least to the possibility of KGB penetration. But when a succession of four-star generals had come from Washington during summer 1951 to compile a report about OSO's preparations for clandestine warfare, which were discussed at special meetings of the Joint Chiefs' 'Ad Hoc Committee on Covert Activities', no one had voiced any doubts about these operations. On the contrary, everyone wanted bigger and more ambitious missions. Washington needed intelligence from inside Russia and ultimately wanted Stalin's removal. In the view of the Joint Intelligence Committee, the most 'vulnerable' target 'to be induced to revolt' was the Baltic States. The best source of agents was the nationalist groups in the DP camps who volunteered to join anti-communist military battalions in the expectation of American support for their independence. After the Pentagon had received $100 million under the Mutual Security Act to fund the paramilitaries, a permanent reservoir of recruits had been established. It was this group of potential agents who were assured, during an inspection by General Eisenhower, that they were vital in any war because the Baltic States were friendly to the West.

In this atmosphere, Truscott's complaints were easily shrugged off by Murphy and Rositzke. Both convinced themselves that their articulate exposition of a proposed operation was the equivalent of success. Truscott's surliness was best ignored, especially his complaints about the losses.

Among those who had just arrived for training in Kaufbeuren were three Latvians who joined Launags from Sweden. Murphy planned their dispatch as soon as possible. As with all proposed missions, the details were forwarded to Washington for approval. George Belic, the new chief of the Baltic Branch at the Agency's headquarters, after perusing the papers, walked them round the organisation for everyone to 'sign off'. The last and most senior official to place his initials in approval was Richard Helms, Director of Operations. Although Helms would like to claim that he was 'always sceptical of this cowboy stuff' and dismissed the operations as 'flea bites', Belic met no resistance from the Son of the American Revolution. Helms signed off the Latvian mission just as he had also approved the Lithuanian landings.

Initially the three Latvians were trained by Launags and Leonids Bromberg, a Latvian associate who had also come from Sweden, and two anonymous Americans, 'Ernest' and 'Paul'. But in March 1952 Paul Hartman, an American of Latvian parents, took charge, using the cover name 'Colonel Kull'. Hartman had been previously employed in the Counter-Intelligence Corps in Europe checking on DPs, and was placed in charge of the Latvian operation with scant experience of intelligence operations. Nevertheless, he was well motivated and proud of his knowledge of security learnt during his years in the DP camps. 'I know all about the Trust,' he told his colleagues, 'and I don't believe anyone. Both the émigrés and the British.' Left to his own devices by Murphy – 'he couldn't care less about the details, he just wants men inside the Soviet Union' – Hartman arranged for the three Latvians to be tested by lie detectors before ordering Launags and Bromberg to leave the camp because he, Hartman, would supervise the final stages of the training. In the interests of security, only he would know the details of the intended landing zone. The three agents were indoctrinated by him to ignore 'nationalist rubbish' and produce raw intelligence. They were not to make contact with partisans or anti-communists but instead should seek to legitimise themselves and lead normal lives. Hartman's self-esteem convinced him that he could not be the victim of deception.

The three, Alfreds Riekstins ('Imants'), Nikolai Balodis ('Boris'), and Edvins Osolins ('Herbert'), were parachuted into Latvia on 30 August with the assurance that at the end of their mission they would either be rescued by boat or could buy their way to the American Embassy in Warsaw or Helsinki using their forged documents and belts full of dollars and gold. Like all American agents, they had been promised a $15,000 bonus on their safe return; in the event of their death, the money would be paid to their next-of-kin. The promise of such a huge sum certainly stimulated their idealism.

Hartman's careful plan misfired within minutes of the agents' landing in the Courland forest near the Lithuanian border. Balodis fell some distance from Riekstins and Osolins and, despite their anxious efforts, could not be found. After burying their parachutes and the heavy equipment, the two agents walked towards a farm inhabited by Riekstins' uncle. Soon after sunrise, both spotted an army patrol on the road ahead. Alarmed, Riekstins dived into the undergrowth and, with Osolins behind, ran through the forest towards the farm. Some days later, a KGB dragnet, helped by an informer, located their hide-out. Riekstins bit on his cyanide pill and Osolins surrendered.

In Riga, General Vevers was initially tempted to run the same deception as 'Operation Lursen-S' against America but on reflection felt constrained by the risk of undermining his own success. The critical obstacle was that the third agent, Balodis, was still at large and able to gather and transmit accurate intelligence to Munich. Vevers naturally believed that the CIA and SIS liaised regularly, comparing intelligence from the Soviet Union. Balodis' reports would inevitably contradict the phoney material prepared by the KGB and transmitted to the SIS via the 'partisans'. Until the American agents' arrival, Vevers was certain that the dearth of queries from London about discrepancies in the intelligence reports already transmitted was eloquent proof that SIS had failed to establish any genuine and independent agents in the Soviet Union. Now, one accurate message from Balodis, especially that there were no partisans in the forest, was the greatest threat posed to the continuing deception of SIS. Under interrogation by Major Bundulis, Osolins could provide no help in finding his colleague. Yet Osolins was the key to Balodis' capture. In his cell, Bundulis offered a choice: execution or co-operation. Osolins chose the latter. The Soviets would later claim that Osolins was a penetration agent codenamed 'Pilot' whom they had infiltrated into OSO, but the evidence is not wholly convincing.

Even before Osolins made his decision, Hartman suspected their capture because no radio signal had been received to confirm the group's safe arrival. The Baltic Branch was plunged into crisis as the knowledge sank in that its security precautions appeared to be worthless. As confirmation, Soviet newspapers and radio began publishing and broadcasting a series of exposés describing the 'top secret' Kempton and Kaufbeuren camps used for training the White Russians, Ukrainians and Balts, and named some of the CIA's officers. Rositzke and Murphy assumed that the information had been extracted from captured agents but Launags and others on the staff became convinced that KGB agents had infiltrated the camps and 'even know what we're having for breakfast'. Four weeks after their dispatch, Hartman effectively wrote off all three agents.

Hartman was not required to subject himself to an inquiry, nor did he suffer any emotional response to the probable loss of his agents. 'It's all part of our mission,' he told Launags. In the course of reviewing the operation, Rositzke speculated that there might be a leak from other Latvians undergoing training or from members of the Latvian Labour Battalion. The Latvian KGB had indeed inserted agents into the battalion but soon after Osolins' arrest their reports ceased. Vevers assumed that his agents had been identified and 'rendered harmless'. In fact, to prevent further leaks, training for future operations was transferred to Washington, beyond the reach of the KGB.

While Hartman arranged the logistics and transport for the move, Bundulis obtained from Osolins a handwritten letter to be sent to a cover address in West Germany. In secret ink, Osolins reported that while he was safe, he had lost contact with the other two agents and asked whether 'Colonel Kull' knew of their whereabouts. Impatient for information, Bundulis sent a second letter and then, using the dead Riekstins' transmitter, posed as Osolins. The KGB officer explained that the radio set had just been repaired and asked whether there was any information about 'Boris' (Balodis). The identical message was repeated according to the schedules several times, but without producing a reply. Hartman remained extremely suspicious until the beginning of November when Osolins wrote that all his money was spent. The same letter contained some intelligence. Hartman agreed that receipt of his message should be acknowledged from West Germany. That first contact coincided with the arrest of Balodis.

During the months when Bundulis had feared that the SIS deception was in danger of exposure, Balodis had not established himself as an agent but instead had been enjoying a luxurious life style. Upon landing in the forest, he buried his equipment and travelled directly to an old girlfriend with whom he spent the huge amount of currency and gold provided by the CIA. The good life had ended abruptly during a routine check at a railway station where his forged identification papers proved to be inadequate. Reassured after interrogation that Balodis had not transmitted any accurate intelligence to Washington, Vevers agreed that Osolins should be used as a magnet for other American agents by sending regular reports. Balodis' subsequent fate remains uncertain.

The receipt of the first letter from Osolins and the radio messages had, by the end of 1952, reassured Hartman that his original fears were partially groundless. By then, Launags and his fellow Latvian training officer Leonids Bromberg were comfortably settled in Bladensburg, Maryland, just outside Washington, enjoying what Launags called 'a gravy train'. Hartman introduced to them two Latvians to be trained for the next mission. The more important was Leonids Zarins, a 25-year-old born in Latvia who had fled West with his parents in 1944. Four years later, he emigrated to America and was educated in engineering at a university in Louisiana. In his graduation essay, Zarins had written a strident polemic denouncing the communist occupation of his homeland. On completion, he forwarded his essay to the White House urging the President to 'take some action'. The letter was passed to the CIA and finally to Hartman who invited the young engineer, by then working for Bell Telephone, for an interview.

The meeting between the youthful, impassioned idealist and the ambitious intelligence officer took place just after Osolins' messages began arriving in Washington. Zarins was easily persuaded to accept the opportunity of fighting for his nation's liberty and was tempted by the promise of a large gratuity. On acceptance, he was moved with another recruit into a farm in Virginia and subjected to intense training by nine instructors, including Bromberg and Launags. Overnight, Hartman's predicament of having no assets in Russia and no recruits to dispatch had been transformed. Twice every week he visited his protégés on the farm, impatiently checking their progress, receiving Launags' assurances that everything was going to plan, but revealing little about his contacts with Osolins.

During that period, the Agency's appetite for clandestine operations had undergone a double somersault, spurred on by the politicians. Dwight Eisenhower had been elected President after a campaign epitomised by a promise made by John Foster Dulles that a Republican administration would 'end the negative, futile and immoral policy of containment towards communism which abandons countless human beings to despotism and God-less terrorism, which in turn enables the communist rulers to forge their captives into a weapon of our destruction'. His brother Allen, the Agency's Deputy Director for Plans, had appealed for 'a spiritual crusade for the liberation of the captive peoples of Eastern Europe'. Senator Joseph McCarthy set such vows in their most emotional context: 'Stalin is Stalin,' said the irascible politician. 'He is masterminding a global communist conspiracy.' The electorate agreed although their support for increased operations coincided with some embarrassing revelations.

In December, Warsaw Radio broadcast a series of programmes exposing the WIN resistance group. At its peak, WIN had attracted enormous support from the CIA and was assessed by Wisner at OPC to command the loyalty of 500 activists and 100,000 sympathisers. Photographs of burnt-out tanks and gun-ravaged police buildings had been 'smuggled' to the West to prove the underground's successes against the communists. Both the CIA and SIS had unquestioningly accepted WIN's credibility until Polish radio proved that the network was from the outset a huge deception operation orchestrated by the KGB. Simultaneously, the latest radio operators sent to the Ukraine by the CIA and SIS went silent. Meanwhile, in London, MI5's internal trial of Kim Philby had ended inconclusively without a confession or prospect for a prosecution although J. Edgar Hoover, the Director of the FBI, was convinced of his guilt and heaped blame upon the British for causing so many abortive American operations. Inside the CIA, James Jesus Angleton had been instrumental in convincing both 'Beetle' Smith and Allen Dulles, before the public embarrassment, that WIN was a ruse identical to the Trust. Deception, Angleton discovered, had been the Russian Intelligence Service's classic tactic since Czarist times.

But the paradox was only evident in retrospect. At the very moment when the overwhelming majority of the CIA's and SIS's covert operations in Russia and the satellite countries was proving disastrous, the politicians were clamouring for more.

Few voices in the intelligence agencies disagreed. Although mocked, penetrated and deceived, there were few in the era before spy planes who doubted the wisdom of continuing. Doubting outsiders like Truscott could be discounted. Nevertheless, after a succession of ferocious rows, Wisner, the head of OPC, acceded to Allen Dulles' demands that he review his operations. The target of the first appraisal was Frank Lindsay who, as Wisner's deputy, was criticised by some as 'riding a tiger with his feet firmly in the air.' Lindsay, a sincere and courageous officer, had shown little obvious discretion when missions were proposed for his approval. Any that suggested a hint of success were cleared because, as he later justified it, 'we thought that we were fighting a war and it was all in the short term'. Lindsay would explain that he was bowing to the pressure from OPC's customers and that he accepted without question the emotional phrase in NSC 68 which described Russia as seeking 'to impose its absolute authority over the rest of the world . . .' OPC's major operations in Albania, Poland and Russia all passed across Lindsay's desk, along with Psychological Warfare material. He worked in the hope that it was possible to provoke nationalist uprisings or, if those failed, to 'directly disrupt the Soviet system' by, for example, flooding the country with 'blank identity and ration cards'.

The first reviews during 1952 changed little. But by the end of 1952 when the disasters were exposed, Lindsay chaired a 'Murder Board' to review each operation and then set off to visit the think-tanks of America to seek alternative methods of collecting intelligence.

On his return, Allen Dulles had become Director of the CIA and C.D. Jackson, the hottest of the Cold War warriors, was ensconced in the White House. Lindsay's report on his inquiries was his obituary: 'Our operations have failed and there is no alternative on offer.' 'Frank, you can't say that,' snapped Dulles who would later justify all the operations by quipping, 'It's given us good experience for the next war.' Lindsay retired from the Agency. Everyone else remained, convinced that if volunteers were forthcoming, their services were certainly required.

A similar but more discreet review of clandestine missions had been undertaken in Broadway. Harry Carr was naturally deeply involved. In the wake of several further unsuccessful drops of Ukrainian teams drawn from Bandera's group, it was agreed that a 'Joint Centre' would be established with the CIA in the I.G. Farben building in Frankfurt to exploit the White Russians who claimed that there was still an active anti-Soviet network operating inside the Soviet Union. At least ten NTS members were being trained in Kaufbeuren at any time and it was agreed that others would be trained in the British Zone. Carr, however, was not to be directly involved. The British liaison officer, Mike Lykowski, alias Mike Peters, who joined George Belic to manage what became an expensive, worldwide operation, reported to SIS headquarters in Germany. Carr did however retain direct control over the Baltic operations which he believed were still highly successful.

During the summer months of 1952, the Roberts and Maxis groups had replied to London's steady stream of requests for intelligence. Their information was circulated, classifed as 'Top Secret' and certified as 'Reliable', to 10 Downing Street and the Foreign Office. As a result, British government policies were being determined partially on the basis of disinformation supplied from Moscow. Yet whenever the demands from London increased, the reply from Russia was snappy: 'We're not spies but freedom fighters. We want to overthrow the communists not gather intelligence.' The snub aroused little concern in London because in late September, with the prospect of longer nights, Silarajs signalled that two Lithuanians and two Latvians would be landed in Lithuania in autumn 1952.

Klose's boat arrived on schedule without any problems. The two Lithuanians were Zigmas Kudirka ('Conrad') and the mysterious 'Edmundes'. Just prior to their departure, McKibbin had given a party for 'Edmundes' at his flat in Hampstead and although SIS still had no clue to the identity of their agent, Zymantas and in turn McKibbin were convinced of his reliability. Kudirka was not told that the first two SIS agents dispatched to Lithuania had been arrested or that Deksnys was now under suspicion. Leaving behind an admirer, Dorothy Collier, Kudirka had been convinced that the operations were wholly safe and the dangers minimal. 'Both Zymantas and John Liudzius assured me that it was safe and I trusted them,' he would repeat to himself in the grim years ahead. The two Latvians were codenamed 'Ledomas', another KGB infiltrator who had spent six months in Britain, and 'Kurt', a radio operator. On arrival, the four were led into the forest while eleven heavy suitcases containing weapons, radios and medicines were hidden in a barn.

Klose took just one passenger on board for the return journey. In response to Silarajs' request that another senior member of the Maxis group should come to London, Lukasevics had selected Janis Klimkans whom Berkis had met at a forest meeting. Klimkans' background mirrored the émigrés' but in stark reverse. Klimkans' father was a peasant farmer who, after the war, while ploughing at the edge of a forest, had been shot dead by 'bandits' or partisans. But Klimkans was an unlikely KGB officer; he had never even considered joining the Communist Party. Clever and charming, he was a senior official in Riga's Education Department when Lukasevics used his considerable powers of persuasion to win his agreement to pass through the partisans' camp posing as a nationalist and meet Berkis. Klimkans was yet another strand in Lukasevics' finely-spun web, put in place on the chance that he might be useful in the future.

Two years later, on board Klose's E-boat, Klimkans was nearing Kiel. In his baggage was a jar of shoe polish. Lukasevics had been puzzled by the special request radioed by 'Gabriel' from London. The KGB's scientific advisers, unable to identify any secrets which the cream might reveal, were similarly baffled. The motives, they would discover later, revealed much about their opponents. An SIS officer in London owned a shoe polish factory and wanted to examine a competitor's product.

Both McKibbin and Silarajs were relieved by Klimkans' arrival. The department had recently been under pressure and Klimkans' presence would give the Special Liaison Centre an opportunity to prove to Carr and Northern Area that their branch was clear of Soviet penetration. Klimkans' own questioning, as he informed Lukasevics a few weeks after his arrival, confirmed that no one was suspicious: 'I have been given identity documents in the name of Leon Blomberg and sent to Old Church Street for three months' training.' In fact, every agent was automatically under suspicion but it was judged best practice to allay the newcomer's instinctive mistrust by proffering friendship. The fatal slip, it was calculated, would unintentionally but eventually emerge. But by Christmas 1952, no hint of suspicion about Klimkans had surfaced. Silarajs was convinced that Klimkans was a genuine partisan and in early 1953, with McKibbin's agreement, he introduced the partisan to the Latvian Ambassador, Charles Zarins.

The outbreak of the Korean war had made Zarins, like so many other East Europeans in London, an even greater focus of attention for British security and military officials who needed information and recruits for special tasks. Their requirements and the outspoken pledges by American politicians to defeat Stalin continued to buoy Zarins' conviction that a new, global conflict was imminent. In his frequent visits to the Legation for an evening's game of bridge, McKibbin encouraged Zarins' belief that the formation of the Baltic brigades in Germany and the importance of the Latvian intelligence network was the preliminary to his country's liberation. Regularly, after a visit by McKibbin or Silarjas, Zarins recorded in his diary his hopes that the resistance movement would strike a blow for freedom.

The Korean war had proved to be a lost opportunity, but similar hopes were rekindled when Stalin died in March 1953. Many in the White House urged the President to exploit the anticipated instability in Moscow to mount a pre-emptive attack. Zarins and McKibbin fed on each other's fantasies about this and were in turn encouraged by Klimkans. By then the KGB had achieved the perfect balance for optimum manipulation. With its own agents on both sides, the 'correct' questions were asked to elicit the 'correct' answers. Klimkans allowed the two London Latvians to persuade him that an early war was inevitable. As proof of their conviction, both

Silarajs and Zarins referred to their conversations with McKibbin. For his part, Klimkans persuaded McKibbin, Silarajs and Zarins that the partisans had resources which could be counted upon in the event of an emergency. Brazenly acting as an *agent provocateur*, Klimkans allowed himself to be convinced that there should be a pact between the volunteers in Latvia and the Legation in London to formalise their relationship.

'The London Agreement' signed by Zarins, Silarajs and Klimkans posing as 'Leon Blomberg' in April 1953 established a framework for Latvia after the Third World War. The contents of the thick document outlined the future nationalist government's policies and agreed who, from the partisans, could expect to hold ministerial rank under Zarins' premiership. Klimkans had successfully insisted that Kipurs, the radio operator, be appointed Minister of Posts, while Alberts Dabols ('Furst') of the Roberts group would become a senior civil servant.

Klimkans expected to return to Russia in May, the following month, but Klose objected. The nights were too short to allow sufficient time safely to approach and leave Soviet territorial waters. Klimkans would have to remain in Britain until the autumn. Lukasevics, who received regular reports from London through the Soviet Trade Mission, was not unduly concerned. On the contrary, having a reliable and stable agent resident inside SIS's organisation promised enormous advantages. The only casualty was Leonids Zarins, the CIA's newest agent, who was parachuted alone into Latvia on 14 May, Hartman's second recruit having pulled out at the last moment.

Leonids Zarins' loyalty to the mission had never wavered even when Hartman had insisted that his priority would be to send back military information: Red Army dispositions, the latest air force bombers and any details about the Soviet atomic programme. Hartman could provide no guaranteed safe house where his agent might live or more than the barest details about Latvian life – Zarins had left Latvia as a young teenager and hardly knew the country. Indeed, Hartman had taken very few precautions to protect his agent from the possibility that the KGB might have mounted a deception operation using Osolins. Zarins' thirty-second parachute fall was literally a drop into the unknown, with one exception. Hartman had given the innocent agent, whose codename was 'Lenny', a packet containing 25,000 roubles, to be given to Osolins.

No post-mission inquiry would ever be established to discover why Hartman had breached a fundamental rule of intelligence operations – maintaining compartmentalisation. By the time an inquiry might have been launched, he had become a counter-intelligence expert working for James Angleton, sharing his chief's obsession that a plethora of suspect KGB moles was working inside the CIA. IN 1953, Hartman was so convinced of his own judgment that, while pouring scorn on British lack of security as exposed by the Burgess/Maclean affair, he signalled Osolins that the money he required would be hand-delivered at a precise rendezvous and included the passwords which would be used. Even before Zarins flew across the Atlantic, Bundulis knew that if he waited patiently, the latest CIA agent would innocently enter the web.

One week later, the inevitable occurred. Zarins, already disturbed by the isolation, danger and sheer impossibility of his task, met Osolins in the centre of Riga and after the exchange of passwords walked into an apartment to be instantly handcuffed. 'So you can't take your cyanide,' was the introduction to his fate. When his confession and debriefing were completed, he was sent to Siberia. 'The man's a fanatic,' Vevers' staff agreed. 'He deserves to die there.' The prediction was fulfilled.

In Germany, Zarins' silence after his initial signal of safe arrival was punctuated by messages from Osolins asking for the whereabouts of his contact and protests about the danger he faced by repeated appearances at the rendezvous point. Hartman was puzzled and the agent's training officer Bromberg was anguished. Zarins' disappearance was inexplicable. Yet, by the end of June, prompted by demands from Osolins for money and material, Hartman accepted that Zarins had been lost and

218

arranged for a businessman who was legally visiting Russia to post a letter to Riga containing money. On its receipt, Osolins signalled his dissatisfaction that it was too little and its method of delivery too dangerous. Vevers' strategy was to maintain the contact between Osolins and Hartman to ensure notification of any more agents. Osolins must seem desperate but brave. Between the repeated demands for money, the captured agent, on the KGB's instruction, wrote an appeal to Bromberg which was posted to Sweden: 'I have often told "Kull" about my desperate plight but he does nothing. Only you understand. Help me now, or else all my work will have been in vain.'

Bromberg was, as intended, provoked. Another $25,000 was sent by courier to enable Osolins to plan his escape. Bromberg, meanwhile, wracked with guilt for dispatching Zarins to his death, decided that he personally would go to Latvia to discover the fate of his network. He stipulated two conditions. First, Hartman should be removed from all connection with the operation. The Agency's replacement was John Austin, a chain-smoking officer who agreed not to interfere in Bromberg's training. Second, Zarins' family should be informed that their son was dead.

It was in early 1954 that Zarins' father, a doctor living in Norway, was unexpectedly visited by a representative of their son's employer, which the family assumed was Bell Telephone. 'Your son,' said the anonymous American, 'was unfortunately killed in an air crash in Vietnam. There were no remains. It's my sad duty to hand you $15,000 provided by the company's insurance policy.' The family would never be told about their son's fate. Their subsequent inquiries in Washington were met by silence. By then Bromberg had been dropped into Russia.

The second $25,000 was successfully delivered to Osolins with the assistance of SIS, who were only too pleased to demonstrate to the Americans that the British service could succeed where the CIA had failed. The courier was Janis Klimkans on his return to Latvia in autumn 1953. Klimkans' farewell from London after one year had been warm and, as testimony to SIS's trust in the two partisan networks, he had returned with a large cache of munitions, medicines, radios, maps, and approximately one million roubles. It was sufficient money for Lukasevics thereafter to boast that SIS actually financed the KGB's deception operation. Travelling with the Latvian on Klose's boat were Ancietas Dukaitis ('Albinas'), a Lithuanian; and Heino Karkman ('Albert'), an Estonian. Both were trained radio operators who were helped by the 'partisans' to reach their destination.

Although Christmas was not celebrated in communist Russia, Vevers, Lukasevics and Bundulis were in a joyful mood as the end of 1953 approached. Their success was in large part due to their observance of the textbook rules conceived by Feliks Dzerzhinsky. Yet their self-congratulation was cut short by the curt announcement on Christmas Eve that Lavrenti Beria, the head of the KGB, had been executed for committing a series of crimes, among them spying on behalf of a foreign power. Inevitably, the police organisation in Riga was directly affected by the upheavals in Moscow. Those KGB officers who had in the past executed fellow officers suspected of deviating from Beria's line were suddenly exposed to retribution. The occupants of Lenin Street became momentarily more concerned about security inside the building than in the republic. Communications with Moscow Centre became slower and more difficult at precisely the moment when, through Klimkans, the partisans had assured London that they would produce more intelligence in return for many new agents, new equipment and much more money.

The anticipated request from Broadway for more intelligence arrived on 2 February 1954. In an unusually long signal, London spelled out to the Roberts group the detailed information which was required about specific factories, shipyards, power stations and ports. But, most important of all, London wanted a sample of water from the River Tobol near Chadrusk in the Urals where it was believed a nuclear reactor had recently been commissioned. SIS wanted to analyse its capabilities. 'Gabriel' (Silarajs) specified in the signal that Janis Erglis, the member of the Roberts network who had spent time with SIS in London, should go to the area, make sketches and, if necessary, mix the litre of river water with alcohol to avert any suspicions. The agent was then to bury the bottle at a specific point near Riga for subsequent collection.

In March, Erglis signalled London that he had accomplished his mission. Broadway in turn ordered the Maxis group to retrieve the flask and hand it to Klose who was due to land more agents within some weeks. Since the boat was due, Maxis passed on the news that the agent Janis Pilsetniks ('Hugo'), who was spending the winter with Remess in his Riga aprtment, had suffered a breakdown. In sharp contrast to Upans, Pilsetniks had become silent, withdrawn and finally too frightened to leave the apartment. 'Gabriel's' reaction was succinct: 'We understand that he is a big burden. Consider that "Hugo" has perished in the cause of the motherland.' Perhaps because Stalin had recently died and the atmosphere in the Soviet Union had relaxed slightly, or possibly because it would enhance the partisans' status, Lukasevics was unwilling to approve an execution initiated by Silarajs. Accordingly, Pilsetniks and the precious bottle of water were loaded onto S208 when it arrived at the end of March.

Less than three weeks later, an unprecedented stream of messages was transmitted to Erglis from London: 'State precisely co-ordinate where sample taken.' 'Were animals grazing in nearby fields?' 'How close nearest village?' Each reply, transmitted according to the schedules, provoked a torrent of further questions. The climax was a signal from Broadway curtly demanding that a representative from Roberts be sent to London immediately. Lukasevics' bewilderment became serious concern when his reply that no one could be spared from Roberts provoked an instant demand for the dispatch of a partisan: 'Unless representative of "Roberts" comes to London, all further contact will be broken off.' Clearly there was a crisis. Lukasevics doubted whether Pilsetniks had discovered the truth about the deception. After reviewing the whole operation, the KGB major thought that maybe it was 'Toms" (Berzins') death that had caused the crisis. Perhaps the agent had been suspicious and had communicated his concern by secret letter before his murder. Or, more likely, Broadway had noticed, as he himself only just had, that more SIS agents sent to Maxis had been either captured or killed than those attached to Roberts. Broadway, Lukasevics reasoned, must have convinced itself that attrition confirmed trustworthiness while safety equalled penetration. The major was unwilling to send the senior officer in Roberts, Peter Reinholds, to London, because the KGB officer knew too much. The risk of an SIS interrogator breaking Reinholds and extracting the truth could not be contemplated. The alternative was to send a skilled but 'ignorant' officer who could absorb the British suspicions about Roberts without being able to reveal much. The KGB agent selected was Margers Vitolins, a 35-year-old artist and doctor who had lived undercover in Riga throughout the German occupation.

In 1947, Vitolins had achieved a considerable coup when, posing as a British agent, he had gone into the forests and contacted the real partisan groups. To each group he announced that a senior British officer was holding a conference in Riga to explain the latest tactics to liberate Latvia. With the Briton, said Vitolins, was the leader of the new Latvian government-in-exile who had recently been smuggled into the country. After calming the partisan leaders' instinctive suspicions, Vitolins also allayed their fears about the guarantees for their safety. 'Don't worry,' he explained, 'the British are well organised and I can obtain for everyone valid identity cards. All I need is a photo of each representative.' About fifteen partisan leaders were duly convinced and Vitolins returned with ID cards which seemed authentic. 'The meeting will be held on 13 October in Riga,' he told each man on parting. On 14 October, after the partisan leaders

222

had spent twenty-four hours briefing the 'British officer' in detail about their individual group's activities, all were arrested and disappeared for ever.

Seven years later, Lukasevics decided that Vitolins was the only man who could travel to London to save Operation Lursen-S. During the month's briefing by Lukasevics and Bundulis, Vitolins was told nothing about the radioactive water or about the crisis. He was told only about a partisan's life in the forest and the procedures they followed to transmit intelligence to London. 'Your task will be to reassure them that the group is secure,' repeated Lukasevics every day. 'You only knew three others in your group and were never in direct contact with any of the radio officers sent from London.'

It was a measure of London's suspicions that for the first time, when S208 arrived in September 1954, Klose delivered no new agents or supplies. Nothing was said when Vitolins clambered into the *Lady Jane Russell*.

Eight

THE WEB DISINTEGRATES

Vitolins stood behind Klose as the S208 edged into the dock in Kiel on 29 September 1954. In the daylight, the Latvian could see a small group – he counted five men – standing on the quayside. Even Lukasevics' meticulous briefing had not prepared the KGB officer for the harsh stares and insincere handshakes which greeted him as he stepped onto the windswept concrete. Silarajs, the first to speak, made little attempt to conceal his suspicion as he introduced 'Alex', who was Berkis, 'Pops', another Latvian, 'Fred', SIS's resident agent in Hamburg, and 'Scott' who was clearly in charge. Few words were exchanged as the party made their way towards two cars which would drive them to 8 Golfstrasse.

As soon as the group stepped inside SIS's requisitioned villa, Vitolins was ordered to undress and take a bath, leaving his clothes in an adjacent room. As he lay in the water, he had little doubt that they were minutely searching through his clothes – 'For secret compartments,' he thought – and even fantasised that he was spied upon through a two-way mirror. Scott's experts were indeed checking Vitolins' clothes for evidence that for the past months the wearer had lived in the damp forests. In anticipation, Vitolins had spent the previous two weeks sleeping in a bunker and his clothes bore the recognisable

224

odour, but the SIS officers nevertheless found a dry box of matches, which was certainly curious.

'We're stuck in Hamburg,' said Scott after the third day. 'There's so much fog, we can't take off.' For nearly two weeks, Vitolins and his hosts spent their days in restaurants and bars. Usually three people ate the meals: Vitolins, Scott and 'Fred'. Silarajs and Berkis were excluded. Occasionally the conversation seemed more like an interrogation but Scott soon noticed the charged atmosphere and smiled to prevent the ice forming. When it was finally decided that they should leave for London, the fog still had not lifted. It was only on the fourth attempt that they could finally land at Fairford. The 'partisan' was driven to his temporary home in London, a small but comfortable flat at 2 Sloane Street, opposite Knightsbridge's fashionable Harvey Nichols department store.

After the tension in Hamburg, Vitolins was pleasantly surprised that the following day he was invited to a party in Hampstead, accompanied by Nora Dashwood, McKibbin's assistant. McKibbin was celebrating his presentation at Buckingham Palace to be awarded the OBE. The discreet citation in *The Times* just mentioned 'Foreign Office'. The party in McKibbin's home also marked the official's retirement. Those at the party who were aware of the circumstances made no mention that the loyal officer's departure from the office was premature. His branch had been in constant crisis since the spring and McKibbin was the first casualty. 'Scott' was presented to Vitolins as McKibbin's replacement. A more serious casualty was Harry Carr who had agreed to a posting in Copenhagen in 1955 to become SIS's resident station officer. Although the hierarchy sought to camouflage the demotion as a senior official's last opportunity before retirement to enjoy the Firm's generous overseas allowances, the younger generation understood that something was amiss in Harry's area. These rumours, however, barely surfaced during McKibbin's party.

The small flat in Aberdare Gardens was packed with

Broadway colleagues and émigrés, in various stages of inebriation, blissfully ignoring the torment of the past decade. Theirs was the generation which had served the demands of the military chiefs to obtain intelligence from behind enemy lines. Their seemingly endless consumption of vodka and whisky was to celebrate their host's commitment to the struggle. Vitolins was drinking with a group who believed that it was still wartime; there had never been peace. While the new generation at Broadway condemned McKibbin for neither accepting nor even understanding that circumstances had changed since 1945, the view of those in Hampstead that night was that the struggle against Bolshevism had never stopped. The war against the Nazis was an unfortunate interruption and even a missed opportunity. Vitolins' presence at the party symbolised their own failure to understand the nature of the ultimate crisis in Ryder Street and Broadway which had arisen after McKibbin emotionally rejected the order temporarily to stop sending agents. One rotten apple, he argued with Carr, should not condemn the whole pile. 'He feels he's let us down,' commented Lozoritis, the Lithuanian Ambassador. The climax of their feud was McKibbin's departure but nobody celebrating in Hampstead that night would ever understand the full circumstances, including McKibbin.

The casual atmosphere ended the following day. Vitolins was escorted to an unnamed office block in Victoria Street to meet Scott and an anonymous lawyer who was starkly introduced as 'your interrogator'. The pace, however, was neither hostile nor hectic, just four hours' questioning daily, interrupted by a break for tea, and then sufficient time for Vitolins to sketch the attractive Nora Dashwood and walk around Knightsbridge. The questions about the Latvian's family, career and friends from the small, bald lawyer were repetitive and delivered slowly. Since the questioner spoke neither Latvian nor Russian, the questions were in German. That he never elicited a single contradiction was a credit to Lukasevics' selection of his emissary. Vitolins just told the truth – with a few omissions. The climax was reached on the ninth day when Vitolins decided to change track dramatically.

'I graduated from the Marxist university,' blasted Vitolins, referring to his degree in art.

'So you're a communist?' asked the lawyer.

'Yes, I'm a communist,' shouted Vitolins raising his voice for the first time in contrived anger, 'and I refuse to be interrogated any more.'

'We know you're a Marxist,' said Scott.

'I'm fed up with your questions,' countered Vitolins. 'If you don't trust me, send me back.'

Silence followed. The two Englishmen exchanged glances and left the room. Scott shortly returned to declare his satisfaction that Vitolins was not a KGB agent and then left the room. His doubts, however, had not been stilled. On the contrary, Scott and the interrogator were convinced that Vitolins was suspect but had decided that there was more to be gained by commencing a deception operation rather than breaking the relationship. The two SIS officers did not confide in Silarajs about their scheme. The émigré would be allowed innocently to reassure his countryman that he had passed the test.

Soon after the interrogators left the room, Silarajs appeared holding a bottle of whisky: 'Let's celebrate.'

'But why were they suspicious?' asked Vitolins.

'The water,' replied Silarajs referring to the specimen collected in the Urals.

'Water?' asked Vitolins, genuinely ignorant.

Silarajs sketched the outline of SIS's request and Erglis' delivery. 'If "August" [referring to Erglis] was too afraid to go into the Urals he could have dipped the bottle into the River Daugava in the centre of Riga. If he wanted to play the fool with us he could have just pissed into the bottle. But instead what he sent us was a sample of water which was so high in radioactivity that anyone who lived in the vicinity of that river would have died instantly. The only people who could have concocted water like that are the KGB.'

Vitolins was puzzled. Unknown to him, Lukasevics had

found it difficult to satisfy SIS's request. Their intelligence that a reactor was located on the Rival Tobal in the Urals was mistaken. There was no operational reactor in the sea. Lukasevics had therefore requested Moscow Centre to prepare a suitable specimen of water. The scientist selected by Moscow Centre to produce the sample, and no internal inquiry would ever be launched to identify the culprit, had taken it upon himself to convince the recipient about the tremendous achievements of Soviet science. Lukasevics had not imagined that Moscow could be so foolish as to endanger the whole operation by exaggerating the strength of the nuclear reactor beyond the point of credibility. In the wake of Beria's execution, Moscow's co-ordination had completely collapsed.

As he drank the whisky, Vitolins assessed Silarajs' attitude. The émigré obviously saw little personal advantage in declaring that either Vitolins or the Roberts group was unreliable. The Latvian exiles needed the partisans to sustain their political hopes and maintain their status in London. Only their continued existence provided a regular source of funds for the Legations from the British government. But there was, Vitolins reasoned, a tactical advantage in confirming Silarajs' suspicions, which had also been voiced by Scott, that possibly the Roberts group was penetrated and Erglis was unreliable, and simultaneously reinforcing the view that the Maxis network remained secure. As Vitolins presented the case, he noticed how Silarajs warmed to the notion, since any other conclusion would lead to further investigation of Maxis and probably the end of SIS's operations in Latvia, Lithuania and Estonia. Zarins and other émigré leaders would never forgive Silarajs were he to initiate any action which led to the cessation of British intelligence activities in the Baltic. Not only would it seal for ever the fate of their nations, but it would dramatically reduce their importance in the eyes of the Foreign Office and the State Department. Silarajs was too self-interested to consider the truth.

Scott approved a training course for Vitolins before his

228

return to Latvia. But rather than Vitolins' moving to the School in Chelsea, the instructors would come to Sloane Street. The reason for his isolation from other agents was not concealed by Scott. 'I believe that you're trustworthy but the KGB has penetrated the partisans.' Now, it was Vitolins who was lulled into self-delusion. Scott was certain that there were flaws in the Baltic operations but needed time to investigate the suspicions without disturbing any arrangements. Berkis, Upans and the other returning agents had all be re-questioned and believed that Maxis was reliable. That opinion seemed to be confirmed by SIS's own experience during the year Klimkans had recently spent in London. Possibly only Roberts was penetrated. There was nothing to be lost in teaching Vitolins some limited tradecraft to maintain appearances. On the contrary, there was much to be gained. Vitolins obviously liked London's carefree atmosphere and the polite hospitality offered by Scott and Nora Dashwood. Indeed, Vitolins seemed to enjoy his life among the capitalists, as was to be expected of an anti-communist partisan. While further investigations were underway, he was shown the rudiments of operating a radio and how to forge passports. An assortment of younger officers played at dead-letter drops in Hyde Park with him and, in Regent's Park, how to deal with surveillance. Unknown to them, their pupil had used these same skills to pass a progress report back to Lukasevics in Riga that all was going to plan.

Vitolins and Silarajs had one delusion in common. Both believed that Scott's suspicions sprang only from the radioactive water. In fact they were based on considerably more solid foundations.

Earlier that year, Paul Hartman, the CIA's Latvian specialist, had reported to George Belic, the Baltic branch chief in Washington, that there were 'problems' about Leonids Bromberg who had been dropped into Latvia on 6 May. Bromberg had insisted that he would personally investigate the fate of Leonids Zarins and would meet Edvins Osolins who, unknown to the CIA, was collaborating with the KGB in Riga. Bromberg's landing, as confirmed by his short radio message, had been perfect and unobserved. After burying some of his equipment, he travelled by train to Riga where old friends, surprised by his sudden appearance, accepted his explanation that he had just returned from deportation in Siberia and offered him a bed. On 12 May, having allowed Bromberg sufficient time to acclimatise, the CIA sent Osolins a telegram through the regular postal service: 'Meet one of ours at the Forest Cemetery.' It was the KGB's first inkling that another agent had arrived.

Osolins was briefed by Bundulis that he should merely identify his contact and arrange another meeting. The stooge arrived melodramatically, walking at the rear of a funeral procession, holding a wreath. He was not expecting to meet Bromberg and his surprise when he saw his former training officer was genuine. Another meeting was arranged, and the two parted. Bundulis was decisive about Bromberg's fate. Since a CIA agent could not be allowed to transmit accurate intelligence which could be compared with the reports sent to SIS, he was to be arrested the following day. Vevers personally supervised the operation to be sure that the agent would not swallow his cyanide tablet.

At the first interrogation, Bundulis' quiet warning to Bromberg of the consequences should the agent refuse to co-operate seemed effective. Bromberg disclosed the hiding place of his equipment, his purpose in coming – to build the network which his trainees had failed to accomplish – and the CIA's future intentions. Between interrogations, Osolins consoled Bromberg, explaining his own predicament, and suggesting that Bromberg might also collaborate. There was, after all, no evidence of Russia preparing to attack the West and life in Latvia was certainly better than they had assumed. Gradually, Bundulis came to believe that Bromberg, despite his reputation as a passionate anti-communist, might be persuaded to collaborate. The CIA would not yet be suspicious about his radio silence since Osolins had written that their meeting had passed safely and that Bromberg's radio was damaged, although repairable.

Bromberg's eventual agreement to co-operate at the end of June aroused neither surprise nor suspicion. The scenario which Bundulis had already prepared for transmission to Washington suggested that both agents were preparing to leave Latvia together and another agent should be sent as a replacement. Bromberg's equipment included several blank passports and a variety of police stamps to forge the permits to enter the harbour at Murmansk. The plan agreed with Hartman was for a freighter to call at a pre-arranged date for the escape.

Bundulis' next hurdle was to prevent Bromberg inserting into the encoding and transmission of his first message any indication that he was under the KGB's control. Every radio operator's style of tapping the Morse key is as recognisable to the receiver as an individual's handwriting. Bromberg's message would be heard and copied in West Germany by a technician who, before his departure, had become acquainted with Bromberg's personal style. The technician would also have agreed with Bromberg the slight variation which the agent would tap out on a certain letter group to warn that he was under KGB control. Aware of that safeguard, Bundulis warned Bromberg before the first transmission not to attempt the ruse.

Bromberg's first messages to the Agency in July contained a short intelligence report prepared by analysts in Lenin Street and the news that he was preparing to leave Russia with Osolins. In Washington, Hartman and other CIA officials, despite the gap between transmissions, believed that Bromberg was still free. By the end of 1953, as Bromberg's co-operation became routine, Bundulis inadvertently relaxed his tight supervision. Very slightly, Bromberg varied the single Morse tap revealing that he was under control. His gambit was not noticed, either in Germany or in Washington. Careful analysis of his intelligence reports, however, did arouse misapprehension. Bereft of any military intelligence or indication that the Soviet Union was mobilising for war, his messages

231

seemed anodyne. Although the same quality of material had satisfied SIS for five years, the CIA expected more. Nevertheless, Hartman sent progress reports to Bromberg on their preparations for extracting the two agents via Murmansk.

Simultaneously, the CIA's Baltic Branch was also receiving intermittent messages from Lithuania. Using the transmitter taken from the bunker before its destruction, the Lithuanian KGB were using Jonas Kukauskus, who had betrayed Luksha, to send intelligence reports and requests for more help. Although one agent, the radio operator Paulus Sirvys, was still free in the forests, the Agency had long been convinced that all its agents were dead and that the radio messages emanated from the KGB. Yet in 1954, one letter from Sirvys did arrive and, although he was betrayed and arrested later that year, the CIA's analysts became uncertain whether their suspicions were after all well-founded. In the wake of losing two more agents who had just been parachuted into Estonia, Belic decided to dispatch Louise Bedarfas, an American of Lithuanian background, to London to compare the Agency's incoming messages from the Baltic with those received by SIS.

Bedarfas spent three weeks in May 1954 at Broadway. The minor contradictions in the messages received by both agencies, the lack of substantial intelligence provided over the whole period and the startling coincidences of similar material coming from both partisans in the forests and Bromberg in Riga were damning. Before she had returned with her report, Belic, Hartman and Vaivada suspected the worst. Nevertheless, Hartman approved a final attempt to extract Bromberg. A message was transmitted to the agent that a small plane was to be sent to a field near the coast. On hearing the plane approach, three fires were to be lit indicating the landing strip. On Bundulis' instructions, Bromberg acknowledged the message and endorsed the plan. On the night, however, he was left in the cells in Lenin Street. At the field, a wire rope was laid across the landing strip and the KGB men waited. On schedule a light plane was heard. The fires were lit and expectations rose. The hidden agents watched as the plane circled, began to descend and then accelerated into the night. In a subsequent exchange of signals, the CIA in Germany signalled that the pilots had reported their failure to see the fires. Bundulis thought that the pilots were afraid and had lied on their return. In fact, they had been ordered not to land. The flight was intended only to keep Bromberg alive.

The CIA's effort to stay in contact with Bromberg, planning his escape via Murmansk, quickly dissipated despite the inevitable consequences to their agent whose life depended upon maintaining the fiction. Hartman was unsentimental about the loss. He was subsequently posted to counter-intelligence under Angleton.

The Agency's termination of its Baltic operations coincided with a public statement by John Foster Dulles to Congress that 'the captive peoples should know that they are not forgotten'. It remained unspoken but understood that the US government would do nothing practical on their behalf. Other attempts to insert agents into Russia across the Finnish, Turkish and Iranian borders had all fallen prey to the overwhelming obstacles that human spies encountered in the country: vast terrain, intolerable weather and unbearable tension. Moreover, the CIA was on the verge of introducing the U2 spy plane which minimised the value of these costly and forlorn attempts.

Once Bundulis saw that the CIA's own messages were 'empty', he terminated the deception. Bromberg was sentenced to twenty-five years' imprisonment and dispatched to Siberia where he would die, apparently of a heart attack while playing basketball. Sirvys was sentenced to twenty-five years' imprisonment. He was released after serving nineteen years.

SIS's predicament was more serious. It would have required special qualities for SIS to condemn five years' 'success'. Although the results of the joint investigation with Bedarfas had raised serious suspicions, the two networks in Latvia and the three in Lithuania still gave the appearance of working freely. Analysis of the Lithuanian operations suggested that the circumstances of one arrest in March 1953 of Paul Janitzkas ('Juras'), who had arrived in 1950 to work for Deksnys, could be written off as an operational misfortune, while the disappearance of another agent, Algis Lechmanas, had seemed unsuspicious. None of those still transmitting had used the code to suggest they were operating under control. Zigmas Kudirka, who had crossed with 'Edmundes' in autumn 1952, had reported that he was living with a blacksmith on a farm. Nothing had changed in the past two years. Hiding during the day in an attic and only leaving the house for air at night, he was replying on schedule to messages from Broadway and transmitting reports delivered by courier from 'Edmundes'. Since Kudirka actually believed that he was free, there seemed little reason for Broadway to think the contrary. Broadway's communications with the two other Lithuanian agents, 'Albinas' (Ancietas Dukaitis) and 'Mike' (Ancietas Pershlotas), who were living in small towns, were similarly satisfactory. Contact with the Lithuanian networks was redirected through Palanga beach. Another representative of the partisans spent six weeks in London, where he was fêted by Zymantas, and was returned with a radio operator. Scott had assumed, in consultation with Carr, that since SIS's experience differed so markedly from the CIA's, it would be wrong to draw dire conclusions although the balance did tend towards increased suspicion.

As a precaution, SIS decided to test the Estonian network. Rebane sent a message to the partisans that one of their leaders should come immediately to London for training. It was a measure of SIS's limited suspicions of the KGB's penetration that when the Estonians' reply arrived that 'Johan' could be picked up by Klose at Saaremaa on 1 November, another agent, 'Harry', was to be dropped on the same trip. SIS clearly still believed that the KGB's penetration was confined to the Roberts group.

Rebane was in Kiel to welcome 'Johan'. After a short stay in Hamburg where the Estonian revealed his identity as Walter Luks, the two flew to London. The partisan was interrogated for several days, not in Russian as the interrogator required, but in Estonian because Luks claimed his Russian was imperfect. Rebane was the interpreter in what became, advantageously for Luks who spoke fluent Russian, a hesitant conversation. The questions followed a familiar pattern about the Estonian's life and family background. At the end of the week, both Rebane and the interrogator declared themselves satisfied and the partisan was sent to a school in Holland Park where, until recently, Ukrainians had been trained.

Scott, like McKibbin, relied upon Rebane's opinion about his countryman. There was every reason to trust his judgment. As a former senior SS officer, he could be expected to smell a communist or a stooge. Rebane held the same opinion about himself. With his lifelong experience, there was little, he believed, which could escape his attention. Following normal practice, he introduced Luks to August Torma, the Estonian Ambassador in London. As required, the visitor bowed to 'His Excellency' and presented the émigré with a small box. Inside was earth. 'From your beloved country,' said Luks. The Ambassador, who was the least realistic of the three Baltic diplomats, was visibly moved and launched into a monologue about the certainty of war in the near future 'which will liberate our country'.

The two men next met at a party held at the Legation on 24 February 1954, to celebrate Estonia's National Day. Rebane stood in the centre of the reception area amid the exiled Estonian community, wobbling on his heels, as usual; he had already consumed a bottle of Scotch. Nearby was Luks who, while utterly discreet about the reason of his presence in London, was talking animatedly to those who spoke of little else but the horrors of communism. It was one of these guests who pulled Rebane to one side.

'You see that man,' he whispered pointing at Luks, 'I

knew him in Estonia. He joined the Red Army in 1941 and became a major.'

'Rubbish,' replied the befuddled SIS employee, 'he was a private who deserted from the rifle corps.'

Luks would stay four months in London.

Similar confidence in the partisans had recently been displayed on the other side of Kensington, at the Latvian Legation. At tea time on several successive Sundays, Vitolins had been invited to meet Zarins and Silarajs. While Marianne Zarins, the Ambassador's daughter, played the piano at one end of the large reception room, the three men discussed the future government of a free Latvia. When, after nine weeks, Vitolins was due to return, neither émigré had the slightest doubt about their guest's credibility.

Scott's own recently held suspicions were by then confirmed but Vitolins remained blissfully unaware of their concealment. In the course of his stay, Scott invited the Latvian to several meals and drove him to Cambridge to show him 'my old college'. Standing in the old town, he said, with what appeared to Vitolins to be honest candour, 'I will always trust you.' Vitolins was willingly convinced of his own success when Scott announced that, after one week's holiday, he would return to Latvia. On the eve of his departure, Silarajs revealed once again his commitment: 'Please take this message back to our men in the motherland.' Vitolins was handed an envelope and a package containing medicines. In Hamburg he was treated to the traditional night on the Reeperbahn and, just before his departure, offered a cyanide pill. It was refused. Dressed once again in his own clothes, he travelled alone on S208 to Bornholm, waited for the unsettled weather to clear and was landed on the Latvian coast.

Vitolins' debriefing in Lenin Street which began in early January 1955 and continued for two months hardly satisfied Lukasevics although the major concealed his unease. While Vitolins certainly seemed to have won Scott's trust, the very reasons for his selection, his ignorance and innocence, were a disadvantage in the debriefing. Although a

236

professional intelligence officer, Vitolins was an artist whose sincerity had perhaps been persuasive in London because it was genuine. But that same sincerity precluded scepticism. Vitolins was sure that his mission had been successful but his return without new supplies or new agents suggested otherwise. Lukasevics could only hope that the damage might be contained by continuing the supply of intelligence and maintaining the deception for the twelve SIS agents still living with the partisans. As an added, but uncertain, touch, he ordered the arrest of Kurt Krumins, an SIS agent who was living with the Roberts group. The arrest, he speculated, might just confuse SIS. But in reality, although neither he nor Vevers could admit the truth, 'Operation Lursen-S' had been radically transformed.

Lukasevics' activities were no longer an exercise to deceive SIS but to limit any damage to the KGB and to discover what mistakes had been made. The boastful aura of success in Lenin Street was becoming corrupted by vanity and frustration. The absence of any new arrivals during the winter and the prospect of similar inactivity in the autumn was compounded by a constant stream of requests to Maxis from Broadway for information which required agents to travel all over the Soviet Union. Moscow Centre correctly suspected that the British were now playing the game in reverse and wanted to analyse the disinformation which the Soviets would contrive. Perceptive analysis of disinformation by SIS could be as damaging as the transmission of correct intelligence. The lack of any reliable information from London complicated the KGB's task. But Lukasevics believed there was a solution: a return to the basic Dzerzhinsky approach of inserting an agent into SIS to recover their trust. The ideal candidate was Klimkans whose well-established relationship with Zarins and Silarajs had produced the 'London Agreement'. Klimkans' presence inside Broadway, Lukasevics calculated, was the only way to re-establish his operation or alternatively to cause SIS everlasting damage.

In the blueprint for such operations, as perfected in the

Trust, at the appropriate moment, when the deception is exposed, the KGB takes another step to intensify the victim's calamity. In 1929 this had been the arrival from Russia in Helsinki of Edward Opperput, a self-confessed Chekist, who applied for asylum. Under questioning, Opperput freely admitted that the Trust was deliberately created by Dzerzhinsky, confirming that Western intelligence agencies had been woefully deceived. Having supplied confirmatory details, the 'defector' suddenly disappeared, to re-surface in Moscow. The Soviets had succeeded in diverting the West's attention from other, genuine defectors, to re-examination of their own fiasco.

In 1955, Lukasevics, following the orders of the Second Chief Directorate in Moscow Centre, directed Klimkans to perform a similar mission. The KGB major's original web was disintegrating but the strands of its successor were being spun. Klimkans' task was finally to destroy the relationship between the émigrés and SIS, divert SIS's attention from other KGB activities and provoke uncertainty about SIS's relations with other informants. The new conspiracy was initiated by a signal in June 1955 from Maxis to 'Gabriel' suggesting that Klimkans return to London with his wife as a long-term 'liaison officer'. On 22 August Silarajs replied: 'Agreed. But danger. "Roberts" has suffered arrests. Boat cannot come to Kurzeme. For security reasons find another route – via Sweden or Germany.' Lukasevics, his judgment clouded by vanity, accepted the reply at face value. The calculations in Moscow Centre were more realistic.

By 1955, the tight security surrounding the Soviet Union's borders had become legendary. Faking an overland escape was impossible and suggesting the hire or theft of a fishing boat to cross the Baltic was no longer straightforward. Nevertheless, Lukasevics calculated that if he allowed time to suggest that the difficulties in obtaining a passage were being overcome, London would be convinced. Maxis therefore signalled to Broadway that Klimkans was seeking a safe route and would remain in contact. In Riga, Lukasevics was confident about his latest strategem. Moscow Centre, still immersed in the reorganisation following the deaths of Stalin and Beria, approved his proposal without comment although he was informed that the Estonian KGB, in an effort to re-establish SIS's confidence in the partisan networks, had allowed Heino Karkman, an SIS agent, to return with Klose when the boat brought Luks back from London. Lukasevics was isolated from the West and failed to grasp the implications of the changes of personnel in Broadway and especially in Northern Area.

Menzies' retirement in 1952 and the disappearance from positions of influence on the fourth floor of Carr, Gibson and others who had joined SIS after the Bolshevik revolution, had terminated for ever the dream of delivering communism a single, fatal blow. Their replacements as Soviet experts – John Bruce Lockhart, Harold Shergold and Jack Easton, eye-witnesses of Soviet power in Germany – were sterner and less emotional than their predecessors. Although all would also be swept up and tainted by KGB-inflicted embarrassments during that decade, they were, like many of the post-war generation, critical of their elders' recent performance. The return of Karkman from Estonia in April 1955 confirmed their suspicions about their predecessors.

Karkman's debriefing in London was a shock for both Rebane and Scott. The agent revealed that he had realised the truth about SIS's whole operation inside the Soviet Union soon after his arrival from Britain: 'The networks are completely penetrated by the KGB.' Throughout his stay in Estonia, he explained, he had concealed his suspicion and persuaded the partisans that, on his return, he would encourage SIS to provide extra help. Luks' arrival and the opportunity for a routine switch was the chance for his escape.

SIS's reaction to Karkman's revelations was hesitant. McKibbin was recalled for detailed questioning and the post mortem suggested that Fred Launags who, at the last moment, had dropped out of the first major landing from Sweden in 1949, was a Chekist. Launags, after all, had also been involved in the disastrous American operations in Latvia. The conclusion was passed on to the CIA who immediately posted the innocent and impassioned nationalist to the equivalent of Siberia: Madrid. Blaming Launags was easy and ignored the skills of the adversary. SIS nevertheless heaped all the blame for the disaster on the CIA agent and also upon McKibbin. Until he died eleven years later, the Scotsman received no comfort for, or recognition of, his protests that Carr deserved equal blame.

At that point, McKibbin's and Carr's successors would have liked to bury the sorry saga. There was little to be gained by continuing the charade. There was also, they decided, no chance of rescuing the SIS agents – of which there were at least eleven – who were still alive in the three Baltic States. Hardly a thought was given by the British officers to those like Zigmas Kudirka, by then living in Vilnius, who, in several letters during 1955, urged his own return. 'I've run out of money,' he wrote to Zymantas, 'and even "Edmundes" has admitted there seems little chance of doing any worthwhile work.' Broadway's reply, sent to 'Edmundes', who was now suspected of being a KGB agent, was emphatic: 'Sea operations no longer possible.' The justification in Broadway for abandoning the agents was that they had volunteered knowing the risks and could not complain about the outcome.

Scott instead focused on Maxis' last suggestion that Klimkans should return to London. His presence would be a heaven-sent opportunity to test all the suspicions, but Broadway feared that the KGB, realising their own undoing, were intending to lure S208 into Soviet waters in order to capture Klose. The risk was unacceptable. But to Scott's surprise, Maxis was insistent that Klimkans travel to Britain.

At the beginning of 1956, Maxis again reported the problems of finding a boat and urged that S208 be sent. 'Politically impossible to send pick-up,' signalled 'Gabriel' in March. The reason given, which has a semblance of

240

authenticity, was the prospective visit of the Soviet leaders, Bulganin and Khrushchev. The Prime Minister's office had told SIS that no operations were to be undertaken that might embarrass the hosts before or during this historic visit. SIS's uncompromising message compelled Lukasevics and Moscow Centre to reconsider how to provoke the British into accepting the responsibility for transport, but his thoughts were interrupted on 22 June 1956 by an unforeseen message from Silarajs: 'We can no longer help you. Will be sending you no further physical or material help. All safe houses are blown. "Viesturs" [Klimkans' SIS codename] should not come but stay at home. Journey too dangerous and would endanger all our other organisations. Destroy or keep radios and codes. This is our last message until better times. We will listen to you until 30 June. Thereafter God help you.' It was a blow to Lukasevics but he began to think of desperate solutions. The terms of Silarajs' message were so friendly, without any suggestion that the truth had yet been discovered, that perhaps there was a glimmer of hope.

Isolated from British affairs, Lukasevics knew nothing of the background to Silarajs' message. SIS was in the midst of another major upheaval. During the visit of the Soviet leaders, SIS had sent Lionel 'Buster' Crabb, an ageing frogman, to examine the hull of a Soviet destroyer at anchor in Portsmouth. Crabb disappeared and, prompted by Soviet protests and leaks, the service was immersed in an unprecedented scandal for disobeying the Prime Minister's instructions. SIS blunders had also been revealed by the Soviet exposure of a potentially huge intelligence success in Berlin where an eavesdropping tunnel had been built from the West under the Soviet headquarters. Finally, there were some major embarrassments in the Middle East. The cost of inept management was finally acknowledged. Irrevocably discredited, Sir John Sinclair was replaced by Sir Dick White: a reluctant transfer for the head of MI5.

The new 'C's' brief was to reorganise the service – its personnel and its methods of operation – to prevent any more embarrassments. Harry Carr, whose focus was still adjusted to the imperial era and was blind to the world's new balance of power, barely met the new director on one of his periodic visits from Copenhagen. The intention was to forestall briefing White about the closing stages of the Baltic operation. Silarajs' final message to Maxis was Broadway's method of sweeping the cupboard clean before the new broom arrived. When that moment occurred, Northern Area would be able to report quite truthfully that its operations in the Baltic were of purely historic interest. Unexpectedly, Lukasevics' perseverance suffocated the plot.

Four days after Silarajs' final message, the first opportunity on the agreed schedules, Kipurs, the Maxis radio operator, replied: 'We've risked a lot of danger and problems but you've knifed us in the back. We're waiting for you to help us. You cannot abandon us. "Viestus" will come alone because of dangers.'

Sending Klimkans under these conditions was, as a pure intelligence operation, reckless but Lukasevics was unable or unwilling to believe that Vitolins had not been at least partially successful. In the early hours of 2 July 1956, Klimkans was dropped on a beach in Gotland. Once ashore, he surrendered to the local police and asked that he be sent to London to meet Charles Zarins. The Swedes, who knew nothing about the background of the 'refugee', would not be hurried. They too wanted to have information about their immediate neighbour and Klimkans was incarcerated for two months for regular if ineffectual interrogation. In September he was allowed to leave for London.

Klimkans submitted himself to SIS for interrogation. Lukasevics believed that the agent's successful year in London would count heavily in his favour, but Vitolins' experience and the past eleven years of SIS naivety had led Lukasevics to underestimate SIS's ruthlessness if the circumstances warranted. The accounts of what followed are divergent but all agree about the first minutes: Klimkans' reception was not warm.

242

Silarajs appeared alternately nervous and sarcastic, and it was evident that the Latvian would have preferred Klimkans to have stayed away from London. If Klimkans was exposed, and Scott was clearly anxious to obtain the truth, Silarajs would be the second casualty. The Latvian suspected that Scott would not treat Klimkans with the same English politeness that Vitolins had enjoyed; Scott had immediately vetoed his request that Klimkans might visit Charles Zarins. Anticipating the worst, Silarajs confided the news to the Ambassador. 'We have been betrayed by prominent Latvian personalities,' wrote Zarins in his diary. 'Some of the young boys have been arrested and killed.'

Scott's exclusive task was to discover how the KGB deception operation worked. Klimkans was escorted to a soundless and airless flat in London where he remained for nearly three months. Daily he was interrogated, and occasionally at night too. There was no physical brutality but the process was well-established. The Russian was to be exhausted and psychologically pounded until he confessed. His physical endurance snapped at the end of the fourth week. The detailed debriefing lasted another eight weeks.

The account of these weeks, which was eventually entered by Lukasevics in his files, was tainted by self-interest. To protect his reputation in front of his subordinates, who had spent hard years in the forests away from their families, his version suggested that Klimkans had been subjected to the harshest form of interrogation possible.

Ensconced in a windowless cell somewhere in London, wrote Lukasevics, Klimkans had been tortured to extract the truth. The interrogations became increasingly remorseless as he was denied sleep, then fed salty food and finally injected with chemicals. Lukasevics even told some of his team that the interrogator had played with a loaded pistol in front of his prisoner. By the end of three months, Klimkans was a physical wreck and, despite his bravery, amid bouts of unconsciousness he could no longer resist making a full confession. 'No man,' Lukasevics told

Kipurs, 'could have withstood what they put him through.' And Kipurs saw for himself that Klimkans, on his return, was severely disoriented and required medical treatment. But the agent had resisted SIS's final offer: to return as a British agent.

The truth was probably somewhat different. Klimkans' resistance had collapsed with relatively little effort. He made a full confession, destroying the last vestige of SIS's trust in the émigrés. Having repeatedly squeezed his limited knowledge of the operation, Scott offered him the chance of working for SIS. While Klimkans pondered whether to accept as a guarantee of his safe return, SIS's links with the KGB web were being broken.

In August, after a radio signal from Luks to Estonia, Rebane travelled to Helsinki for a rendezvous with the agent. Accompanying him was Heino Karkman, who had first exposed the KGB's deception. The meeting did not take place. Instead, Rebane received another signal from Luks asking him to come to Estonia or at least meet at sea. The KGB's crudity betrayed their intention and Rebane returned to London, abandoning at least four SIS agents in Estonia. After sending a final message closing down the radio contact, he left SIS. Karkman remained in Scandinavia and joined a Swedish merchant ship as a radio officer. He was murdered shortly afterwards.

The operation in Lithuania was also closing. In reply to Zigmas Kudirka's pleas to be rescued, Zymantas had signalled in July, 'We cannot organise return. Chin up. Your situation is not that bad. Try your own escape through Sweden.' In September, soon after Klimkans' arrival in London, Kudirka was arrested.

Sick with fear, he faced his two interrogators, General Gormonramoff and Pietyor Karpuchin, determined to follow SIS rules and offer only his cover story and denials. His chain-smoking audience smiled. 'We know everything,' said Karpuchin. 'Have a cigarette and listen.' For nearly fifteen minutes, the KGB officer explained every detail of Kudirka's career in the SIS. ' "Edmundes" was our man. Make a full confession and it will help you at the trial. Fighting is useless.'

'All I wanted,' said Kudirka, 'was to help my country and study at university.'

The prosecution at his trial demanded twenty-five years' imprisonment. The court sentenced him to fifteen years.

Klimkans' ordeal ended much earlier. In November, when he was fed and rested, Scott bade him farewell. According to Lukasevics's legend, the SIS officer said: 'We're sending you back to Russia and we'd like you to take a message. Tell your masters that we're grateful for the lessons but we're not complete fools. And finally tell them to treat our people as well as we've treated you.' There was no suggestion of a deal or of exchanging British agents for the KGB officer. SIS, understandably fearful that a public trial of its agents in Russia would cause an embarrassing international scandal, lacked any muscle to negotiate. It was fortuitous that the final denouement in London coincided with the Twentieth Party Congress in Moscow where Nikita Khrushchev was denouncing the crimes of Stalin's KGB. The new Soviet leadership would see little advantage in extolling a triumph of Beria's regime.

Accordingly, Klimkans was taken by SIS officers to a military airfield outside London. Apprehensively, the Soviet agent waited as his plane gained altitude to see its ultimate direction. He relaxed as it flew due east. At Stockholm airport a limousine drew up at the stairway. With its passengers comfortably seated it drove at speed into the city and stopped at the Russian Embassy at Villagatan 17. 'Here we are,' said Klimkans' escort cheerfully. 'This is where we say goodbye.' Klimkans got out and knocked at the Embassy door. The car had driven off before he heard a lock click and he could enter the building. On his return to Russia, Klimkans, who remained in hospital for some weeks, was awarded the Red Star and invited to join the Communist Party. Kipurs, who proposed him, was awarded two Red Stars.

The fate of the British agents was mixed. While some

were executed and others served a full twenty years in prisons outside Moscow, some were treated leniently. Paul Janitzkas, the Lithuanian sent as a radio officer to Jonas Deksnys, was released without trial after one year in prison. Zigmas Kudirka, although sentenced to fifteen years, was released after just two years. Unexpectedly, 'Edmundes' met him as he stepped onto the platform in Vilnius after a fourteen-hour train journey from Moscow. They walked to a nearby park and 'Edmundes' explained his early release. 'You didn't kill anyone and you weren't bad,' said the KGB officer. 'A lot of people died in the years after the war, so you are lucky to have only suffered imprisonment. The only way to end the war was for us to control those who were fuelling the flames.' Kudirka left the park to meet his girlfriend, who had never been told of his arrest, and to see for the first time his son who had been born after his arrest. During his years of rehabilitation, his anger was not directed at the KGB but at the British. 'They put me into the web,' he repeatedly told his family, 'and abandoned me. Completely abandoned me. They haven't even returned my personal possessions.'

The three SIS émigrés met mixed fates. All of them were dismissed from the service at the end of 1955. Silarajs at first considered opening a shop in Beaconsfield but finally followed the trail of many East Europeans who, fearing KGB revenge, sought a new life and new identity in Canada. He died in the late seventies. Zymantas, the Lithuanian, rejected the offer of a teaching post at Oxford University and emigrated to Los Angeles. Spiritually and emotionally he had been destroyed by the revelations of failure, death and deceit. For the next eleven years he worked as a gardener and grave digger in a local cemetery. He died distraught in 1973. Alphons Rebane also left Britain soon after his dismissal to settle in Augsburg, West Germany. As a former German SS officer, Rebane was automatically entitled to a military pension. Just before he died in 1966, the victim of alcoholism, he managed to burn systematically all his private papers in

246

the hope, as he told an associate, that his disaster would be concealed from the KGB.

Lukasevics was promoted to general and spent the 1960s in Moscow Centre. In December 1972 he arrived in London as a First Secretary at the Soviet Embassy, under the name of Yakov Konstantinovich Bukashev. For eight years, he directed the KGB's counter-espionage operations in Britain. No one in SIS made the connection between Bukashev and the Baltic disaster. Ironically, his home was at 43 Holland Park, a mere stone's throw from the Legations of the three Baltic States which had become ghosts of a forgotten era. Occasionally, taking an evening stroll, he walked past the forlorn stucco buildings, monuments to his success.

On his return to Riga in 1980, Lukasevics filled a suitcase with mementos of Britain. Until he died in 1988, the walls of his comfortable apartment bore witness to an enjoyable stay in London. Lukasevics, it was said, had become an Anglophile. In his retirement, he embroidered the legend of his great success and claimed that the last message from Broadway which announced Klimkans' return in 1955 read, 'In the name of the Queen, we beg you to keep this affair silent.'

In November 1987, Kim Philby visited Lukasevics in Riga. Seventy-five years old, frail and shaking, Philby made his first visit to Latvia partly to pay homage to the home of his KGB controller in Spain, Janis Berzins; partly as a political ploy to suggest on local television that the nationalist demonstrations which were sweeping the Baltic States were inspired by the British secret service; and partly to appear in a special television programme which Lukasevics was organising to celebrate the KGB's seventieth anniversary. 'They're doing just the same now as in my day,' Philby told his Latvian audience about the nationalist protests in the streets. 'And I know all about that.' But as Philby later confided to Lukasevics in the course of a conversation which, at Lukasevics' request, was also tele-recorded, he was never involved in Carr's Baltic operations after 1947. He could claim no credit for their failure. The indirect claims in his KGB-approved autobiography of having caused the arrests of British agents were yet another attempt by his masters to obfuscate his true role, which was to keep Moscow Centre informed about the success of their deceptions.

Accompanied by Lukasevics, Philby toured the city before returning to Moscow, leaving the Baltic citizens unconvinced that the street demonstrations in favour of self-determination were caused by capitalist provocateurs. Not even Lukasevics believed that explanation. Indeed, the KGB officer whispered to his colleages that he favoured the new Glasnost. Some even suspected that he favoured some resurgence of Latvian independence. However, no one, apparently, answered that forty years earlier the SIS agents and their sponsors sought precisely the same objectives as the nationalists in the era of Glasnost which he welcomed.

In his Surrey retirement home, Carr drew little comfort from the news in the Baltic States. At the age of eighty-eight, he was having an unpleasant struggle merely to survive the day. Moreover, unlike Lukasevics, he could not enjoy reminiscing about the past. The former Director of Northern Area had retired in 1961 without receiving further honours. Surrounded by mementos from his childhood in Russia and sporting trophies from school, he could only listen to the songs of Pyotr Leschenko and puzzle endlessly over where and why his operations had unravelled. Invariably his answer was Philby, whose refuge in Moscow was a satisfactory explanation for all his disasters. 'He had a particular detestation for Philby,' wrote *The Times* obituarist, 'whose treachery was responsible for the deaths of many whom Carr had known in Russia.' Whether Carr truly believed that erroneous excuse is unknown. When the young historians from the office came to fill in the missing details of his personal record, Carr found it convenient to obfuscate and fall back upon his reputation for being obsessively secretive. The Firm was so different now from in his day. It had even moved from St James's to a dreadful monolith called

Century House. No one in that place understood the Red Web; not even he did fully. He had served his country and his cause faithfully, honestly and with passion. That was all the world needed to know.

Carr died on 19 March 1988 and was cremated after a private and unostentatious ceremony in Guildford. *The Times'* obituary was the first inkling his two sons and brother had of his career and his private torment over the previous thirty years. But they could barely grasp the nature of the wounds. Two months later, Kim Philby died in Moscow. Amid theatrical pomp, one nation's traitor was publicly honoured as a hero. Carr was spared the ordeal. Six months later, on 10 November 1988, Janis Lukasevics died in Riga. Seventy years after the Bolshevik revolution, the spinner of the web passed the legacy of the Trust to a new generation of perpetrators. Undoubtedly they would find a new generation who would become their victims.

GLOSSARY

CIA	Central Intelligence Agency
CIC	Counter-Intelligence Corps
DP	Displaced Persons
FBI	Federal Bureau of Investigation
JCS	Joint Chiefs of Staff
KGB	Committee of State Security (USSR)
LCC	Latvian Central Council
NKVD	Soviet Secret Police
NSC	National Security Council
NTS	National Labour Alliance (USSR)
OGPU	Russian Internal Security (forerunner of KGB)
OMGUS	Office of Military Government (US)
OPC	Office of Policy Co-ordination
OSO	Office of Special Operations
OSS	Office of Strategic Services
OUN	Organisation of Ukrainian Nationalists
OUNR	Organisation of Ukranian Nationalist Revolutionaries
PCO	Passport Control Office
PHPC	Post-Hostilities Planning Committee
SIS	Secret Intelligence Service (later renamed MI6)
SMT	Swedish Military Intelligence Service
SOE	Special Operations Executive
SSU	Strategic Services Unit
VLIK	Supreme Committee for the Liberation of Lithuania
WIN	'Freedom and Independence' Movement of Poland

ACKNOWLEDGMENTS

Of the many people who gave me assistance in writing this book, and did not request anonymity, I am grateful to the following:

In Britain: Rt Hon. Julian Amery, PC, MP, Christopher Carr, Edward Carr, Richard Davies of Leeds University, Sir James Easton, Ed Harriman, Colonel Seamus McGill, Einar Sanden, Sir Peter Tennant, Nikolai Tolstoy and Captain Derek Wyburd, RN.

In the USA: George Belic, Nijole Brazenas-Paronetto, John Bross, William Coffin, Paul Hartman, Burton Hersh, Fred Launags, Franklin Lindsay, Stasys Lozoritis, Tom Polgar, Thomas Powers, Brunius Raila, Harry Rositzke, Elmars Skobe, Thomas Bell Smith, Anthony Sova, Al Ulmer, Anthony Vaivada, Stanley Vardys and Walter Zilinskas.

I am especially grateful to Robert Fink for his extremely thorough research in the archives, and to Michael Kinsella and Bob Royer for their hospitality and friendship in Washington. Thanks also to John Taylor and Wilbert Mahoney in the National Archives.

In Sweden special thanks to Janis Zalkans and Karlis Kangeris, who were very generous with their help. In addition, thanks to His Excellency Leif Leifland, GCVO, Ieva Leshuska, Helene Lööw, Janis Lukins, Juris Kaza and Leonid Silins.

In Finland many thanks to Jukka Rislakki.

In West Germany thanks to Kestutis Girnius, Heinz Hoehne and Jan Trapans.

In Moscow Boris Semyonov, Vitali Sufan, and Yuri Startsev of Gostelradio gave invaluable assistance. In Riga very special thanks to Andris Trautmanis and Janis Leja of Latvian TV. Thanks also to Sylvia Lename for translations and research, and to Kazimirs Kipurs, a KGB officer who, had he been born elsewhere, would have willingly served in any other intelligence agency. In Lithuania thanks to Algimantas Jokubenas of Lithuanian TV and to Zigmas Kudirka.

Finally, at BBC Television, talks to Jill McCloughlin, Pete Wane and Lorraine Hodges.

SOURCES

The principal sources for this book were interviews with over 200 people, a limited number of relevant documents in the national archives in London, Washington, Stockholm and Helsinki and the records of the émigré movements.

The provisions of the new Official Secrets Act could render former SIS officers speaking about these matters – which are well-known to the Russians – liable to prosecution. Although such harsh constraints do not apply to former CIA officers, American law does oblige its former servants to apply for permission to give interviews. Those former officers who did apply are cited, but others would speak (many for the first time) only on condition of anonymity. Their request has been respected, although it understandably leaves the reader somewhat dissatisfied about the source of a quotation.

More serious issues inevitably arise concerning the nature of the information provided by KGB sources. The history of the book was such that I would not know until nine months after starting the research that I was to be given access to the KGB officers and their archives. Accordingly, I had travelled extensively in the West, speaking to those directly involved in the operations, before arriving in the Baltic States.

Those interviewed in the West, even those who had occupied senior positions, could recall or knew only limited details about the whole pattern. Many people, however, were able to supply names of agents who were known to have survived in the West or in Russia, or the names of the senior KGB officers involved. On arrival in the Baltic States, I was denied access only to former agents who, having served long terms of imprisonment, felt bitter towards the British and wanted no reminder of their disturbed past. There were others who were less resistant.

Unfortunately, just before my arrival in November 1988, General Janis Lukasevics died suddenly. In preparation for my research, however, he had collected a wealth of material and approved access to the KGB's files by a senior Latvian television correspondent. He had also given a lengthy television interview. Several of his staff who were involved in the operation were also still alive. I was allowed access both to the material and the people. During that first, and the subsequent two visits, I was able to check and cross-check with Western sources all the information provided by the KGB, before returning to request-ion the KGB officers. For example, the KGB provided the dates of arrival of S208. By questioning former agents, and those who staffed S208 who live in the West, it was possible to corroborate those dates. Similarly, the early escapes from Sweden in the post-war years could be corroborated by survivors in the West and by some written records. Klimkans' visit to London was confirmed by Charles Zarins' diary, the London Agreement and those surviving Latvians who recall the man whom they knew as 'Leon Blomberg'.

It was also possible to corroborate the CIA's operations. Two former CIA-sponsored agents have survived in Lithuania and one in the West, and many CIA officers are still alive. KGB officers expressed their own interest in certain aspects of the Agency's motives and operations (they also voiced similar interest in SIS) and asked for information from their rivals. Those exchanges confirmed the veracity of most of the KGB's account. Some of the doubts which surfaced in my mind, how-ever, could not be answered, because of the death of Lukasevics and other officers directly involved.

In all the instances where my doubts were not satisfied, I have either completely omitted the details or introduced a caveat into the narrative.

The notes which follow are therefore somewhat unconven-tional. In general, I have not cited KGB material because it is included only when it was corroborated by a Western source. However, many of those interviewed could not be named and a citation of any value was therefore often impossible.

FO is the Foreign Office, London
PRO is the Public Records Office, London

RG is the Records Group at the National Archives, Washington
SD is the State Department, Washington

page 2 'Carr was born': Carr recorded some memoirs, which are kept in the Russian Department of the University of Leeds. His family and friends provided other material.

page 4 'the author W. Somerset Maugham': Nigel West, *MI6*, Weidenfeld & Nicolson, 1983, page 14.

page 5 'in all the major Russian banks': Michael Kettle, *The Allies and the Russian Collapse*, Deutsch, 1981, page 176ff.

page 8 'in Lenin's household': Allen Dulles, *The Craft of Intelligence*, Harper & Row, 1963, page 24.

page 8 'The Cheka does not judge': Paul Blackstock, *The Secret Road to World War Two*, Quadrangle Books, 1969, page 20.

page 9 'unfit for duty in France': George Kennan, *The Decision to Intervene*, Princeton, 1958, page 373.

page 10 'forestall the German advance': *ibid.*, page 276.

page 11 'Britain should "do all we can"': Richard Ullman, *Britain and the Russian Civil War*, Oxford University Press, 1968, page 12.

page 11 'crusade against Bolshevism': *ibid.*, page 11. PRO GT 6050; Cab 24/67–20.10.1918.

page 11 'Mr Churchill's Private War': William Manchester, *The Last Lion*, Michael Joseph, 1963, page 682.

page 11 'Civilisation is being completely extinguished': *ibid.*, page 676.

page 11 'break up their power': Ullman, *op. cit.*, page 90.

page 11 'the "mad enterprise"': *ibid.*, page 126; Lloyd George, *Truth About the Peace Treaties*, vol. 1, page 371.

page 11 'cause a revolution in Britain': Manchester, *op. cit.*, page 677.

page 11 'a culture of typhoid': *ibid.*, page 680.

page 13 'the riff-raff of Tsarism': Ullman, *op. cit.*, page 22.

page 13 'fighting for their lives': *ibid.*, page 60.

page 13 'against Bolshevism': *ibid.*, page 55.

page 14 'Gough followed Churchill's orders': *ibid.*, page 260ff.

page 14 'That foe is Soviet Russia': Phillip Knightley, *The Second Oldest Profession*, Deutsch, 1986, page 55.

page 15 'A not very creditable enterprise': Ullman, *op. cit.*, page 253.

page 17 'Ironside recommended Carr to Cumming': Carr tapes, Leeds University.

page 18 'His being was organised': Geoffrey Bailey, *The Conspirators*, Gollancz, 1961, page 16.

page 19 'Bolsheviki will never sleep in peace': *ibid.*, page 89.

page 19 'The most probable [cause of] war': Anthony Verrier, *Through the Looking Glass*, Cape, 1983, page 12.

page 20 'though at an increased price': John Whitwell, *British Agent*, Kimber, 1966, page 59.

page 20 'Meiklejohn sent London': West, *op. cit.*, page 27.

page 22 'had accepted the Trust's credibility': Blackstock, *op. cit.*, page 44.

page 22 'We are watching this second Russia': Bailey, *op. cit.*, page 11.

page 24 'a movement of considerable power within Russia': Blackstock, *op. cit.*, page 89.

page 24 'very intelligent youngster': *ibid.*, page 91.

page 24 'I am leaving tonight': Bailey, *op. cit.* page 51.

page 26 'terrific anti-Bolshevik': Andrew Boyle, *The Climate of Treason*, Hutchinson, 1979, page 132.

page 27 'the Kremlin's suspicions': Blackstock, *op. cit.*, page 166.

page 27 'the monarchists living abroad': *ibid.*, page 175.

page 28 'it is impossible to gain even an inkling': Hinsley *et al.*, *British Intelligence in the Second World War*, HMSO, 1979, vol. 1, page 46.

page 28 'Nobody gave me any tips': Whitwell, *op. cit.*, page 20.

page 32 'His optimism was shared by Lt Col Vale': Jukka Nevakivi, *The Appeal That Was Never Made*, Hurst, 1972, page 84.

page 33 'any real importance to the continued existence of Finland': *ibid.*, page 171.

page 34 'was often wrong': McGill interview.

page 34 'would attack Russia in spring 1941': Hinsley, *op. cit.*, page 441.

page 37 'Blunders, indiscretions and crimes': Charles Cruickshank, *S.O.E. in Scandinavia*, Oxford University Press, 1986, page 20.

page 37 'more pro-Swedish than the Swedes themselves': Olsen papers, Roosevelt Library, 7.2.1944, page 5.

page 39 'Falk obtained access': West, *op. cit.*, page 169ff.

page 41 'products of the Slavic imagination': Tom Bower, *Blind Eye to Murder*, Deutsch, 1981, page 43.

page 41 'we paid the penalty accordingly': Victor Rothwell, *Britain and the Cold War 1941–47*, Cape, 1982, page 77.

page 41 'robbed the Balts of their independence': Stanley Vardys, *Lithuania Under the Soviets*, Praeger, 1965, page 62, quoting Sumner Welles.

page 41 'much sooner than you expect': *ibid.*, page 62.

page 42 'the glorious family of the Soviet Union': R. Misiunas, *The Baltic States*, Hurst, 1983, page 25.

page 44 ' "acid test" of British intentions': Rothwell, *op. cit.*, page 89.

page 44 'almost accidental': *ibid.*, page 93.

page 44 'undermine the force of the whole document': Hugh Thomas, *Armed Truce*, Hamish Hamilton, 1986, page 317.

page 45 'can use force to get them out': *ibid.*, page 317.

page 45 'What I want to explain to you': SD 760A. 02/10-2753 February 1954.

page 47 'In summer 1943': Elisabeth Barker, *The British Between the Superpowers 1945–50*, Macmillan, 1983, page 6ff.

page 48 'a radical departure from Foreign Office policy': Rothwell, *op. cit.*, page 120; Thomas, *op. cit.*, page 209, footnote 122.

page 49 'a very restricted circle': Rothwell, *op. cit.*, page 123.

page 49 'special security treatment': *ibid.*, page 123.

page 49 'the shadow of the Bear': Thomas, *op. cit.*, page 212.

page 49 'gather information from inside the Soviet Union': Phillip Knightley, *Philby*, Deutsch, 1988, page 125ff.

page 52 'Born in Moscow in 1891': McKibbin's biography was supplied by his nieces and stepdaughter who live in Finland, and by Walter Zilinska and several Balts who live in Sweden.

page 53 'passed on to McKibbin': Vardys, *op. cit.*, page 64.

page 53 'had joined the "police battalions" ': *ibid.*, page 41.

page 54 'Zilinskas suggested to McKibbin': Zilinskas interview.

page 54 'a "satanic practice" ': R. Harris Smith, *OSS. The Secret History of America's First Central Intelligence Agency*, New York, 1972, page 200.

page 54 'a quarter of a million dollar budget': Bradley Smith, *The Shadow Warriors*, Basic Books, 1983, page 222.

page 55 'all operations must cease': Thomas, *op. cit.*, pages 163–4; cf. footnote 183.

page 55 'oral approval from the Joint Chiefs': Anthony Cave Brown, *Wild Bill Donovan*, Michael Joseph, 1982, page 418.

page 55 'Intelligence to be Furnished to the USSR': *ibid.*, page 424.

page 55 'Olsen secured from the Swedish government': Olsen papers, *op. cit.*, Roosevelt Library. Olsen also described the Latvians as 'unreliable . . . trouble-makers': *ibid.*

page 60 'a rising star in the Party's Central Committee': Vardys, *op. cit.*, page 102.

page 60 'by the late summer, Suslov admitted': Thomas Remeikis, *Opposition to Soviet Rule in Lithuania*, Chicago, 1980, page 40.

page 60 'claimed the lives of twenty per cent of the population': Misiunas, *op. cit.*, page 72.

page 67 'condemned their communications as "pathetic appeals"': FO 371/47043, 21.9.45.

page 68 'render the opponents harmless': FO 371/47061, 29.10.45.

page 69 'the larger ones will have to be offered tomorrow': SD 860M 01/2-1545, 15.2.45.

page 70 'Algirdas Voketitis': personal interview.

page 71 'the Russians were "a scurvy race, Mongolian and permanently drunk" ': Thomas, *op. cit.*, page 151.

page 73 'Vaivada typed out a three-page memorandum': SD 860M.01/7-3145, 19.9.45.

page 74 'I would be loath to hazard American lives for purely political purposes': Thomas, *op. cit.*, page 149.

page 77 'Lukasevics': the general died eleven days before our arranged meeting. Nevertheless, he had made available his files and a series of filmed interviews and had given permission to his subordinates to co-operate fully with me.

page 81 'You can never . . . deal with the Russians': Thomas, *op. cit.*, page 198.

page 81 'They just bombed us': Barker, *op. cit.*, page 33.

page 81 'smiling granite': Thomas, *op. cit.*, page 15.

page 82 'personally congratulated Ribbentrop': Rothwell, *op. cit.*, page 75.

page 82 'The depressing thing is': *ibid.*, page 238.

page 82 'the ideological imperialists': Thomas, *op. cit.*, page 197.

page 82 'planning world conquest': *ibid.*, page 124.

page 83 'a tremendous revival of orthodox Marxist ideology': Rothwell, *op. cit.*, page 250.

page 84 'addicted to the study of history': *ibid.*, page 248.

page 84 'We should be unwise': *ibid.*, page 256ff.

page 85 'a "vigilance committee" on Bolshevism': Thomas, *op. cit.*, page 532.

page 85 'a "full-dress anti-communist campaign" ': Barker, *op. cit.*, page 47.

page 85 'The Russia Committee's first meeting': JCS SM: 5062.

page 85 'George Kennan . . . dispatched an 8,000-word telegram': Thomas, *op. cit*, page 489.

page 86 'Molotov was "madly offensive, even crazy"': Rothwell, *op. cit.*, page 317.

page 87 'could be easily issued again to the German soldiers': Anthony Cave Brown, '*C*', Michael Joseph, 1987, page 664.

page 87 'had come across thousands of Russian-speaking soldiers': Nicholas Bethell, *The Last Secret*, Deutsch, 1974, page 17.

page 89 'They robbed like bandits': *ibid.*, page 108.

page 89 'Many of them had British decorations': *ibid.*, page 128.

page 90 'were transferred across the Alps to a British POW camp in Rimini': Tom Bower, *The Times*, 20 and 21 August 1987.

page 90 'Valdmanis . . . sent a plea': FO 1032/2242, 30.8.45.

page 91 'I was their commander': FO 371/407052, 17.8.45.

page 91 'did not deserve the fate': FO 371/47051, 8.9.45.

page 91 'It is impossible to distinguish': FO 371/47052, 31.10.45.

page 91 'most had volunteered to join the SS': FO 371/47053, 23.11.45.

page 91 'The majority were forced to join': FO 371/47052, 27.9.45.

page 91 'a "very high percentage of former collaborationists" ': FO 371/55975, 18.2.46.

page 91 'the Moscow Declaration of 1943': Bower, *Blind Eye to Murder*, page 59ff.

page 92 'demand for transfer to Russia of Colonel Arvids Kripens': FO 371/47063, 10.12.45.

page 92 'an honest and good man': FO 371/47053, 29.11.45.

page 93 'During the night of 6 August 1946': the sources for this saga were four participants: Skobe, Lukins, Launags and Tomsons, as well as the KGB officers.

page 97 'On 17 December, as Skobe made': based on interviews with Skobe and other participants and on the Swedish intelligence report of the incident, available from the Swedish National Archives, Stockholm.

page 99 'Danielsson': Danielsson's own report is available in the Swedish National Archives.

page 102 'Sebris found a suitable candidate': Rumnieks interview.

page 106 'a castle outside Osnabrück': the account is based on Zilinskas, Voketitis and two others. Markulis' history is described by Luksha in Juozas Daumantas, *Fighters for Freedom*, Manyland Books, 1975 and in Russian publications.

page 108 'Brimelow advised the minister': FO 371/65753, 29.5.47. *page 84* 'had only been the absence of the Soviet ambassador': FO 371/65753, August 1947.

page 109 'firm and vigilant containment of Russian expansive tendencies': John Gaddis, *Strategies of Containment*, Oxford University Press, 1982, page 4.

page 110 'No one was more frustrated than Harry Rositzke': personal interview and Rositzke's memoirs.

page 110 'devious, monstrous, incalculable and inscrutable': Harry Rositzke, *The CIA's Secret Operations*, Reader's Digest Press, 1977, page 14.

page 111 'the agency was given extra legal authorisation': John Prados, *Presidents' Secret Wars*, Morrow, 1986, page 26.

page 111 'propaganda with covert psychological warfare': John Ranelagh, *The Agency*, Simon & Schuster, 1986, page 115.

page 111 'part of the American crusade against Stalin': Rositzke, *op. cit.*, page 13.

page 111 'to defeat the European recovery program': Ranelagh, *op. cit.*, page 177.

page 112 'that mobilisation was being planned': Christopher Simpson, *Blowback*, Weidenfield & Nicolson, 1989, page 60.

page 112 'would reach the English Channel': RG 319 1946–48 P&O TS Files 091 Russia TS (sec 2) Case 26, 16.9.46.

page 112 'war was unlikely': Jean Edward Smith, *The Papers of General Lucius Clay*, vol. 2, Indiana, 1974, page 568.

page 112 'the CIA's was a voice of some reason': Trevor Barnes, 'The Secret Cold War', *The Historical Journal*. And see report on the Jigsaw Project, 7 December, 1948, RG 319 Army Intelligence Decimal File 1949–50, 334 Jigsaw Committee.

page 113 'the consensus of 2,000 CIC officers': Simpson, *op. cit.*, page 55.

page 114 'I want an agent': Rositzke, *op. cit.*, page 34.

page 114 'directive NSC 10/2'; Modern Military, National Archives. Policy paper files.

page 115 'preferable . . . as rulers of Russia': Simpson, *op. cit.*, page 82ff.

page 115 'The top-secret programme was called Bloodstone': SANACC 395, 1948, on microfilm at the National Archives, Washington. 'Utilization of Refugees from the Soviet Union in US National Interest.' See also discussion on the treatment of Baltic nationals.

page 115 'targeted refugees from the "Soviet World"': Simpson, *op. cit.*, page 100.

page 115 'SANACC 395 empowered Wisner to recruit foreigners': National Archives, *op. cit.*, and cf. Simpson, *op. cit.*, page 108.

page 116 'under Bloodstone were Gustav Hilger': Simpson, *op. cit.*, page 114.

page 116 'the "special operations" ': JSPC 891/6. See 'Proposal for Establishment of a Guerrilla Warfare School' RG 319 Records of Army Staff, 1946–8 P&O TS Files P&O 352 TS (Sec 1) Case 2.

page 116 'Kennan had written to Forrestal on 29 September 1947': JSPC 891/6.

page 116 'Staff studies were cited': JSPC 891/6, 20.9.48.

page 117 'covert warfare, sabotage and assassination': JSPC 862/2 Appendix C page 27. Note that it is hard to see a link between Bloodstone and JSPC 862/3, as some have claimed.

page 91 'clandestine warfare as "excellent" was Lithuania': RG 319 Records of the Army Staff 1946–8 P&O TS Files P&O 352TS (Sec 1) Case 2.

page 117 'We cannot really profess indifference': RG 319 JCS 1903/1, 27.8.48 NSC 20. 'Appraisal of the Degree and Character of Military Preparedness Required by the World Situation', 12 July 1948, is available at RG 319 Records of Army Staff, 1946–8 P&O TS – Entry 154 – Box 26. P&O 091 Russia TS (18 Aug 48) F?W 15/3.

page 118 'George Belic': personal interview.

page 121 'Operation Whiskey': obtained under Freedom of Information Act from Forte Meade, Maryland.

page 122 'Colonel Antanas Sova': personal interview.

page 122 'dispatches from the US Embassy': SD 860N.00/1–1448, 14.1.48, & SD 860N.00/6–348, 3.6.48.

page 123 'Foreign Office officials doubted the strength': FO 371/71244, 6.7.48.

page 124 'a decisive struggle': Alan Bullock, *Ernest Bevin*, Oxford University Press, 1985, page 594.

page 124 'Russians will be in Paris by August': *ibid.*, page 537.

page 126 'Sveics arrived at Tepfers' home': Launags interview and KGB officers.

page 128 'free from the terror of bandits': SD 860N.00/6–1347, 13.6.47, and see SD 860N.00/1–1448, 14.1.48.

page 128 'memorandum written in mid-1947 called "Lithuania's Underground" ': SD 860N.00/6, May 1947.

page 134: 'Russia Committee which on 25 November 1948 had discussed a proposal to start "offensive operations"': FO 371/71687 & FO 371/77623.

page 134: 'mirrored SOE's operations three years earlier': Bethell, *op. cit.*, page 36.

page 134: 'we should aim at winning the "cold war"': FO 371/71687.

page 134 'to liberate the countries within the Soviet orbit by any means short of war': FO 371/71687.

page 135 'exposed the absence of any co-ordination': RG 319 Army Intelligence Dec File 1949–50, 334 Jigsaw Committee.

page 135 'Wisner's judgment was endorsed by Frank Lindsay': Lindsay interview.

page 139 'deliberate exclusion in 1948 of the Ukrainians from covert operations': RG 319 JCS 1903/1, 27.8.48; NSC 20.

page 139 'to bring about the elimination of Soviet power from the satellite states': Gaddis, *op. cit.*, page 68; NSC 58/2.

page 141 'be asked to confine his attentions': FO 371/66714.

page 141 'in no way to be regarded as political dissidents': FO 371 66604, 66605, 66700, 66710, 66711, 66712, 66713, 66714.

page 143 'His SIS code name was "Kranja"': Berkis told his life story to a Latvian émigré, Anslavs Eglitis, who was living in Los Angeles and published the story in Latvian. Berkis moved to the USA in the mid-1950s. Before his death in a road accident, he also gave his brother every detail of his activities.

page 146 'The three agents and their British escort': the journey and the whole operation inside the Baltic States became the basis of a six-part drama broadcast by East German Television in 1971 under the title *Rottenknecht*.

page 152 'Kipurs was selected': Kipurs interview.

page 153 "British put up a stubborn rearguard action': Kim Philby, *My Silent War*, Panther, 1969, page 40.

page 154 'NSC 68': Modern Military, National Archives, 14 April 1950.

page 156 'share experiences': Belic interview.

page 157 'Monsignor Krupavicius . . . had visited Washington': SD 860M. 00/2-249 4 March 1949. See also 00/5-2049 for details of the visit.

page 157 'The American's promises had been expansive': Sova interview.

page 160 'hearings on "Communist Aggression"': US House of Representatives, 1954.

page 161 'Sirvys heard Luksha swear': Sirvys interview.

page 164 'Both SIS and CIA had their Baltic puppets': Philby, *op. cit.*, page 144.

page 165 'War is certain to break out soon': interviews with Kudirka and three other Lithuanian agents.

page 172 'always handsome, always articulate and always wrong': Polgar itnerview.

page 172 'NSC 68': Modern Military, National Archives.

page 173 'world-wide revolutionary movement . . . the inheritor of Russian imperialism': NSC 68.

page 187 'Bolislav Pitans, a radio operator': Pitans interview.

page 191 'Elmar Remess, a 30-year-old journalist': Remess interview.

page 199 'both agencies needed to produce forgeries': Thomas Bell Smith, *The Essential CIA*, private publication.

page 201 'Socially as well as professionally': William Colby, *Honourable Men*, Simon & Schuster, 1978, page 86ff.

page 203 'running self-importantly to fat': Philby, *op. cit.*, page 141.

page 204 'I'm going over to Germany': Polgar interview and others.

page 205 'in an atmosphere of impatient tension': Rositzke interview and memoirs.

page 206 'the most "vulnerable" target "to be induced to revolt"': RG 218 records of JCS. CCS 385 (6.4.46) Sec 25 (JCS 1735/84).

page 207 'I know all about the Trust': Hartman interview.

page 213 'Lindsay's report on his inquiries was his obituary': Lindsay private papers.

page 213 'It's given us good experience for the next war': Rositzke, *op. cit.*, page 141.

page 216 'Zarins and McKibbin fed': Besides Zarins' diary, which is in the possession of his daughter, there are many who survive who witnessed the relationship between the two men.

page 217 'The London Agreement': an original exists in Riga and is mentioned by Zarins.

page 222 'Margers Vitolins': Vitolins interview.

page 226 'McKibbin emotionally rejected the order': among McKibbin's confidants were the wife of Zymantas and the son of Stasys Lozoritis, who is the present Lithuanian representative in Washington.

page 233 'the captive peoples should know that they are not forgotten': US House of Representatives, 30 November 1953, The Select Committee on the Captive Nations – Baltic States.

page 249 '*The Times* obituary': 22 March 1988.

BIBLIOGRAPHY

This is a selective bibliography of books which were helpful in researching this book.

AGAR, AUGUSTUS, *Baltic Episode*, Conway, 1963.

BAILEY, GEOFFREY, *The Conspirators*, Gollancz, 1961.

BARKER, ELISABETH, *The British Between the Superpowers 1945–50*, Macmillan, 1983.

BARNES, TREVOR, 'The Secret Cold War', *The Historical Journal*, vol. 24, no. 2 (1981); part 2, *ibid.*; vol. 25, no. 3 (1982).

BETHELL, NICHOLAS, *The Last Secret*, Deutsch, 1974.

—— *The Great Betrayal*, Hodder, 1984.

BLACKSTOCK, PAUL, *The Secret Road to World War Two*, Quadrangle Books, 1969.

BOWER, TOM, *Blind Eye to Murder*, Deutsch, 1981.

BOYLE, ANDREW, *The Climate of Treason*, Hutchinson, 1979.

BRUCE LOCKHART, R.H.., *Memoirs of a British Agent*, Macmillan, 1974.

BULLOCK, ALAN, *Ernest Bevin*, Oxford University Press, 1985.

CAVE BROWN, ANTHONY, *Wild Bill Donovan*, Michael Joseph, 1982.

—— *'C'*, Michael Joseph, 1987.

COOKRIDGE, E.H., *Gehlen*, Hodder, 1971.

CRUICKSHANK, CHARLES, *S.O.E. in Scandinavia*, Oxford University Press, 1986.

DAUMANTAS, JUOZAS, *Fighters for Freedom*, Manyland Books, 1975.

DULLES, ALLEN, *The Craft of Intelligence*, Harper & Row, 1963.

GADDIS, JOHN, *Strategies of Containment*, Oxford University Press, 1982.

HARRIS, JOHN, *Farewell to the Don*, Collins, 1970.

KENNAN, GEORGE, *The Decision to Intervene*, Princeton, 1958.

KETTLE, MICHAEL, *The Allies and the Russian Collapse*, Deutsch, 1981.

—— *The Road to Intervention*, Routledge, 1988.

—— *Sidney Reilly: The True Story*, Corgi, 1983.

KNIGHTLEY, PHILLIP, *Philby*, Deutsch, 1988.

LEWIS, JULIAN, *Changing Direction, British Military Planning for Post-war Strategic Defence 1942–47*, Sherwood Press, 1988.

MANCHESTER, WILLIAM, *The Last Lion*, Michael Joseph, 1983.

MISIUNAS, R., *The Baltic States*, Hurst, 1983.

NEVAKIVI, JUKKA, *The Appeal That Was Never Made*, Hurst, 1972.

PHILBY, KIM, *My Silent War*, Panther, 1969.

POWERS, THOMAS, *The Man Who Kept the Secrets*, Knopf, 1979.

PRADOS, JOHN, *Presidents' Secret Wars*, Morrow, 1986.

RANELAGH, JOHN, *The Agency, The Rise and Decline of the CIA*, Simon & Schuster, 1986.

READ, A. & FISHER, D., *The Deadly Embrace*, Michael Joseph, 1988.

REMEIKIS, THOMAS, *Opposition to Soviet Rule in Lithuania*, Institute of Lithuanian Studies Press, Chicago, 1980.

ROSITZKE, HARRY, *The CIA's Secret Operations*, Reader's Digest Press, 1977.

ROTHWELL, VICTOR, *Britain and the Cold War 1941–47*, Cape, 1982.

SIMPSON, CHRISTOPHER, *Blowback*, Weidenfeld & Nicolson, 1989.

SMITH, THOMAS BELL, *The Essential CIA*, private publication.

TAURAS, K.V., *Guerrilla Warfare on the Amber Coast*, Voyages Press, 1962.

THOMAS, HUGH, *Armed Truce*, Hamish Hamilton, 1986.

TOLSTOY, NIKOLAI, *Victims of Yalta*, Hodder, 1977.

ULLMAN, RICHARD, *Britain and the Russian Civil War*, Oxford University Press, 1968.

VARDYS, V. STANLEY, *Lithuania Under the Soviets*, Praeger, 1965.

VERRIER, ANTHONY, *Through the Looking Glass*, Cape, 1983.

WEST, NIGEL, *MI6, British Secret Intelligence Operations 1909–45*, Weidenfeld & Nicolson, 1983.

—— *The Friends*, Weidenfeld & Nicolson, 1988.

WHITWELL, JOHN, *British Agent*, Kimber, 1966.

WYMAN, DAVID, *Abandonment of the Jews*, Pantheon, 1985.

YERGIN, DANIEL, *Shattered Peace*, Houghton Mifflin, 1977.

INDEX

Brimelow, Thomas, 83–4, 91, 92, 107–8, 141
Britain: and Baltic independence, 40–1, 44; British tradition of covert action for political agents, 6; declaration of war against Germany, 32; and Finland, 33; and Nazi atrocities, 40–41; possible post-war alliance with Germany, 48; and Russia, 4, 5, 9, 10, 11, 14, 19, 26, 48, 83; support for anti-communist groups, 84; *see also* Foreign Office; MI5; SIS
British Baltic Volunteers, 89
Bromberg, Leonids, 207, 210, 218–19, 230–33
Brooke, Sir Alan, 47–9
Bruce Lockhart, John, 239
Bruce Lockhart, Robert, 7
Brunius, Klemensas, 76
'Bukashev, Yakov Konstantinovich' 247; *see also* Lukasevics, Major Janis
Bulganin, Nikolai, 241
Bunakov, Nikolai, 24
Bundulis, Major Alberts, 78, 79, 148–9, 150–3, 208, 209–10, 218, 230–3
Burgess, Guy, 176
Burke, Michael, 173, 204
Butenas, Julijonas, 161, 175
Byrnes, James, 82

Canada: Soviet spy ring, 86
Carr, Harry Lambton:
  career: army service, 3; awarded CMG, 62–3; contacts with Philby, 49–50, 67, 177, 248; as Controller of Northern Area of SIS, 63; in Copenhagen, 225; early life, 2–3; in Helsinki, 17, 19, 24, 32; as interpreter and translator, 12, 16, 17; plan for penetration of Russia through Baltic States, 39–40;

in retirement, 248–9; in SIS review of clandestine missions, 213–14; in Stockholm, 36, 50; training 28; visits to USA, 153–6, 163
  characteristics: hatred of communism, 13, 16, 33, 239; hypochondria, 37; lack of contact with others, 201, 242; limitations and errors of judgment, 17, 27, 38–9, 102, 122, 128, 137, 163–4, 177, 179, 198, 201–2, 239; memorabilia, 1; obsession with security, 25, 38, 138, 142, 145, 179, 192; social abilities, 29, 37; successes, 33, 34, 62–3; suspicion of Baltic operations, 234
  relationships: with colleagues, 38; with Falk, 38–9; with Finnish intelligence services, 29, 33; with McKibbin, 52–3, 67, 142, 178; with Mallet, 37; with Menzies, 64; with Reilly, 24; with Rositzke, 154–6, 163–4, 170; with SOE, 64; with Ukrainian nationalists, 30
Caucasians: return to Russia after Second World War, 87–8
Cavendish, Anthony, 146
Cavendish-Bentinck, Victor: on Babi Yar, 41
Cecil, Lord Robert: on 'Crusade against Bolshevism', 11
Central Intelligence Agency (US) *see* CIA
Chamberlain, Neville, 30–1
Cheka (Soviet secret service), 8, 78; *see also* OGPU; Okhrana
Churchill, Winston, 5, 11, 13, 14, 15, 18, 37, 41, 43, 44, 46–7, 48, 86–7, 124
CIA: Baltic operations, 173, 229, 233; conference with SIS, 169; foundation, 111; and

imminence of war with Russia, 112; joint centre with SIS, 213–14; lack of co-ordination and leadership, 135; and Maclean and Philby, 176–7; meeting with Hayter's team, 134–5; officers named by Soviet press, 209; production of forged USSR passports, 199–200; reassessment by Truscott, 204; recruitment of Launags, 138–9; and Russia's atomic bomb, 136; and 'special operations', 117; Special Procedures Group, 111; support for WIN, 212; *see also* Office of Strategic Services; USA, National Security Council

Clay, General Lucius, 74, 112

Cockerton, Peggy, 142

codes: Finnish decryption agency, 33, 55

Coffin, Bill, 88

Cohen, Kenneth, 63

Colby, William, 201

Collier, Dorothy, 214

Collier, George, 143

'the Colonel', 98, 100

'Colonel Kull', 207; *see also* Hartman, Paul

Communist International: forged letter, 23

Communist Party, British, 23, 49

'Conrad', 201; *see also* Kudirka, Zigmas

Conservative Party: election victory and Zinoviev letter, 23

Cossacks: independence claim, 13; return to Russia after Second World War, 87–9; war crimes by, 89

Courland resistance, 57–8, 96

Courtney, Commander Antony, 130–1, 146

Cowan, Admiral Sir Walter, 13, 15

Cowgill, Felix, 49

Crabb, Lionel 'Buster', 241

Cripps, Sir Stafford, 83

Crofton, John ('Little John'), 144, 146, 178, 201

Cromie, Captain Francis, 6, 7

Cumming, Captain Mansfield, 6, 14, 17, 20–1, 22, 23

Cunningham, Sir Andrew, 47–49

Czar *see* Nicholas II, Czar

Czarists *see* White Russians

Dabols, Alberts, 185, 217

Daggett, Eileen, 30, 36, 37

Daily Mail: forged letter published in, 23

Danielsson, Kommissar Otto, 99

Dashwood, Nora, 142, 225, 226, 229

Davis, Walpole, 204

Deksnys, Jonas, 76, 93, 104–7, 123–4, 127, 133, 159, 163–4, 169

Deniken, General Anton, 12, 13, 15

Deuxième Bureau *see* France, Deuxième Bureau

Disraeli, Benjamin: quoted, 5

Donovan, William ('Wild Bill'), 55, 109

Dukaitis, Ancietas, 220, 234

Dukes, Sir Paul, 7, 14–15, 15, 33

Dulles, Allen, 61, 172, 203, 211, 212, 213

Dulles, John Foster, 211, 233

Dunderdale, Wilfred 'Biffy', 25, 65, 178

'Durba Zigmas' *see* Kudirka, Zigmas

Dzerzhinsky, Feliks, 8, 22, 25, 78, 148, 179, 238

Easton, Air Commodore James 'Jack', 64–5, 135, 136, 177, 239

Eden, Sir Anthony, 44, 48–9, 60

'Edmundes', 197, 200, 214, 234, 245, 246

communism in, 108; USA and, 108, 112
'Gregory' (Volga German agent), 20
Gubbins, Colin, 12
'Gustav' (Estonian), 182–5
Gylys, Vytautas, 53, 55

Hagbard, 97, 98
Hall, Rear Admiral Reginald 'Blinker', 10, 14
Hallamaa, Reino, 33, 55
Hamburg: Reeperbahn, SIS in, 146, 187, 198
Hardinge, Lord, 15
'Harry', 234
Hartman, Paul, 173, 207, 209–10, 210–11, 218–19, 229, 231, 232, 233
Haselmann, Erwin ('Lilia'), 57, 59
Hayter, William, 134, 135
Helms, Richard, 119, 207
Helsinki *see* Finland
'Herbert', 207; *see also* Osolins, Edvins
Hilger, Gustav, 116
Hill, Captain George, 7
Hillenkoetter, Roscoe, 111, 136
Hiss, Alger, 86
Hitler, Adolf, 30–1, 43
Holland: SOE in, 64
Holman, Major General H.G., 13
Hoover, J. Edgar, 55, 212
'Hugo', 197; *see also* Pilsetnieks, Janis
Hull, Cordell, 44

'Imants', 207; *see also* Riekstins, Alfreds
Iran: CIA operations in, 233
Ironside, General Edmund, 12, 13, 16
Italy: CIA activity in, 111–12
Izvestia: reports Reilly's death, 24

Jackson, C.D., 213
Janitzkas, Paul, 164, 234, 246

Jebb, Gladwyn, 134
Jellicoe, Lord, 109, 134
Jessup, Peter, 204
'Johan' *see* Luks, Walter
Johannson, Captain, 56
Johnson, Colonel Leonard, 100
Johnson, Hershel, 54
Joyce, Robert, 135
'Jungle' operations, 142
'Juras', 234; *see also* Janitzkas, Paul

Kalnins, Bruno, 56
'Känt', 190
Kaplan, Dora, 8
Karkman, Heino, 220, 239, 244
Karpuchin, Pietyor, 244
Katek, Charlie, 118, 169
Keightley, General Charles, 89
Kell, Vernon (head of MI5), 17
Kennan, George, 9, 85–6, 109, 110, 114–15, 116, 117, 118, 139
Kerensky, Aleksandr, 4
KGB: arrest of Arnitis, 77; in Baltic area, 60; Beria execution, 220; lack of co-ordination, 184, 228; in London, 79; monitoring by Western intelligence, 66; Operation Lursen-S, 148–9, 168, 169, 179, 180, 181, 184, 191–2, 194, 198, 199, 215, 220, 220–3, 237, 238, 241; Philby's contacts, 59; radioactive water incident, 227–8; response to increased Western espionage, 125; and Soviet Ministry of Defence, 194; tactics, 104–5, 144; and WIN, 212; *see also* Lukasevics
Khrushchev, Nikita, 30, 241, 245
Kipurs, Kazimirs, 152, 168, 183, 188, 190, 193, 197, 217, 242, 244, 245–6
Klibitis, Peter, 56
Klimkans, Janis, 215–17, 220, 237–8, 238, 240, 241, 242–4

275